RIGHTS, RACE, AND

What is the source of rights? Rights have been grounded in divine
agency, human nature, and morally justified claims, and have been
used to assess the moral status of legal and customary social practices.
The orthodoxy is that some of our rights are a species of unrecognized or natural rights. For example, black slaves in antebellum
America were said to have such rights, and this was taken to provide
a basis for establishing the immorality of slavery. Derrick Darby
exposes the main shortcomings of the orthodox conception of the
source of rights and proposes a radical alternative. He draws on the
legacy of race and racism in the United States to argue that all rights
are products of social recognition. This bold, lucid, and meticulously
argued book will inspire readers to rethink the central role assigned
to rights in moral, political, and legal theory as well as in everyday
evaluative discourse.

DERRICK DARBY is Associate Professor of Philosophy, University of
Kansas.

RIGHTS, RACE, AND RECOGNITION

DERRICK DARBY

University of Kansas

CAMBRIDGE
UNIVERSITY PRESS

CAMBRIDGE UNIVERSITY PRESS
Cambridge, New York, Melbourne, Madrid, Cape Town, Singapore, São Paulo, Delhi

Cambridge University Press
The Edinburgh Building, Cambridge CB2 8RU, UK

Published in the United States of America by Cambridge University Press, New York

www.cambridge.org
Information on this title: www.cambridge.org/9780521515405

First published 2009

Printed in the United Kingdom at the University Press, Cambridge

A catalogue record for this publication is available from the British Library

Library of Congress Cataloging-in-Publication Data
Darby, Derrick, 1967–
Rights, race, and recognition / Derrick Darby.
p.   cm.
Includes bibliographical references and index.
ISBN 978-0-521-51540-5 (hardback) – ISBN 978-0-521-73319-9 (pbk.)
1. Human rights–Philosophy. 2. Natural law. 3. Slavery–United States.
4. Race discrimination–United States. 5. Slaves–Legal status, laws, etc.–United States.
6. African Americans–Civil rights. 7. Civil rights–United States. I. Title.
JC571.D3327 2009
323.01–dc22

2008045754

ISBN 978-0-521-51540-5 hardback
ISBN 978-0-521-73319-9 paperback

For my teachers

Contents

Preface

The seeds for this project were planted during my time as a graduate student in philosophy at the University of Pittsburgh. One of the best things about life in that storied department was that it not only allowed for philosophical creativity and curiosity—it demanded them. One of my first serious intellectual curiosities was about the relationship between personhood and the law. How was it that things as diverse as human beings, slaves, corporations, animals, trees, ships, works of art, and national symbols like the stars and stripes could come to be legal persons or nonpersons? And how was this legal status different from philosophical conceptions of personhood?

After cutting my teeth on traditional philosophical problems in metaphysics concerning personhood and personal identity during my early years as a graduate student, I decided that John Locke's observation that person was a "forensic" term held part of the solution to the problem that I set for myself. I eventually came to believe that persons were first and foremost bearers of rights. Moreover, I believed that if being a bearer of rights was a matter of being recognized or treated as such—as the law teaches us—then being a person must in the final analysis also be a matter of being recognized or treated as such, or so I was prepared to spend my precious dissertation years arguing until Kurt Baier intervened. He convinced me that this task posed too great a summit to climb for the purposes of writing a dissertation. Alternatively, he proposed that I focus instead on the less daunting (or so he assumed) task of defending the thesis that being a rightholder is a matter of being recognized or treated in a certain way. This seemed sensible enough to me back then; after all, defending this thesis was necessary to acquire the real prize, namely the thesis that personhood was a matter of recognition or a matter of decree, as I was wont to put it back in those days. And so my philosophical quest began in earnest.

Although he never tipped me off, I suspect that Baier knew that my quest would be arduous and would meet with ridicule and skepticism.

After all, what philosopher in his or her right mind, with a passionate concern for social justice, and a working knowledge of the history of political philosophy, and of race relations in the United States of America, would endeavor to reject the venerable fighting doctrine of natural rights and to argue instead that all rights were a species of unnatural rights? And how could such a philosopher account for the wrongness of slavery and other historical injustices? Admittedly, on several occasions I came very close to giving up on this project as I struggled to carry out a research project that was so contrary to "philosophical" common sense and that aimed to challenge and to propose a conceptual alternative to a long-standing philosophical outlook that many people believed to be unimpeachable. But I am glad that I persevered. It has been a wonderful intellectual quest and the results have been bountiful. The seeds of this project would not have had the chance to bloom without a skillful dissertation director and thesis committee. I simply cannot imagine having had a better thesis director than Joseph Camp, a philosopher's philosopher. Nor could I have worked with anyone better than John McDowell at telling you exactly what you believed, why you believed it, and why what you believed was wrong-headed.

Rights, Race, and Recognition is a comprehensive and systematic philosophical articulation and novel defense of a theory of rights that I am now quite convinced of. Parts of the theory have been developed and refined in peer-reviewed journal articles for almost a decade after graduate school. Portions of this book have appeared previously in the *Southern Journal of Philosophy, Social Theory and Practice,* the *Canadian Journal of Philosophy, Res Publica,* the *Journal of Social Philosophy,* and *Law, Culture, and the Humanities.* And I am grateful to the publishers for permission to draw from these articles. During this period I have taught at several research institutions: Northwestern University, Texas A & M University, and the University of Kansas. I am grateful for the good colleagues I have had in each of these places and for the ways in which they have enriched and challenged my thinking about the nature and value of rights. I am grateful for the many wonderful students I have taught over the years who were gracious enough to allow me to test my views on them and who offered me thoughtful criticism. I am also grateful for the support of the Friends of the Hall Center for the Humanities at the University of Kansas for their generous book subvention award.

To my dismay I cannot name all of the friends and colleagues who have entertained my ideas and provided useful feedback and inspiration over the years. Nor can I name everyone who has provided me with emotional and other kinds of support, encouragement, and all kinds of advice over the years. But I am deeply grateful to all of them with special thanks to Linda Martín Alcoff, James A. Anderson, Timothy Boyce, Bernard Boxill, Carl Preston Brown, Stephen Daniel, Ernest Darby, Daniel Dennett, Douglas Dorsey, my brother Johnny Edwards, Mitchell Green, Michael Hanchard, William Johnson, Ron Kennedy, John McDermott, Howard McGary, Lucius Outlaw, Gregory Fernando Pappas, Ronald Ross, Jerry Wallace, and Mark Wallace. There are a few people who have had a profound impact on my thinking about rights—largely through frequent and often spirited philosophical exchanges over the years—whom I must single out for special thanks: John Deigh, Thomas McCarthy, Charles Mills, and Robert Gooding-Williams. And there are a few people who have set the high standard for philosophical work on rights that I have aspired to emulate. While I leave it to them to judge how successful I have been, I thank Loren Lomasky, Rex Martin, and Carl Wellman for setting the standard so high. I am grateful to numerous audiences who have entertained my ideas in the United States and abroad, particularly in Brazil, France, Greece, Italy, Portugal, South Africa, and the United Kingdom, where parts of this project have been presented on various occasions over the years. I also owe special thanks to the generous referees for Cambridge University Press who strongly supported the publication of this book, and to my editor, Hilary Gaskin, for embracing the project and giving it such a fine home.

One of my greatest debts of gratitude is to my brother, Tommie Shelby. His philosophical acuity, calm and steady spirit, compassion, and wise counsel have helped sustain me as a professional philosopher, as a man, as a husband, and as a father. My greatest debt is to my wife, Angela, for sharing me with philosophy for nearly two decades. I can never repay you for your sacrifices but hope that the goodness of the good times have outweighed the many trials and tribulations. You are forever, come what may, my sunshine.

My mother often reminds me that from when I was very young, she knew that I was attracted to the life of the mind. She was my very first teacher and I have been blessed with wonderful teachers during my early childhood and secondary education in the New York City public school system as I grew up in Queensbridge public housing projects. Their concern, encouragement, and ability to inspire confidence have been essential to my academic success. My years as a Colgate University undergraduate presented me with more wonderful teachers. I am grateful to Manning Marable and Josiah Young for introducing me to the study of

African and African American history and the contribution of people of color to the world of ideas. I am especially grateful to Anne Ashbaugh for letting me know even before I did that I would be a philosophy major. And I am deeply grateful to Jerome Balmuth who insisted that I abandon my aspiration to become a Supreme Court Justice one day, and instead attend graduate school in philosophy and become a professional philosopher (a more lofty plan of life, I am sure he thought). As a small token of my appreciation for their profound impact on me, I dedicate this book to all of my teachers, with abiding love and admiration.

Introduction

This book addresses a perennial question in the philosophy of rights. If we have any moral rights at all how do we acquire them? The reader may wonder why we should care about this question. Well, the short answer is that we should care because considerable normative weight is placed on having rights and because the prevailing response to how we come to have them is overvalued. It will become clear why I think that these two concerns are related as the argument of this book unfolds. Suffice it to say for now that the prevailing conception of how we acquire moral rights is overvalued largely because too much normative weight has been placed on having them. I substantiate this charge in large part by attending to the legacy of such rights as instruments of racial subordination, particularly in the United States of America prior to the abolition of black chattel slavery. Specifically, I argue that we have reason to diminish the normative weight assigned to moral rights—as they are understood according to the prevailing philosophical view—and that this paves the way for grounding moral rights not in facts pertaining to how subjects are constituted but in facts pertaining to whether subjects have been afforded a certain kind of social recognition. Hence the main claim defended here is that taking the legacy of race and racial subordination into account gives us good reasons for taking moral rights to be acquired by virtue of some form of social recognition.

I believe that there are no rights that exist prior to and independent of social recognition of ways of acting and being treated. So insofar as natural rights, human rights, and presocial moral rights are understood in this manner, my thesis is that there simply are no such rights. All rights including moral ones are products of social recognition. To be sure, many readers may find this thesis shocking and some may even find it morally pernicious. But once we appreciate the shortcomings of the prevailing view, and see that grounding rights in recognition has more to recommend to it than meets the eye and does not leave us morally impoverished, as some critics charge, this thesis will not only be less shocking but will appear more sensible and attractive as well. Of course, some critics may still insist that the thesis is false even though they cannot prove the point in any satisfactory way. But rendering it less shocking and more sensible and attractive will constitute a substantial victory nonetheless. Therefore, I shall leave the eminently more difficult task of establishing the "truth" of my thesis to a more skilled philosopher, or perhaps to one that has unfettered epistemological access to the Platonic form of Truth.

What I accomplish in this book, somewhat more modestly though no less importantly, will suffice to inspire us to rethink the central role that we have assigned to rights in moral, political, and legal theory as well as in our everyday normative practices of guiding, justifying, and criticizing individual and collective conduct. Furthermore, it will make us more amenable to the suggestion that giving up the idea of unrecognized rights may ultimately result in a more ideal democracy, which would certainly be ironic given that the United States, hailed by many as the greatest democracy in history, was founded on natural rights.[1] And most importantly the book will yield a philosophical conception of what having rights amounts to that takes a wider view of the historical facts regarding the infamous legacy of black chattel slavery and black subordination in the United States by taking the perspective of the racially oppressed as a point of departure for philosophical reflection.

Obviously this is not the only perspective from which we might theorize about what having rights amounts to, and we certainly need not presume that the perspective of the racially oppressed is monolithic. Yet there is ample cause to develop a philosophical conception of the source and value of rights from a perspective that is as widely shared and as well represented as the one considered here. A defining aspect of this perspective is that it rejects the conventional wisdom of asserting that individuals have rights of any kind—moral or otherwise—in the absence of being able to reckon on acting in certain ways with impunity or to reckon on certain kinds of treatment. So whether it be engaging in nonviolent civil disobedience protesting an unjust law or whether it

---

[1] For an engaging discussion of the impact of rights on deliberative democracy, see Mary Ann Glendon, *Rights Talk: The Impoverishment of Political Discourse* (New York: The Free Press, 1991). And for an illuminating perspective of the role of natural rights in the establishment of the American Republic, see Michael P. Zuckert, *The Natural Rights Republic* (University of Notre Dame Press, 1996).

be taking a seat on the front of a public bus in the once racially segregated Jim Crow south, to have a moral right to do these things, while certainly distinct from having a mere legal right to do them, nevertheless also demands, at least in part, that one can actually act in these ways or count on these ways of acting being reliably and systematically maintained and enforced by recognized authorities when resistance is encountered. Admittedly, embracing this position rules out arguing that individuals can have a presocial moral right to act in these ways but I will argue that we can manage just fine without such arguments. That is, we can manage just fine from the moral point of view even if we cannot suppose that blacks had a presocial moral or natural right to sit in a designated whites only seat of a racially segregated bus in the US south during the Jim Crow era.

The utility of rights discourse in normative theory and debate is undeniable. A particularly influential book in contemporary political philosophy opens with the observation that "individuals have rights and there are things no person or group may do to them (without violating their rights)."[2] And from this seemingly unassailable normative bedrock the book argues for a libertarian minimal state. Another influential legal and political philosopher characterizes rights as "political trumps" and observes that politicians appeal to the rights of people to justify a great part of what they want to do (whether this be to use less or more state power or public resources to deliver what citizens are owed).[3] And in describing the uncompromising character of rights, another prominent rights theorist implores us to view rights as staking out chunks of moral turf that others are forewarned not to trespass on and with which they must comply.[4] Countless other works, philosophical and otherwise, routinely observe or assume that rights protect their bearers and are of great value to them in many other respects. Although the details concerning the alleged value of rights vary, all of these ruminations on rights invite the same general conclusion—that having rights matters a great deal. Indeed, given the considerable normative weight typically assigned to having rights in everyday moral and political discourse as well as in some of the most sophisticated and influential work in moral and political philosophy—particularly in the United States where fondness for rights is perhaps greater than anywhere else in the world—it is plausible to

---

[2] Robert Nozick, *Anarchy, State, and Utopia* (New York: Basic Books, 1974), p. ix.
[3] Ronald Dworkin, *Taking Rights Seriously* (Harvard University Press, 1977), pp. xi and 184.
[4] Loren E. Lomasky, *Persons, Rights, and the Moral Community* (Oxford University Press, 1987), p. 5.

claim that being a rightholder is arguably one of the most valuable normative statuses that something can possess.[5]

The purported value of having rights undoubtedly accounts for the proliferation of rights and rightholders in moral and political discourse. Many intensely debated issues such as abortion, capital punishment, gay marriage, affirmative action, the basis of our obligations to animals, to the environment, to future generations, and to poor and embattled nations are routinely framed and debated using the language of rights. Furthermore these and other debates illustrate that moral rights are attributed not exclusively to human beings in full possession of their rational capacities and capable of acting morally and pursuing projects but also to human beings capable of considerably less, such as the severely mentally disabled, infants, psychopaths, the unborn, and even the dead. What is more, they are also commonly attributed to many subjects that are anything but human such as nonhuman animals, trees, ecosystems, future generations, corporations, cultural minorities and other groups, and even to works of art.

Of course any of these attributions can be—and most are—contested. Many people have been critical of appeals to rights in general precisely because of this phenomenon of overusing them and thereby devaluing the currency of rights discourse. But be that as it may, ascribing or refraining from ascribing rights to things is intensely debated precisely because the status of being a rightholder is assigned such considerable normative importance. To establish something's status as a rightholder is to establish that we should think seriously about how we should or should not act toward it. To be sure, failing to establish a subject's status as a rightholder does not entail that it gets no consideration at all, as rights are not the

---

[5] The great fondness for rights in the United States notwithstanding, one could plausibly say that being a rightholder may well be one of the most valuable statuses that citizens of the world can possess. To the extent that US foreign policy is purportedly driven not merely by national security interests but by promoting and protecting human rights around the globe, and that the exercise of state power and influence is often deployed in the name of doing these things, then one could take this to be evidence for saying that the value of having certain rights extends far beyond the territorial borders of the United States. But if this is the case, then US citizens are not the only ones who should take a keen interest in a philosophical accounting of how we come to acquire rights. Other citizens of the world may have their lives impacted in concrete ways either by US action or inaction that pertains to presumptions about the existence (or non-existence) of certain presocial or prepolitical rights. For example, US imposed economic sanctions against another country or military aggression may be justified in the name of such rights, or, in contrast, failures to provide various forms of humanitarian assistance to citizens of some nations may be justified by denying that human needs for medicine, food, and minimal standards of health have the status of presocial or prepolitical rights and thus do not have the same kind of primacy.

whole of moral discourse; however, it certainly gets considerably less consideration than full-fledged rightholders, according to the prevailing view. Hoping to preserve the integrity of rights discourse in the face of so much jockeying to exploit the value of rights for various purposes, some of the best recent work in the theory of rights has aimed to distinguish real rightholders from alleged rightholders.[6]

Although this strategy is not without difficulties, we certainly can distinguish different kinds of rightholders, and it is important to do so for present purposes. In particular, we can distinguish between legal rightholders and nonlegal ones, a distinction that sheds a peculiar light on the above debates. In view of this distinction it might be held that these debates merely amount to debates over whether certain things have been afforded special legal consideration, in which case we can determine how we should or should not act toward them legally. Admittedly many of these debates have been framed in precisely these terms. But many of them have also been framed in other terms. For example, in many instances it is claimed that various subjects possess certain nonlegal rights, that is, certain rights that they possess prior to and independent of whether they have been recognized by law or by existing nonlegal yet social conventional rule systems. And, in the most general terms, the reason why being this kind of rightholder is taken to afford subjects considerably greater normative status than possessing mere legal or conventional rights is because we can point to something's status as a bearer of nonlegal or nonconventional rights to criticize existing legal and social practices and institutions.

To take a rather vivid example, consider the case of legally sanctioned chattel slavery as it was practiced in the antebellum United States. Enslaved blacks were without many legal rights of free blacks and whites and this permitted certain ways of treating and acting toward them. But to the extent that enslaved blacks were held to possess certain nonlegal or more generally certain nonconventional rights, and this normative status trumped their legal status, then this status could be cited to condemn black enslavement and to argue for abolishing existing legal and social practices that licensed ways of treating and acting toward blacks which were taken to be incompatible with their status as nonconventional rightholders. A similar observation has been made in describing the situation of blacks in South Africa prior to the abolition of apartheid: "We say that

---

[6] Carl P. Wellman, *Real Rights* (Oxford University Press, 1995).

black South Africans have the moral right to full representation even though this right has not been accorded legal recognition, and in saying this we mean to point to the right as a moral reason for changing the legal system so as to accord it recognition."[7]

By the same token, when we consider some of the hotly contested debates mentioned above we observe a similar strategy of ascribing these nonconventional rights to certain subjects to both condemn and argue for abolishing existing legal and social practices. We see, for example, anti-abortion advocates claiming that the unborn have such rights either at conception or at some later stage of development to argue for abolishing laws that permit women to have abortions, or at least to restrict lawful abortions to very limited cases such as rape. On the other side we see abortion advocates arguing that the unborn have no such rights but that women do and that these rights outweigh any considerations that might be brought to bear in calling for the abolition of abortion or for too narrowly restricting when women can have an abortion. Given the entrenchment of rights in the abortion debate, it is certainly plausible to think that "it requires an act of imaginative dexterity to conceive how the abortion issue might be recast in language that avoids all invocation of rights."[8] But perhaps the same can be said of many other familiar debates. This heavy reliance on rights discourse in general, and moral rights discourse in particular, clearly accounts for why some philosophers insist that "moral rights are not some esoteric construction of otherworldly philosophers, but common parts of the conceptual apparatus of most if not all of us when we make moral and political judgments."[9]

To be sure, one need not invoke something's status as a nonconventional rightholder with an eye toward arguing for or against existing legal or conventional practices. For example, someone might concede that homosexuals have a nonlegal right to marry the person of their choosing yet insist that current legal practices need not make this a legal possibility. In this case, one might believe that other considerations outweighed legally sanctioning this right to marry. On the other hand, one can deny that homosexuals have a nonlegal right to marry yet still argue that they ought to be afforded a legal right to do so on the basis of other normative considerations. This observation notwithstanding, some advocates of

---

[7] L. W. Sumner, *The Moral Foundation of Rights* (Oxford: Clarendon Press, 1987), p. 13.

[8] Lomasky, *Persons, Rights, and the Moral Community*, p. 4.

[9] Joel Feinberg, *Freedom and Fulfillment: Philosophical Essays* (Princeton University Press, 1992), p. 199.

these nonconventional rights will demur that even though we can arrive at these conclusions on the basis of other normative considerations, e.g. consequentialist ones, the conclusions will not be as weighty as if we had appealed to nonconventional rights. It will be objected that these other normative considerations do not take individuals seriously enough.

Hence the main case for positing the existence of nonconventional rights can be summarized as follows. We need ways to guide, justify, and criticize individual conduct and conventional practices and institutions that are reliable and serviceable across cultures and national borders. Insofar as the status of mere legal rightholder does not afford this possibility we need a status that transcends existing legal and conventional practices. And we get this by positing the existence of certain nonconventional rights. Yet for this normative status to yield a reliable and universal critical standard that is serviceable across cultures and national borders it must be acquired or possessed by virtue of something that makes a subject's status as a rightholder secure and not subject to the contingencies of legal or other conventional practices. I take this to be the main rationale for positing the existence of rights secured prior to and independently of any and all forms of social recognition.

To get to the bottom of why such rights are taken to matter so much—not only more than mere legal or conventional rights but more than other kinds of normative considerations such as duty and utility—we would need to undertake a genealogy of rights. We could proceed by first determining the historical origins of rights discourse beginning perhaps with a debate about whether the ancient Greeks had any, or with whether rights originated much later during the middle ages, or even later still during the age of European Enlightenment.[10] Although I certainly cannot undertake this project here, I suspect that wherever we locate their origins we shall find that rights were introduced for some normative purpose or other and that there will be a connection between this purpose and conceptions of how subjects come to acquire rights. In the next two chapters I will shed some additional light on why nonconventional rights are taken to matter so much nowadays by elaborating on why many people doubt that we can manage without them. In the meantime I simply want to emphasize that for many people rights matter a great deal.

---

[10] For a good place to start on the question of whether the ancient philosophers had a conception of rights, see Fred D. Miller, *Nature, Justice, and Rights in Aristotle's Politics* (Oxford University Press, 1995). And for a defense of the claim that natural rights originated in medieval Europe, see Richard Tuck, *Natural Rights Theories: Their Origin and Development* (Cambridge University Press, 1979).

Because so much has been taken to turn on whether something is or is not a rightholder, philosophers have devoted significant attention to accounting for how rights are acquired. In other words, because the demands on rights for normative service have been so plentiful and widespread, philosophers have been compelled to address the full range of theoretical and normative questions to which they give rise, including but not limited to the following questions. What are rights? How do we come to have them? What rights do we have? Who or what can have rights? What is the value of having rights? What is the relationship between rights and other normative concepts? And at least in some cases these questions are addressed with the hope that the currency of rights can be redeemed from the devaluation that has accompanied the proliferation of both rights and rightholders. Some have addressed these questions with the hope of clarifying certain normative matters pertaining to how we ought to act, what kind of people we ought to be, what is or is not morally permissible, or what our flourishing consists in. And still others have done so for a variety of other reasons. While I certainly think that this philosophical attention to rights has been merited, I also think that the prevailing philosophical conception of how we come to acquire moral rights is unsatisfactory. The task of this book is to explain why this is and to defend a different conception of how subjects come to acquire moral rights.

Consequently, this book has both a critical and constructive dimension. But a particularly striking aspect of my case is that in relying on the legacy of black enslavement and black subordination both to cast doubt on the prevailing view and to motivate my alternative I am using this legacy in a way that is completely contrary to the way it is typically used, which is to invoke it in arguing for some version of the rights without recognition thesis and to cast doubt on grounding moral rights in social recognition. My reasons for this will become readily apparent in chapter 4 after taking a closer look at the dual legacy of natural rights discourse to defend as well as to attack black enslavement and black subordination.

Some philosophers may wonder what kind of philosophical project this book engages in. To the extent that rights can be claimed or asserted in ethical discourse pertaining to what ought or ought not be done—a distinctively normative project—and that we can also raise meta-questions about rights and ethical discourse generally—a distinctively metaethical project—the reader may wonder what kind of project is being undertaken here. Is it a normative or a metaethical project? Although I am not entirely happy with the tacit presumption that we can neatly distinguish these two projects, I suppose that there is no harm in saying that this book aims to make a distinctive philosophical contribution to "the grounding theory on which first-order rights claims are ultimately based."[11] It aims, in other words, to offer and defend a way of answering a particular foundational question in the theory of rights, one that can be raised given our practices of claiming or asserting rights. Why do we have rights? In this regard, it is clearly a metaethical or second-order project. Accordingly, I do not aim to claim or assert or even presume that subjects have certain rights and then go on to spell out the normative implications of having them. Instead I develop a view about how subjects come to have certain rights. Of course, this is compatible with concluding that subjects do not have any rights at all, if we become convinced of my conception of what having them amounts to, and we believe that the conditions for rights possession articulated by this conception do not obtain. But this is neither surprising nor worrisome since it is true of any conception of what having rights amounts to.

As for my unease with detaching the normative from the metaethical project, what concerns me most is that this may obscure the fact that the two projects can and should inform one another, which is certainly the case in this book. More specifically, my grounding conception of what having rights amounts to is informed in part by attending to the legacy of first-order rights discourses involving the claiming of rights and the denial of rights claims in the historical context of chattel slavery in the United States, where the classification of individuals by race factored into both the claiming of rights and the denial of rights claims. I believe that attending to these normative practices can and should inform the shape of our grounding conception of what having rights amounts to. And in the other direction—from the metaethical to the normative—I believe that we can test the adequacy of prevailing grounding theories of rights by considering how they strike us when certain first-order rights discourses are brought into sharper focus. Thus it is imperative to appreciate that I aim to make a contribution to the theory of rights that is partly critical, insofar as it challenges a prevailing theory, and partly constructive, in that it offers an alternative by attending to first-order rights discourses shaped by the legacy of slavery and racial discrimination.

The book will unfold as follows. In the second chapter I discuss the nature and shortcomings of the prevailing conception in greater detail, paying special attention to the two most popular ways of spelling out the "rights without recognition" thesis. The third chapter develops and defends

---

[11] Lomasky, *Persons, Rights, and the Moral Community*, p. vii.

my alternative conception. The fourth chapter further develops the case against the prevailing view and the motivation for my alternative by considering the connection between race and rights. Chapter 5 develops an argument that establishes the wrongness of slavery without relying on the idea of rights without recognition. And chapter 1, to which we now turn, offers a detailed overview of the plan and argument of the book. It proceeds by explaining in greater detail why many people will be loath to accept the claim that we can manage just fine without presocial moral or natural rights in our normative arsenal.

CHAPTER I

Having rights

The history of humanity is rife with moral atrocities. State-sponsored ethnic cleansing and chattel slavery are especially poignant examples. In a graphic description of the former in Dostoevsky's *The Brothers Karamazov*, the Turks are reported to have burnt Slav villages, raped Slav women and children, nailed prisoners by their ears to fences, cut unborn children from the womb, and to have tossed babies in the air and caught them on bayonets. And a century later virtually the same script could be written to describe the atrocities committed against Bosnian Muslims by Serbian forces under Slobodan Milosevic in the former Yugoslavia: many people, including women and children, are reported to have been killed, burnt alive, tortured, and raped.

With regard to chattel slavery as practiced in the antebellum United States of America, in his autobiography Frederick Douglass vividly recalls the first time he witnessed a slave beating, a central means of maintaining order under the slave system. He provides a chilling description of how his Aunt Hester was brutally beaten by her master:

Before [the master] commenced whipping Aunt Hester, he took her into the kitchen, and stripped her from neck to waist, leaving her neck, shoulders and back, entirely naked . . . After crossing her hands, he tied them with a strong rope, and led her to a stool under a large hook in the joist, put in for the purpose. He made her get upon the stool, and tied her hands to the hook . . . after rolling up his sleeves, he commenced to lay on the heavy cowskin, and soon the warm, red blood (amid heart-rending shrieks from her, and horrid oaths from him) came dripping to the floor.[1]

And a little more than a century later, if Douglass had still been alive he could have crafted an equally chilling description of the torture of Abner

---

[1] Frederick Douglass, *Narrative of the Life of Frederick Douglass, An American Slave* (New York: The Library of America, 1994), p. 19.

Louima, who was brutally sodomized with a plunger by New York City police officers in Brooklyn while his hands were handcuffed behind his back.

The torture of Louima, the beating of Douglass's Aunt Hester, the torture of Jews, Muslims, Protestants, and other alleged heretics during the sixteenth-century Spanish Inquisition, the atrocities suffered by the Slavs at the hands of the Turks, by the Muslims at the hands of the Serbs, the lynching of blacks during Reconstruction, and the genocide of Jews by the Nazis in Germany and of the Tutsis by the Hutus in Rwanda in the mid-1990s are all disturbing instances of moral atrocities.

While these are paradigmatic examples of moral wrongs, they are by no means the only kind of moral wrongdoing. Acts of omission constitute another kind of wrongdoing. For example, we can contend that failing to help others in need when one is able to do so without risking harm to oneself is not merely something that it would be nice or kind to do but something that it would be morally wrong to refrain from doing. By the same token, failing to attempt to save a drowning baby, to call for help to assist a mugging victim, to feed the hungry, to notify the police authorities that altar boys are being sexually abused by priests, and failing to disclose evidence that would set free someone condemned to die can all be considered moral wrongs as well. And many more such cases can be marshaled to make the point that acts of omission, failures to aid or assist or to permit, are no less moral atrocities than where agents take a more active role in wrongdoing.

Hence a broader understanding of what counts as committing a moral wrong for which blame and punishment can be assigned that includes both acts of commission and omission is very much a part of everyday moral thought and discourse. But whether we embrace a narrow or broad view about what counts as a moral atrocity is of no consequence for present purposes.

Moreover, comparatively speaking, we need not assume that murder, slavery, rape, or torture are the worst instances of moral wrongs. Instead we could contend that all moral wrongs are equally wrong whether it be torturing a prisoner or failing to try to save a drowning baby; there is no substantive difference in degree between them. Accordingly, one might propose that less gut-wrenching acts, perhaps of the sort that Douglass describes elsewhere in his autobiography, be added to the list of moral atrocities. Elsewhere he associates the inhumanity of slavery not merely with floggings but with methods of attempting to "disgust [slaves] with freedom" by encouraging them to plunge into the lowest depths of dissipation. In addition to adopting various plans to make slaves drunk, Douglass recalls how masters would make slaves overeat to the point of sickness to discourage them from asking for more food than their regular allowance.[2]

To this list of moral wrongs we can also add other acts such as depriving someone of their nationality on unsubstantiated charges of treason or without due process, compelling someone to submit to a nonconsensual marriage, and depriving someone of necessary social services in the event of unemployment, sickness, disability, or old age, or any other act or omission by government or by an individual or community that we might find listed on an international charter of human rights. Thus we can embrace a broad conception of what counts as a moral wrong to include atrocities that take the form of omissions and we could also embrace the view that these are no less moral wrongs than those that take the form of commissions. Furthermore, we can even include commissions that are not as gut-wrenching as murder, slavery, and torture.

For present purposes I need not take a stand on what counts as an atrocity. Although I believe that murder, slavery, rape, and economic exploitation of the poor are atrocities, there will certainly be some who disagree with my list, either by rejecting things that I include or including things that I would not. What acts or omissions actually end up on the list of atrocities and what moral weight is assigned to them is beside the point of the present discussion. To emphasize this let me add that we need not rule out the possibility that what we take to be atrocities could be described as virtues in some imaginable worlds. Perhaps someone with a more creative mind than mine could imagine a world in which murder, slavery, rape, and torture were not atrocities but practices to be pursued and valued, and that generally called forth approbation.

Perhaps one could imagine a world diametrically opposed to the one that David Hume envisioned, where it was the case that the human species was constituted so that whatever contributed to the good of humanity produced pain and disapprobation and that whatever contributed to human misery produced pleasure and approbation; moreover, in this world (of what some might call devils), what were classified as moral virtues and vices were inverted so that what we consider atrocities were considered virtues and what we consider virtues were considered vices. Although I have difficulty imagining how such a world could sustain

---

[2] *Ibid.*, p. 67.

human life and human flourishing, present purposes do not require ruling out this possibility. It need only be assumed that there are atrocities and that whatever they turn out to be—murder, torture, slavery, or what have you—they can be correctly described as moral wrongs.

Appealing to the concept of a right, a presocial right in particular, serves as a longstanding and rhetorically powerful way of accounting for what makes something a moral wrong; the atrocities described above can be described as violations of rights possessed by the subjects that are wronged. But defenders of such rights would add that not only do perpetrators of these atrocities act wrongly, they wrong someone in particular. And this puts the individuals wronged in a certain position of moral authority that they would not have been in if the perpetrators had merely acted wrongly; those wronged would, among other things, have a legitimate claim against the perpetrators and they would have a basis for self-respect even in the face of their unspeakable treatment. This presumed special significance of rights has inclined many people to suppose that worlds without rights, natural or presocial moral rights in particular, would be morally impoverished in various respects. The victims of the Serbian atrocities, Douglass's Aunt Hester and other victims of chattel slavery, as well as victims of the abuse of police or religious authority, would all be left without a certain kind of moral authority were we not to view them as bearers of presocial moral rights. I shall rebut this thesis in chapter 2, and advance a normative argument against chattel slavery without supposing that slaves have a presocial moral or natural right to be free in chapter 5.

Readers can embrace my general view that social recognition of ways of acting and being treated is necessary for possessing moral rights without also embracing my normative argument against slavery. Although my defense of this argument is not half-hearted, I offer it cautiously as I wish to be somewhat pluralistic about how normativity can be salvaged save for ruling out appealing to presocial moral or natural rights for this purpose.[3] Yet I realize that some readers may be disinclined to take the social recognition step with me if they cannot imagine what our

---

[3] I first made this point in my article "Unnatural Rights," *Canadian Journal of Philosophy* 33 (2003), 49–82. And I have been criticized for remaining too neutral about this matter; see Paul Patton, "Foucault, Critique and Rights," *Critical Horizons* 6 (2005), 267–87. My argument against slavery in ch. 5 will suffice to address this objection. Yet it is important to appreciate my reasons for not wanting to build a particular normative theory into the exposition of my theory of what having moral rights amounts to.

normative capabilities would look like in the absence of such rights. My argument against slavery is meant to show that other normative resources allow us to make a rather potent argument against slavery (and other atrocities). But long before we get to that point defenders of the prevailing conception of what having moral rights amounts to must come to terms with the deficiencies of their own view.

THE PREVAILING CONCEPTION OF RIGHTS

Appeals to rights abound in moral, political, and legal discourse. Hotly debated social issues like abortion, capital punishment, gun control, same-sex marriage, pornography, reparations for African Americans, affirmative action, immigration reform, the basis of our obligations to animals, the environment, and to future generations are routinely framed and debated in the language of moral rights in particular. These debates illustrate that moral rights are ascribed not only to human beings in full possession of their rational capacities, possessing moral personality, and capable of pursuing projects, but also to human beings capable of considerably less, such as the severely mentally disabled, infants, psychopaths, the unborn, and even the dead. They also show that moral rights are ascribed to many subjects that are anything but human, such as animals, trees, ecosystems, future generations, corporations, ethnic and cultural minorities, nations, and even to works of art. By the same token we sometimes find parties to these debates rejecting the ascription of moral rights not only to animals, plants, and the unborn but to human beings as well. Of course, all of these positions can be and usually are contested. Yet any effort to contest or defend them presupposes a background theory of rights, or a conception of the conditions that must be satisfied for a subject to possess moral rights. Unfortunately parties to these debates do not always give serious thought to the nature and implications of their background theory of rights, which often impedes productive debate over the issues.

An important philosophical problem raised by positing the existence of moral rights is articulating the conditions that license their ascription. By virtue of what do we possess moral rights (if we possess any at all)? One might be tempted to frame the question in this way: what aspect of our nature or being endows us with moral rights?[4] But this presumes too much at the price of begging the main question at issue. It presumes that

---

[4] See, for example, A. I. Melden, *Rights and Persons* (Berkeley: University of California Press, 1977), ch. 6.

we have moral rights merely by virtue of having a certain nature or being constituted in a certain way. Moreover, it suggests that the real work in delineating the realm of moral rightholders lies in determining the relevant moral right-endowing nature. But these questions are not equivalent. The temptation to replace the former question with the latter must be resisted to avoid begging the main question, which leaves open the possibility of rejecting the view that we have moral rights merely by virtue of having a certain nature or being constituted in a certain way. Indeed, the main question invites two distinct general approaches to the problem: to construct a position that renders the possession of *moral* rights entirely independent of facts about a subject's social milieu or, alternatively, to construct one that denies this.

I emphasize the word "moral" to head off a possible source of misunderstanding. One might suppose that this distinction failed to note the difference between what we call moral and what we call legal (or conventional) rights, where the former are possessed entirely independently of what goes on in the social world while the latter are not. Furthermore, one might suppose that if I were aware of this distinction, then the latter position would be essentially the same as Jeremy Bentham's—that there are no moral rights, only legal (or conventional) ones. Rest assured, however, that I am well aware of the distinction and that I do not intend to adopt Bentham's view of the matter. Contrary to the conventional wisdom I intend to defend the view that moral rights possession does indeed share this social component with legal rights possession, though the former is not completely accounted for by it.

The prevailing conception of moral rights holds that the possession of moral rights is entirely independent of facts about a subject's social milieu. And there are two main ways of elaborating on the sense in which they are held to be so. One maintains that possessing a certain moral nature or constitution is necessary and sufficient for possessing unrecognized moral rights. The other appeals to the idea of a morally valid claim (to act or be treated in a certain way), and maintains that having such a morally valid claim is necessary and sufficient for possessing a moral right. As I will make clear, the two views are not unrelated. Yet those who defend the former approach spend much of their time making a case for their preferred right-conferring nature. Among the most commonly proposed candidates are included being rational, being sentient, having moral personality, being a project pursuer, and being human, among others.

Yet both approaches presume that the possession of moral rights can be accounted for without making reference to social setting or, more specifically, without taking account of whether the subject has been afforded any form of social recognition. As one proponent of the prevailing view puts the matter: "Moral rights (in the relevant sense) are rights whose existence depends on principle and fact, not on social recognition or enforcement."[5] After exposing shortcomings of both ways of explicating the moral rights without recognition view—and thereby undermining the prevailing conception—I develop and defend my conception in chapter 3, a conception that links moral rights with social recognition.

RIGHTS AND RECOGNITION

The widespread and largely uncritical acceptance of the prevailing conception of moral rights is understandable given the longstanding and very familiar role that such rights play in political and moral discourse. For many, these rights are valuable normative tools for evaluating, guiding, and justifying individual and group conduct. When Robert Nozick begins *Anarchy, State, and Utopia* by affirming the existence and value of individual rights and by posing the question of how much room such rights leave for state action, he concisely captures the primary function of moral rights within political philosophy—to mark the scope and limits of political authority.[6]

A defining element of the prevailing conception (embraced by libertarians and nonlibertarians alike) is that moral rights are taken to be rights that individuals can have against the state, possessed prior to legislation or other conventional practices or institutions. Hence they are sometimes characterized as natural rights, in the sense that they are not the product of legislation, convention, or hypothetical contract. The so-called naturalness of moral rights is crucial. It accounts for why these rights can serve as "political trumps" or "side constraints," which can be invoked to challenge state action or inaction that imposes a loss or injury on an individual in the name of a collective goal or in the name of legal or otherwise conventional rights. Presumably moral rights could not serve this seemingly indispensable purpose if their existence depended upon social practices of any kind.

The normative value of moral rights thus understood undoubtedly accounts for why so many people take the existence of such rights for granted, and get on to the "real" business of exploring the implications of

[5] David Lyons, *Rights, Welfare, and Mill's Moral Theory* (Oxford University Press, 1994), p. 3.
[6] Nozick, *Anarchy, State, and Utopia*, p. ix.

having them. Nozick takes the existence of natural rights for granted and proceeds to defend the need for a minimal state—limited to the narrow functions of protection against force, theft, fraud, and the enforcement of contracts—to guarantee respect for these rights. But he is not the only one to proceed in this fashion. After acknowledging that the prevailing conception of moral rights has not been universally accepted and that some philosophers (most notably Bentham) have rejected natural rights and opted for a positivist conception of rights, Ronald Dworkin maintains that a positivist conception of rights is philosophically unorthodox and that politicians (and others) appeal to prior moral rights all the time to justify what they want to do. Consequently, in *Taking Rights Seriously*, he opts not to defend the thesis that individuals do have such rights against their government but instead to take this for granted and explore the implications of having them, arguing, contrary to Nozick, that the most fundamental of rights, namely a right to equal concern and respect, demands much more state action than libertarians allow.[7]

Rejecting the orthodoxy, I refuse to take the prevailing conception of moral rights for granted despite the seemingly irreproachable utility of relying on natural rights to evaluate, guide, and justify individual, group, and government conduct. We are long overdue for a conception that takes a wider view of the historical facts. From this vantage point a fruitful point of departure for philosophical reflection on the source and value of moral rights is consideration of the everyday social world as it is and has been historically rather than as we would like or hope it to be. To be sure, this is not to recommend that the philosopher must completely defer to the historian, the social scientist, the economist, or the legal theorist. But it does suggest that her theoretical philosophical output runs a greater risk of being dismissed as irrelevant or insignificant if she totally disregards or is ignorant of what these empirically informed scholars tell us about the past and present realities of the social world. And many of these scholars tell us that appealing to the concept of race has been (and continues to be) a way of classifying individuals in the social world, and that racism is still a pervasive social reality in the United States and abroad. Although we must certainly admit that there are conflicting interpretations of these social realities, some of these interpretations can nonetheless provide inspiration and guidance for philosophical reflection.

---

[7] Dworkin, *Taking Rights Seriously*, p. 184.

For instance, taking our cue from an observation made by John Rawls in *A Theory of Justice,* we could opt to embrace the prevailing conception and assume that individuals do indeed possess moral rights solely by virtue of some fact about how they are constituted, say, by virtue of having moral personality. And from here we can infer that all individuals have moral rights, and have always had them, since no races lack, or have ever been thought to lack, this attribute.[8] Alternatively, taking a wider view of the historical facts demands that we take account of the fact that some individuals and designated racial groups have indeed been taken to lack this attribute, and that this provided a philosophical justification for constructing conventional practices in which these groups could be treated in certain ways predicated on the assumption that they were not moral rightholders. Of course, one could simply view this as an occasion to select another attribute as the relevant right-conferring property, perhaps one that is thought to be universally shared and minimally sufficient for possessing moral rights. But I shall take it as an opportunity to call the prevailing conception of moral rights into question. More specifically, I shall draw on past and present realities pertaining to race and racism not to reject the concept of a moral right altogether but to advance an alternative conception of what having such rights amounts to that rejects the naturalness of such rights in favor of a positivist grounding.

As we have seen, according to the orthodoxy moral rights are taken to differ from legal and other conventional rights whose existence is not tied to the nature of subjects but is instead the product of human design. In defending the unorthodox thesis that moral rights are products of social recognition I am rejecting the conventional wisdom that subjects possess moral rights merely in virtue of their natures. So my objective is not to deny that subjects possess moral rights. Rather it is to propose and defend an alternative account of what possessing these rights comes to. And what is distinctive about this account, which I shall refer to as rights externalism, is that it assigns certain social practices an essential role in grounding moral rights, or, more precisely, in accounting for what is required for having such rights.

According to a weak interpretation of this thesis, to say that certain social practices play an essential role in grounding moral rights is merely to say that we cannot effectively enjoy the moral rights that we already possess independently of these social practices unless these social practices

---

[8] John Rawls, *A Theory of Justice* (Cambridge, MA: Belknap Press, 1971), p. 506.

are in place. On this interpretation the relevant social practices are necessary for the exercise or enjoyment of moral rights though not for their existence or possession. According to a strong interpretation the relevant social practices are not merely essential for the exercise or enjoyment of moral rights; they are essential for the very existence or possession of moral rights. Were these social practices not to obtain subjects who merely had morally valid claims to act or be treated in a certain way would not possess moral rights, though they would indeed possess morally valid claims. The point is that more than moral validity is required to convert a claim into a right. Insofar as I embrace the strong interpretation I contend that there is a conceptual connection between moral rights possession and the instantiation of certain social practice conditions that include the authoritative social recognition and enforcement of morally valid claims. Hence the rights recognition thesis is that social practices play an essential role in grounding moral rights in this strong sense.

It is imperative to appreciate the way in which this position is very different from Bentham's, one of the most influential critics of natural rights, who held that the postulation of such rights was both logically absurd and morally pernicious.[9] For Bentham neither God, nor natural law, nor rational nature as such, was the source of rights. On the contrary, he held that all bona fide rights were products of positive law.[10] Were we to accept this constraint we could pursue the extreme option of denying that moral rights (as opposed to merely conventional rights) are bona fide rights insofar as they are not products of positive law, or we could pursue the less extreme and more attractive option of rethinking what possessing moral rights must amount to if they are to satisfy this constraint. Because I favor this latter strategy I take a slight modification of Bentham's constraint as my point of departure with an eye toward developing and defending a conception that assigns certain social practices an essential role in grounding moral rights. A consequence of the thesis that moral rights are products of social recognition is that possessing moral rights is similar to possessing legal and other conventional rights in that social

---

[9] Jeremy Bentham, in John Browing (ed.), *The Works of Jeremy Bentham* (Edinburgh: William Tait, 1843), vol. III, p. 221. For illuminating reconstructions of Bentham's critique of natural rights, see H. L. A. Hart, *Essays on Bentham: Studies in Jurisprudence and Political Theory* (Oxford: Clarendon Press, 1982), ch. 4; John Deigh, "Rights and the Authority of Law," *The University of Chicago Law Review* 51 (1984), 668–99; and Sumner, *The Moral Foundation of Rights*, ch. 4.

[10] Bentham, *Works*, III, p. 221. Several commentators on Bentham's work have rightly pointed out that this view is too strong, since nonlegal conventional practices can also give rise to rights that are not natural. For instance, see Hart, *Essays on Bentham*, p. 84 and Sumner, *The Moral Foundation of Rights*, p. 113. My modification of Bentham's constraint accommodates this insight.

practices play an essential role in grounding them as well. However, it is imperative to appreciate that where moral rights are at issue, another condition must be satisfied so that this social constraint is necessary but not sufficient for moral rights possession.

To be sure, my solution to the moral rights ascription problem will encounter spirited and perhaps even hostile resistance. As suggested earlier, the most serious resistance will come from those who are loath to give up the critical normative power typically associated with a peculiar understanding of the source and value of moral rights: by taking moral rights to be possessed independently of whether or not they have been afforded any sort of social recognition we can call upon them to make moral criticisms of both individual and social conduct not recognizing or acknowledging these rights. In this regard rights are alleged to constitute indispensable normative weapons for championing the value of individual persons. Hence advocates of this objection will conclude: to the extent that taking some sort of social recognition to be a necessary condition of possessing a moral right rules out this invaluable normative use of such rights it must ultimately be rejected for fear that we would be left morally impoverished.

However, this conclusion is somewhat extreme unless of course one can argue that moral rights so understood are the only normative resource at our disposal, that all other normative resources are really moral rights-based at bottom, or that they are the best available normative resource for critical purposes. But indisputable arguments for these claims have not been offered. Nevertheless, moral rights do indeed serve this critical role for many people in their normative theorizing. Hence to allay this worry and thereby neutralize a major source of resistance to a social recognition-based account of moral rights, it is incumbent upon me to propose an alternative means of salvaging normativity, which I do in chapter 5. But first, in chapter 4, I call into question the presumption that appealing to presocial moral rights is the best ideal for critical purposes by reflecting upon the dual legacy of rights, thus conceived, to both attack and defend black chattel slavery and post-bellum black subordination.

TAKING RACE AND RACISM SERIOUSLY

Reflection on the social realities of race and racism provides a main source of inspiration for my rejection of the prevailing view and for my preferred alternative. Although carrying out my primary objectives does not require me to be an expert on these matters, or even to provide an overview of recent philosophical treatments of race and racism, I do wish to identify two related justifications for expounding an alternative conception of what possessing moral rights amounts to. This alternative conception will reflect a deeper appreciation for the past and present social realities of race and racism than does the prevailing conception.[11] The first pertains to the interplay between race and rights in antebellum American political thought and practice, and the second to a general methodological orientation within contemporary political philosophy to take race and racism more seriously for purposes of philosophical reflection.

During an early nineteenth-century debate in the House of Representatives over whether Missouri would join the union as a slave or free state an antislavery advocate made the following appeal:

> you have proclaimed, in the Declaration of Independence, "That all men are created equal; that they are endowed by their Creator with certain inalienable rights; that amongst these are life, liberty, and the pursuit of happiness;" and yet you have slaves in your country.[12]

However, by the time of the Missouri controversy America was far enough removed from the revolutionary era for this appeal to be ineffective. Not only was Missouri admitted to the union as a slave state; the Missouri legislature was permitted to bar the immigration of free blacks and mulattos into the state.

Although this appeal to the philosophy of natural rights caused significant disruptions in the slave system just before and after the American War of Independence from Great Britain, several decades into the nineteenth century defenders of slavery were no longer largely reduced to conceding that slavery was incompatible with this philosophy, nor to arguing for slavery as a matter of practical necessity. Many of them began to argue more boldly that slavery was perfectly compatible with the normative ideals expressed in the Declaration of Independence and the preamble to the US Constitution. Arguably the most lucid and memorable summary of this widely held proslavery perspective came several

---

[11] For several useful collections containing current philosophical thought on race and racism, see Susan E. Babbitt and Sue Campbell (eds.), *Racism and Philosophy* (Cornell University Press, 1999); Bernard Boxill (ed.), *Race and Racism* (Oxford University Press, 2001); Michael P. Levin and Tamas Pataki (eds.), *Racism in Mind* (Cornell University Press, 2004); and Andrew Valls (ed.), *Race and Racism in Modern Philosophy* (Cornell University Press, 2005).

[12] Philip A. Klinkner and Rogers M. Smith, *The Unsteady March: The Rise and Decline of Racial Equality in America* (University of Chicago Press, 1999), p. 133.

decades after the Missouri controversy in the infamous *Dred Scott* decision, where Supreme Court Chief Justice Roger Taney maintained:

it is too clear for dispute, that the enslaved African race were not intended to be included, and formed no part of the people who framed and adopted this declaration; for if the language, as understood in that day, would embrace them, the conduct of the distinguished men who framed the Declaration of Independence would have been utterly and flagrantly inconsistent with the principles they asserted . . . Yet the men who framed this declaration were great men . . . incapable of asserting principles inconsistent with those on which they were acting. They perfectly understood the meaning of the language they used, and how it would be understood by others; and they knew that it would not in any part of the civilized world be supposed to embrace the negro race . . .[13]

Hence one of the first and most pressing problems the newly formed United States of America faced was the problem of reconciling its commitment to natural rights with the practice of slavery and racial subordination. Abolitionists appealed to the natural rights of slaves to critique slavery and ultimately to argue for its demise, while proslavery theorists appealed to these same rights to defend slavery. Recent scholarship on race and racism in various disciplines gives us reason to reconsider the dual legacy of natural rights as a conceptual instrument for combating racial subordination as well as for defending it.[14] More specifically, this ever growing body of scholarship gives us reason to question whether so-called natural rights have been the best ideal for safeguarding the value of persons (humanity), where racial ideology and social practice have conspired to reject the personhood (or humanity) of individuals falling under certain socially constructed categories, with race and gender being the most politically salient. Upon a closer examination, which I will undertake in chapter 4, we shall find that the prevailing conception of moral rights was equally well suited to justifying slavery and to dispelling the apparent anomaly between a thoroughgoing commitment to the existence of natural rights and the practice of slavery and racial subordination.

---

[13] *Dred Scott* v. *Sandford* 60 U.S. 393 (1857). Reprinted in Derrick A. Bell (ed.), *Civil Rights: Leading Cases* (Boston: Little Brown & Company, 1980), pp. 1–25.

[14] See, for example, Rogers M. Smith, *Civic Ideals: Conflicting Visions of Citizenship in US History* (Yale University Press, 1997); Winthrop Jordan, *White Over Black: American Attitudes Toward the Negro, 1550–1812* (University of North Carolina Press, 1968); George M. Frederickson, *The Black Image in the White Mind: The Debate on Afro-American Character and Destiny, 1817–1914* (New York: Harper and Row, 1971); and Charles W. Mills, *Blackness Visible: Essays on Philosophy and Race* (Cornell University Press, 1998).

Hence both then and now the social realities of race and racism in America provide a catalyst for contesting the meaning and implications of the American creed that all men are created equal and have natural rights to life, liberty, and the pursuit of happiness. Therefore it is fitting that we take these realities into account if we are interested in arriving at a more mundane and historically sensitive conception of what possessing moral rights amounts to. One of the things we stand to gain if we accept that what moral rights we have is, at least in part, a matter of how things are in the social realm rather than how we wish them to be is a deeper appreciation for the importance of eternal vigilance in securing and safeguarding all of our rights, including our moral ones.

Within contemporary political philosophy, especially among philosophers of color and an increasing number of Anglo American philosophers, there is a powerful trend of criticizing orthodox political philosophy for not taking race and the history and practice of white supremacy and black subordination in the United States seriously as material for informing and enriching philosophical reflection about core problems and questions in philosophy. It is widely and rightly assumed that if these matters were taken seriously then political philosophy would be transformed in important respects. For one thing, this transformation would force the expansion of the canon within political philosophy to include African American political thinkers (e.g. Frederick Douglass, Martin R. Delany, W. E. B. Du Bois, Anna Julia Cooper, Booker T. Washington, and others). Fortunately, there is a growing body of scholarship within contemporary philosophy that has taken up this task. For too long mainstream Anglo American political philosophy has ignored the valuable contributions that these thinkers make not only to African American political philosophy but also to political philosophy in general.

In addition, as matters of race and racism come to the forefront of political philosophy, our understanding of traditional political categories (e.g. democracy, justice, freedom, equality, political authority, political legitimacy, political solidarity, and so on), traditional problems and traditional modes of analysis will have to be rethought. It is widely assumed that the concept of rights is the most important category in Anglo American political philosophy. Accordingly, my contribution to this important and ongoing collective transformation within political philosophy is to articulate and defend a way of rethinking the source and value of moral rights that takes the past and present social realities of race and racism seriously for the purposes of philosophical reflection. The end result is rejecting the discourse of natural rights and defending instead a socially oriented conception of moral rights that takes moral rights possession to be partly a matter of individuals being afforded a certain sort of social recognition.

I am well aware of the fact that the concept of race has come under attack in recent years, with critics arguing against it both as a viable empirical category and on the grounds of it being morally pernicious and politically divisive.[15] Of course, many others still argue for conserving the concept of race for purposes of political solidarity even in the face of criticisms of the empirical viability of the concept.[16] But my purposes in this book do not require me to take a stand on this broader debate over the viability and utility of the concept of race, though I will take it for granted that the problem of racial discrimination is still a serious problem in the United States and elsewhere. So in what sense does race and racism matter for my purposes? My methodological orientation is to defend a solution to the moral rights ascription problem that reflects a high level of "race consciousness," as it were, consciousness of the way in which the concept of race, racial thinking, and practices of entrenching racial supremacy and subordination have shaped past and present social realities. And one can certainly adopt this orientation without waiting for the debate over the viability and utility of the concept of race to be settled.

TAKING INDIVIDUALS SERIOUSLY

The philosopher Cornel West makes a perceptive observation about the identity of black philosophers that provides the broader context for my methodological orientation. He contends that "[black philosophers] read history seriously and voraciously."[17] Moreover, our work tends to embody forms of cultural criticism and political engagement, and often traverses and cuts across disciplinary divisions in seeking sources that serve our philosophizing. While this observation certainly applies to philosophers who are not of African descent, it accurately characterizes the intellectual orientation of numerous contemporary black philosophers, many of

---

[15] For leading advocates of the philosophical case against conserving race for political purposes, see Kwame Anthony Appiah, *In My Father's House: Africa in the Philosophy of Culture* (Oxford University Press, 1992), and Tommie Shelby, *We Who Are Dark: The Philosophical Foundations of Black Solidarity* (Harvard University Press, 2005).

[16] For leading advocates of the case for conserving race for political purposes, see Lucius T. Outlaw, Jr., *On Race and Philosophy* (New York: Routledge, 1996), and Linda Martín Alcoff, *Visible Identities: Race, Gender, and the Self* (Oxford University Press, 2005).

[17] Cornel West, "Philosophy and the Urban Underclass," in Bill E. Lawson (ed.), *The Underclass Question* (Philadelphia: Temple University Press, 1992), p. 192.

whom bring aspects of the black experience (as it has been contemplated within various disciplines) to bear on addressing various philosophical problems. And it certainly captures my intellectual orientation. For as I have made clear, the theory of rights that I articulate and defend in this book is inspired by serious critical engagement with the past and present experiences of African Americans in a country where rights, race, and racism share the same legacy. Indeed, this project could not get off the ground were it not for taking seriously interdisciplinary and what West calls "dedisciplinary" modes of knowledge.

That said, some critics might express surprise that a self-described student of history has managed to overlook an aspect of the history of philosophy that pertains to my project at least as much as the history of race and racism when it comes to thinking about the nature and value of rights—namely, the history of the liberal political tradition within philosophy. It might be objected that political philosophers conversant in this tradition would appreciate the seriously unorthodox nature of an attempt to ground all rights in some form of social recognition. In particular, they would realize that this was an inherently "illiberal" endeavor. So if offering a theory that is compatible with this longstanding philosophical tradition is a constraint on any theory of rights, then a recognition-based theory of moral rights cannot be acceptable.

Although I cannot offer a complete reply to this objection here, as it would require another book to address the question of what being a liberal entails, I shall explain why the objection is misguided. In this section I address the following concern, viz. that rejecting natural rights, or denying that individuals possess certain rights prior to all forms of social recognition, renders us unable to capture the deeper normative significance of the liberal political philosophical tradition. In addressing this concern I will make quite clear that I have not ignored the significance of the liberal tradition within political philosophy. On the contrary, I have closely followed recent scholarship in political theory pertaining to the history of liberalism that calls our attention to thinkers within this grand tradition, such as Thomas Hill Green, Bernard Bosanquet, David George Ritchie, Henry Jones, and John Atkinson Hobson, not typically studied in philosophy departments, to provide the historical orientation for the rethinking of the source and value of rights that I offer in this book. And this is clear evidence of my taking history seriously—not just the history of race and racism but the history of liberal political philosophy as well.

Liberalism is widely heralded as a political tradition that takes individuals seriously. Indeed, proponents and critics alike take this to be one of its defining characteristics, although there has been considerable debate concerning both when liberalism came to be a distinct tradition of political thought and how (and whether) liberalism can be defined. Some scholars claim that strictly speaking the term "liberalism" should not be used before the early nineteenth century, while others locate its first use in the second quarter of the nineteenth century.[18] Nevertheless, there is broad agreement that the roots of liberalism can be traced at least as far back as the seventeenth century to the English Whig political tradition and John Locke's philosophical expression of its core themes in his political writings, most notably the *Two Treatises of Government* and *Letters of Toleration*.

Obviously there is good reason for tracing the roots of liberalism back to the seventeenth century. In Locke's political philosophy we find crucial elements of early liberal political thought; most notably, we find the doctrines of individualism and natural rights as well as the presumption that natural rights can be used to articulate the precise nature of the relationship between individuals and political authority. The term "natural rights liberalism" has been used to capture this early liberal perspective; however, I shall use the designation classical liberalism. For my purposes, classical liberalism represents an amalgamation of the doctrine of individualism (the emphasis on individuals as the fundamental unit of political value), the doctrine of natural rights (the view that individuals possess certain presocial natural rights that mark the scope and limits of political authority), and the distinctive manner in which these doctrines are blended to articulate a certain conception of what taking individuals seriously amounts to that continues to dominate mainstream Anglo American social and political philosophy.[19] The upshot of this view is that individuals are taken seriously when (and only when) they are viewed as bearers of (negative) natural rights that are possessed prior to and independently of all social relations and that are taken to establish the limits of both state and individual conduct.

But classical liberalism is just one of a family of liberalisms. And while Locke, Bentham, John Stuart Mill, Herbert Spencer, T. H. Green, Leonard Trelawny Hobhouse, and Isaiah Berlin have all been characterized as

---

[18] For the former claim, see Robert Leach, *British Political Ideologies* (London: Philip Allan, 1991), p. 56. For the latter, see William Sweet, *Idealism and Rights: The Social Ontology of Human Rights in the Political Thought of Bernard Bosanquet* (Lanham: University Press of America, 1997), p. 10, n. 2.

[19] See e.g. Nozick, *Anarchy, State, and Utopia*; Dworkin, *Taking Rights Seriously*; Joel Feinberg, *Rights, Justice, and the Bounds of Liberty* (Princeton University Press, 1980); and Lomasky, *Persons, Rights, and the Moral Community*.

liberals, all of these political philosophers cannot be deemed natural rights liberals or classical liberals. Liberalism has undergone various transformations during its long history, partly in response to changing social and political circumstances. While we must remain vigilant against anachronistic interpretations of the history of liberalism, resisting the temptation to select certain figures as most central to the tradition or to appraise certain ideas as having the greatest importance, we certainly cannot avoid generalizations altogether in articulating what makes the family of liberalisms part of a single genus.[20] Accordingly, if we follow the widely shared consensus that the roots of liberalism can be traced back to Locke, then we must note how individualism and the natural rights philosophy were combined in early liberal political thought to articulate a certain understanding of what taking individuals seriously amounted to. From this early liberal perspective individuals were taken to possess certain natural rights in prepolitical society, but since the enjoyment of these rights was rendered insecure due to various inconveniences, e.g. want of a common judge to determine what rights individuals had and to enforce and adjudicate conflicts of rights, individuals were compelled to form a social contract to establish political authority for the sole purpose of making the enjoyment of their prepolitical natural rights more secure than it could be in the absence of government.[21]

From this starting point we gain a general and peculiar perspective on the liberal tradition as it moved from Locke through to late nineteenth- and early twentieth-century political thinkers; this gives us a plausible basis for classifying the various strands of liberalism as part of a single genus. Each strand offers us a general conception of what taking individuals seriously amounts to, variously emphasizing prepolitical natural rights (classical liberalism), utility and the greatest good (utilitarianism), socially grounded rights and the common good (new liberalism), positive rights and active state intervention (welfare liberalism), negative rights and minimal state intervention (libertarianism), and equality (egalitarian liberalism). Yet the influence of classical liberalism remains strong in contemporary political philosophy notwithstanding the fact that many strands of liberalism are in play. Contemporary understandings of what it

---

[20] For more on this point, see Avital Simhony and David Weinstein, "Introduction," in Simhony and Weinstein (eds.), *The New Liberalism: Reconciling Liberty and Community* (Cambridge University Press, 2001), p. 8.

[21] John Locke, in Peter Laslett (ed.), *Two Treatises of Government* (Cambridge University Press, 1960).

means to take individuals seriously are largely identified with philosophers who come closest to holding the classical liberal position. But be that as it may, only an anachronistic understanding of the liberal tradition prevents us from seeing that within the family of liberalisms not all liberals emphasize natural rights and nor do they all emphasize the value of the individual at the expense of, or in opposition to, community and the common good. And most importantly for present purposes, not all liberals maintain that taking individuals seriously requires the postulation of negative natural rights that exist prior to political society and all social relations.[22]

To be sure some critics will contend that individuals are not really being taken seriously unless they are viewed as bearers of natural rights that are possessed prior to and independently of all social relations. But this is merely one of two great dogmas of classical liberalism. The other dogma is that the rights individuals do possess are purely negative in nature. A commendable exception to this unfortunate tendency to understand liberalism predominantly through the lenses of classical liberalism can be found in the work of an increasing number of political philosophers and political theorists who propose that we view the liberal tradition through the lenses of the mid- to late nineteenth- and earlier twentieth-century British political philosophers, most notably Green, Ritchie, and Hobhouse. Among the valuable insights gained by turning our attention to these thinkers, especially Green, is that we can capture the common core of liberal theories that individuals are to be taken seriously but without taking individuals to be bearers of rights that preexist all forms of community and are purely negative in nature. Thus we find historical precedent within the tradition for rejecting the two dogmas of classical liberalism. Although new liberalism and classical liberalism agree that individuals ought to be taken seriously, they offer us very different perspectives on what this amounts to; the latter assigns presocial natural rights a prominent role in the explanation while the former does not.[23] Furthermore, the latter is generally loath to posit the existence of positive rights but the former is not.

---

[22] For an illuminating comparative discussion of liberal individualism in Bentham, Mill, Spencer, and Bosanquet, see Sweet, *Idealism and Rights*, ch. 1.

[23] Michael Freeden contends that until the nineteenth century liberalism was first and foremost associated with the doctrine of natural rights. See Freeden, *The New Liberalism: An Ideology of Social Reform* (Oxford: Clarendon Press, 1978), pp. 22–3.

More specifically, Green demonstrates that new liberals can also embrace "natural" rights as evidence that they too take individuals seriously provided that they rethink what having such rights amounts to. In Green's political philosophy, as developed in his posthumously published *Lectures on the Principles of Political Obligation*, his influential new liberal attempt to reconcile respect for individuals as such with emphasis on the value of community and the common good takes shape around a rejection of what he calls "prior natural rights"[24] and around the articulation of a social recognition-based conception of rights, as well as a serious commitment to the existence of positive rights and freedom. As will become apparent as the argument of this book is developed, Green's political philosophy has inspired my defense of rights externalism in many important respects.[25] But for now I simply wish to make the point that articulating what it means to take individuals seriously and rethinking the source and value of rights are mutually supporting philosophical endeavors. The former opens up conceptual space for a social recognition-based conception of rights, and rethinking rights in this manner undermines classical liberalism's monopoly on how to conceptualize what taking individuals seriously amounts to.

The main themes animating Green's political thought include the importance of self-development and its relationship to the common good, the moral function of the state to provide the preconditions for this development (which is taken to be indispensable for securing the common good), the development and defense of a social as opposed to atomistic conception of rights, and above all a preoccupation with the themes of a social self and community in articulating a more dynamic and less dualistic conception of the relationship between individuals and political authority.[26] Hence if classical liberalism can be broadly characterized as being preoccupied with individuals as the main unit of political value, then Green's version of liberalism can be broadly characterized as preoccupied with breaking down the individual–community dualism by

---

[24] T. H. Green, in P. Harris and J. Morrow (eds.), *Lectures on the Principles of Political Obligation* (Cambridge University Press, 1986), §23.

[25] Here I owe a great debt to Rex Martin for sparking my interest in Green and in the British Idealist philosophical tradition more generally.

[26] For studies that pay special attention to the British Idealists' preoccupation with the social self and community, see Sandra M. Den Otter, *British Idealism and Social Explanation: A Study of Late Victorian Thought* (Oxford: Clarendon Press, 1996), Sweet, *Idealism and Rights*, and A. J. M. Milne, *The Social Philosophy of English Idealism* (London: George Allen & Unwin, 1962).

placing the value of community and individual on equal footing and by demonstrating the interdependence of the two in political society.[27]

It has been argued that the various social and economic circumstances of *fin de siècle* Victorian Britain provided the impetus for a broader rejection of the individual/society dualism in much British political thought of the time; chief among these circumstances were the forces of industrialization, urbanization, poverty, depression, dislocation, and crime. These forces conspired to create worries that free market individualism as defended by the likes of Spencer and other *laissez-faire* classical liberals—leaving individuals to fend for themselves in a modern industrialized capitalist society and being guaranteed societal protection only from loss of life, liberty, or property—had destroyed traditional forms of association and the stability of social conditions. This created nostalgia for lost community and a preoccupation with underscoring the interrelatedness of the well-being of individuals and the well-being of society.[28]

Thus, broadly speaking, these circumstances contributed to a progressive, and many would say, radical revision of liberal philosophical thought that later generations would use to defend even more radical reform of liberal social policy and a more interventionist state to deal with the pressing social problems of turn-of-the-century Victorian Britain. This deconstruction of the individual–society dualism, to which Green made important contributions, supplied a philosophical justification for a greater role of the state in social and economic life to secure individual welfare that went far beyond the state's purely protective role under classical liberalism and thereby paved the way for what we would now describe as the modern welfare state in which the promotion of positive as well as negative rights are taken to fall within the proper authority of the truly liberal state.

We see, therefore, that while Green's political philosophy is not exclusively individualist insofar as it takes community and common good seriously, it does not eschew liberalism's emphasis on the value of

---

[27] In this regard, Green and other Idealists take some inspiration from Hegel, which accounts for why they have been characterized as "British Hegelians." Peter Robbins, *The British Hegelians 1875–1925* (New York: Garland Press, 1982).

[28] Den Otter, *British Idealism and Social Explanation*, p. 5 and pp. 149–50. This nostalgia for lost community and attempt to get contemporary liberalism to place greater weight on its importance survives in contemporary communitarians, who have inherited the Idealist and new liberal legacies; see Alasdair MacIntyre, *After Virtue: A Study of Moral Theory* (University of Notre Dame Press, 1981); Michael Sandel, *Liberalism and the Limits of Justice* (Cambridge University Press, 1982); and Charles Taylor, *Sources of the Self: The Making of Modern Identity* (Cambridge University Press, 1989).

individuals. In fact, I propose that by taking community and common good seriously he affords us a conception of what it means to take individuals seriously that departs substantially from the classical liberal conception. For present purposes one important difference is that we see that liberals can express their commitment to taking individuals seriously in the language of rights without embracing classical liberalism's understanding of natural rights. To be sure, we will want reasons for rejecting this understanding and embracing the alternative. But these reasons are not difficult to come by.

As observed above, according to classical liberalism individuals are taken seriously when viewed as bearers of natural rights that mark the scope and limits of political authority. Both past and contemporary liberals suggest that we simply cannot take individuals seriously without attributing presocial rights to them (whatever we choose to call these rights). But many liberals routinely ignore, dismiss, or simply do not see the force of ongoing critiques of such rights, many of which can be traced back to the scathing criticisms of the doctrine of natural rights by Jeremy Bentham, Edmund Burke, Karl Marx, and D. G. Ritchie. One familiar line of criticism made by contemporary communitarians and others is that rights are too individualist. They encourage us to think of ourselves as apart from and threatened by a society, state, or government that is constantly seeking to intrude upon or invade our rights. The adversarial spirit wrought by rights blinds us to the extent and importance of our reliance on others. We fail to realize how we depend upon communities that not only give meaning to our lives but also partly constitute our social identities. We are more focused on what is owed to us than we are on our responsibilities to others and the need to act virtuously with the good of community in mind.

One strategy for dealing with this line of criticism would be for liberals to reject rights altogether and place nonrights-based normative concepts at the center of social, moral, and political thought, as some critics have urged. These critics contend that because liberal individualism is to be rejected for ignoring community, sociability, the common good, and the like, and because liberal individualism is usually cashed out in terms of rights, then liberals must ultimately reject rights as well. But abandoning rights would be difficult given that they are so deeply ensconced in the liberal tradition. Moreover, it would require considerable intellectual dexterity for liberals to totally abandon a concept that has been intimately associated with the view that individuals matter and must be taken seriously—a cornerstone of liberal thinking. Hence one way to frame the challenge that the critique of rights poses for liberals is this. How to accommodate communitarian concerns with community, the common good, and sociability within a liberal framework while remaining committed to individual rights? How can liberals articulate a conception of what taking individuals seriously amounts to without subscribing to the doctrine of presocial natural rights?[29]

In keeping with the overall concern with themes of sociability, we see in Green and other late nineteenth-century British liberal progressives a social conception of taking individuals seriously. Maintaining that classical liberalism's conception of what it means to take individuals seriously was impoverished because industrialization and accompanying social problems suggested that we must do more to take individuals seriously than merely leave them alone and respect their presocial natural rights, these liberal philosophers rejected the model of the autonomous, unencumbered individual and argued for a conception of the individual embedded within a social milieu.[30] And the resulting social conception of the self brought with it the idea of an individual whose value was not tied to having natural rights but to having capacities that could only be developed by being socially recognized in the form of rights, which the state had the responsibility for maintaining, promoting, and enforcing.

Hence, as one theorist aptly observes, according to these thinkers, "true individualism" is the self-realization of one's capacities in the context of society.[31] Rejecting atomistic individualism, they endorsed a kind of holism that has been described as "relational organicism," which embraces "the interdependence of the self-development of individuals, the interdependence of individuals and society, and the mutual recognition of each as a personality."[32] Relational organism characterizes the manner by which Green and others moved from atomistic individualism to social individualism and thereby reconceptualized liberalism's conception of what it meant to take individuals seriously. On this socially oriented conception, social relations are constitutive of individual identity and

---

[29] Compare this formulation to similar ones. For example, Sweet, *Idealism and Rights*, p. 242; Den Otter, *British Idealism and Social Explanation*, p. 204; Simhony and Weinstein, "Introduction," *The New Liberalism*, p. 17; and Rex Martin, "T. H. Green on Individual Rights and the Common Good," *The New Liberalism*, p. 67.

[30] For an illuminating discussion of idealism, individualism, and social ontology, see Sweet, *Idealism and Rights*, pp. 236ff.

[31] David Boucher, *The British Idealists* (Cambridge University Press, 1997), p. xxiv.

[32] Simhony and Weinstein, "Introduction," *The New Liberalism*, p. 19.

well-being, the value of self-development is a common good, and the state has the moral function of helping to realize this good by removing obstacles that would impede self-development.[33]

Rethinking what taking individuals seriously amounts to in a social manner clears conceptual space for rethinking rights along a social dimension. This is the key to answering the challenge of articulating a conception of what taking individuals seriously amounts to without subscribing to the doctrine of presocial natural rights. Green is arguably the greatest source of inspiration for answering this challenge within the liberal tradition of political philosophy, since he supplied the first systematic socially oriented conception of rights. Being liberal, he and other Idealists wanted to retain rights; however, they also wanted to bring their understanding of rights into line with their alternative social vision of what taking individuals seriously amounted to—rejecting atomistic individualism in favor of social individualism as part of their overall effort to place community and society on equal footing with individuals in their social and political thought.

Perhaps the most compelling evidence of Green's attempt to reconcile individual liberty and the value of community in his political philosophy lies in his theory of rights, which takes social recognition to be necessary for any right properly understood. And herein lies the key to meeting the challenge posed by the critique of rights. If taking individuals seriously amounts to seeing them as members of community, and rights are to be accommodated rather than discarded, then one way to do this is by taking rights to be constituted by social recognition. By imposing a social constraint on rights possession, Green affords us a theory of rights that departs substantially from classical liberalism's presocial natural rights conception. By making social recognition a necessary element of rights possession, Green explicitly rejected classical liberalism's view that individuals possessed presocial natural rights in a state of nature that were retained in political society and that marked the scope and limits of political authority.

Obviously, proponents of such a theory of rights need to work out the details of this social recognition element, which I shall do in this book. But suffice it to say for now that Green affords us ample philosophical resources to answer the challenge of how liberals can articulate a

---

[33] These ideas are fleshed out in my normative argument against slavery in ch. 5.

conception of what taking individuals seriously amounts to without subscribing to the doctrine of presocial natural rights.

Of course, proponents of such a conception must argue for the social recognition component and this is no easy matter.[34] Although I will not attempt to develop this particular argument in more detail, let me sketch a rather general argument for embracing the connection between rights and recognition that I find somewhat compelling. Classical liberalism certainly provides one expression of what taking individuals seriously entails. But new liberalism provides another, which is more attractive insofar as it constitutes a more judicious attempt to reconcile liberty and community. Many contemporary liberals admit that this is a worthwhile pursuit, as countless efforts to defend liberalism against communitarian critics suggest. I suppose that some contemporary liberals will want to resist reconciliation by holding hard and fast to atomistic individualism, but this certainly goes against the current of much of liberal and nonliberal political thinking, where considerations of community and other civic virtues loom large and suggest that atomistic individualism is outdated. A Green-style theory of rights that joins rights with recognition would seem to be more attractive for the same reasons. If the general theory of rights is not updated with the introduction of the social thesis then it appears that new liberalism cannot yield an account of taking individuals seriously. To make good on the claim that it yields such an account the social thesis must run all the way through to the theory of rights.

Let me conclude this section by saying why I take the foregoing argument for retrieving the new liberal social conception of rights to be partly historical and partly normative. Presocial natural rights have been espoused by canonical figures in the liberal tradition to articulate and underscore the value of individuals (e.g. Locke, Spencer, Mill). Defenders of such rights who invoke these thinkers all too often suggest that individuals are not or cannot be taken seriously if they are not viewed as bearers of presocial natural rights. While they may disagree over the precise explanation of the source of these rights, they commonly agree on the general point that individuals possess certain rights prior to and independently of social recognition. Hence it is concluded that

---

[34] Martin argues that Green gives a negative defense of the social recognition component, not a positive one, by seeing the recognition theory as integral to classical liberal social contract theory. See Martin, "Green on Natural Rights in Hobbes, Spinoza and Locke," in Andrew Vincent (ed.), *The Philosophy of T. H. Green* (Hants: Gower Publishing, 1986).

individuals are not or cannot be taken seriously if they are not viewed as having rights prior to and independently of social recognition. This argument is partly historical because it defers to canonical figures in the liberal tradition and the fact that they posited such rights in their political philosophies. And it is partly normative because it claims that there is an overarching normative reason for positing these rights, namely to articulate a way of taking individuals seriously and marking the scope and limits of political authority. From this vantage point individuals are viewed as isolated with interests that need to be protected from the state, from communities, and other potential adversaries.

Hence the plausibility and attractiveness of presocial natural rights are defended as part of our best theoretical effort to take individuals seriously normatively speaking, as reflected in the work of canonical figures. This could be read as a reconciliation of liberty and community in favor of strong individualism—a reconciliation that would be challenged by utilitarians, Marxists, conservatives of a Burkian orientation, new liberals, and contemporary communitarians. But this normative historical argument can be used to positively defend the new liberal social conception of rights as well. And this particular deployment of the normative historical argument gets off the ground by denying that individuals are not or cannot be taken seriously if they are not viewed as bearers of presocial natural rights. As we have seen, new liberalism provides its own articulation of what it means to take individuals seriously. And in its canonical representatives (e.g. Green and Ritchie) this is linked with a recognition-based conception of rights. Hence the plausibility and attractiveness of this conception can be defended as part of our best theoretical effort to take individuals seriously normatively speaking, as reflected in the work of other equally important canonical figures within the liberal tradition.

Classical liberalism and new liberalism represent distinct conceptions of what it means to take individuals seriously. If modifications of liberalism to accommodate communitarian concerns are indeed progressive and ultimately yield a more attractive liberal conception of what it means to take individuals seriously, then because this conception is not only compatible with the idea of socially recognized rights but also requires that rights be rethought along these lines, it yields a more attractive conception of rights than the one associated with classical liberalism. Hence retrieving new liberalism and its conceptions of individualism and rights can enrich contemporary liberal thought by showing contemporary liberals that they can safely dispense with presocial natural rights without giving up moral rights altogether.[35] And this is a fairly pressing matter not only in view of longstanding and very recent forceful criticisms of presocial natural rights that have yet to be rebutted convincingly, but because the emphasis on community looms large in contemporary political philosophy and theory and cannot be ignored by any reasonable and open-minded liberal.

So we see that the accusation that grounding rights in social recognition is "illiberal," and demonstrates an insufficient grasp of the liberal philosophical tradition, is impaled on its own sword. A broader view of the liberal philosophical tradition—one that includes a reading of philosophers that offered liberal political philosophies reconciling respect for individuals with concern for community and common good—supports viewing all rights as products of some form of recognition and positing the existence of positive as well as negative rights, thereby revealing that one need not embrace the two dogmas of classical liberalism to fall within the ambit of the liberal tradition. In this regard, my defense of rights externalism can thus be viewed as the product of not only taking the history of race and racism seriously but of taking a broader view of the liberal tradition seriously as well. Let us now consider in greater detail the substance and shortcomings of the prevailing conception of what having moral rights amounts to.

---

[35] Sweet, *Idealism and Rights*, p. 241, also makes the general points that we can and should acknowledge the force of longstanding objections to natural rights liberalism but that we need not get rid of rights altogether so long as they can be rethought to meet these objections.

CHAPTER 2

Rights without recognition

One of the so-called self-evident truths proclaimed in the United States of America's Declaration of Independence is that all men are endowed by their creator with certain unalienable rights. Many people still follow the founders in affirming the naturalness of these rights even though nomenclature has varied over the years. But in what sense are these rights natural? And what exactly is the source of these unalienable natural rights which have played such an important role in explaining why governments are instituted among men, what function they serve, and what they must do to guarantee their continued existence?

The answer to the first question—in what sense are these rights natural—appears to be relatively clear. They are "natural" in the sense that human beings are taken to possess them prior to and independent of formal as well as informal governmental or societal recognition. As such they are the product of neither legislative nor customary practices and can thus serve as independent grounds for judging and guiding both legislation and custom, which is the primary reason for positing such rights in the first place. Another way to put the point is to say that natural rights exist prior to and independently of the actions of all positive authority, both governmental and nongovernmental. Although these rights may be independent of all positive law and authority, if men were indeed endowed by their creator with these rights, as the founders proclaimed, then they would not be natural in the sense that human beings possessed them entirely independently of all law and authority. On the contrary, they would be the product of divine agency and thus could not serve as independent grounds for judging and guiding divine legislation and authority. This would be a relatively comfortable position to maintain on the naturalness of unalienable rights for those not troubled by the required theological commitments. But in the aftermath of the Enlightenment and Bentham's penetrating critique of this way of accounting for the source of natural rights, this is clearly a dead option for many in secular philosophical circles.

Be that as it may, the normative attractiveness of natural rights—as suitably independent standards of normative criticism and guidance—has proven too overwhelming to abandon them altogether.[1] Hence what has emerged in secular philosophical circles generally and in rights theory in particular is a way of accounting for the naturalness of these rights that renders their existence entirely independent of all agency and authority, whether it be human or divine. One way to render divine activity less significant in accounting for the source of natural rights is by claiming that, if the creator did indeed endow all men with unalienable natural rights, this was accomplished by creating them with a particular right-endowing nature; consequently, the fact that they have this nature (and not the fact that God endowed them with it) becomes the more direct explanation of the source of these rights. From this perspective natural rights are "natural" in the sense that they are possessed by human beings prior to and independent of the actions and laws of both man and the creator insofar as human nature itself or some specific aspect of it is their source. Some people will give the creator final credit by insisting that the creator bestowed this right-endowing nature upon man and is therefore the true source of their natural rights, while others will reject this explanation in favor of a more naturalistic one.

Throughout this book I shall assume that the prevailing conception affirms the existence of natural rights in a theologically neutral sense, that is, it takes these rights to be possessed prior to and independent of either human or divine agency and authority.[2] I shall also assume that the terms "natural rights," "human rights," "rights of man," "basic rights," and "moral rights" are sometimes used interchangeably to designate rights that are taken to be possessed prior to and independent of both human and divine agency and design, and in this regard are generally contrasted with legal and other conventional rights whose existence are products of human agency and design.

To be sure, defenders of these rights acknowledge that they can be enshrined in legal and other conventional rule systems and can thereby

---

[1] For a very penetrating explanation of the reluctance and inability to abandon natural rights and their various incarnations, see Raymond Guess, *History and Illusion in Politics* (Cambridge University Press, 2001), ch. 3.

[2] And this is not due to a prejudice against the theological position. In fact, my position is much closer to the spirit of this view since both are positivist theories.

become legal or conventional rights themselves. In fact, some people even argue that positive law should always or at least sometimes aim to make moral rights legal ones. Yet they insist that these rights—by whatever name they are called—constitute a distinct class of rights that exist prior to and independent of such rule systems and other products of human contrivance. Individuals are taken to possess them even though they may not be codified in law, custom, or otherwise acknowledged or recognized by individuals or society. The most pressing challenge for proponents of the prevailing conception is to account for how individuals come to possess these prior prepolitical and presocial rights without making recourse to human or divine agency.[3] This chapter exposes several serious shortcomings of the two predominant ways of answering this challenge, which will suffice to undermine the attractiveness of the prevailing conception and to clear the way for my alternative conception of the source of moral rights.

RIGHTS AND ONTOLOGY

Assuming that we do indeed have at least some moral as distinct from merely legal or conventional rights—and setting aside the question of which moral rights we have (an important question that I will not address in this book)—how can we explain their source if we depart from the founders' theological explanation? If we reject the view that our rights are within the gift of a human or divine external authority, then we could look within ourselves or to our natural constitution, so to speak, for the basis of these natural rights. If the creator endows individuals with natural rights by creating them with a suitable nature (e.g. a rational nature), then the more basic explanation for why we possess these rights is not divine agency *per se* but having a particular right-endowing nature. Hence, if men do indeed possess such rights, they possess them merely by virtue of having this nature. This is the core idea behind the ontological approach and it is widely held by both philosophers and laypersons.

---

[3] Not surprisingly, accounting for the source of these rights is the same problem that earlier defenders of natural rights had to face and made recourse to natural law to handle. Yet in explaining how individuals come to possess prepolitical rights their most conscientious contemporary defenders have sought to avoid the metaphysical and epistemology difficulties that plagued the eighteenth-century conception of natural rights, difficulties which were intimately linked with the claim that natural law was their source, and difficulties which lead Bentham to dismiss natural rights as "simple nonsense."

One contemporary rights theorist captures the point this way: "If I have rights, it is because of something about me, not something that resides in the messy world outside."[4] And another makes the point this way: "basic moral rights are possessed by their possessors independently of other beings. My moral right to autonomy and integrity springs from my nature and being; it depends on no one else, and is conferred by no one else . . ."[5] Throughout this book I shall use the term "rights internalism," or "internalism" for short, to characterize this version of the prevailing view. Although advocates of rights internalism disagree about what it is about a subject that makes it a moral rightholder, they all agree that it is solely facts about the subject or, more generally, facts about the subject's nature that ground this status. From this perspective, for any moral right to be correctly ascribed to some individual, that individual must possess a certain nature or some property, the possession of which is taken to confer the right. Hence, if we adopt this perspective the real philosophical work involved in accounting for the source of moral rights lies in determining the relevant moral right-endowing nature. Is it being human? Is it agency? Is it rationality? Is it sentience? Is it being a project pursuer? Is it having interests? Is it the capacity to make claims, or is it some other property?

To be sure, the relevant nature need not be reduced to a single property: several properties could be individually necessary and collectively sufficient. Nor for that matter need the relevant nature be understood just in terms of nonrelational properties, i.e. those that a subject could possess if it was the only thing that existed. Accordingly we find some internalists grounding moral rights in nonrelational properties such as sentience or rationality as well as in relational properties such as citizenship, socioeconomic status, or group identity. Furthermore the relevant nature need not be one that is commonly invoked by more universalist-minded rights theorists. Although a subject's race, gender, class, national identity, or sexual preference are usually taken by some people to be irrelevant for determining whether it possesses moral rights, some rights theorists have recognized, and rightly so, that these facts about

---

[4] Lomasky, *Persons, Rights, and the Moral Community*, p. 153. It should be noted that Lomasky's view does not exclusively rely on ontological considerations to ground rights. He proposes what he describes as a "multivalent" theory of rights in which certain things that fail to possess the relevant right-endowing property can "piggyback" their way into the moral community of rightholders by virtue of the relationship in which they stand to bona fide members of the community. But I remain skeptical about this view as I believe that the ontological and the social grounding are mutually exclusive ways of grounding rights.

[5] H. J. McCloskey, "Moral Rights and Animals," *Inquiry* 22 (1979), 27.

a subject have as much claim to grounding moral rights as do humanity, rationality, and other familiar categories.[6] This fact will loom large in chapter 4, where I call attention to the use of race as an ontological ground for rights in the antebellum as well as post-bellum United States to challenge the presumption that rights internalism presents us with an unassailable strategy for combating racial subordination. If it does not, then a primary motivation for embracing rights internalism disappears.

Proponents of rights internalism should be troubled by the absence of consensus in practice about what constitutes the relevant moral right-endowing property. One reason why this is so, which I shall develop in the next section, bears on the unsatisfactory solution to the problem of rights proliferation that it affords us. It might be thought that there was no real controversy here since humanity seems to be the obvious candidate for the relevant moral right-endowing property.[7] But this is far from obvious. If we did believe that being human was the relevant moral right-endowing nature, it would be fair to ask what it was about human beings that made them uniquely eligible for membership in the realm of moral rightholders. If it was their humanity or, more generally, the fact that they were members of a natural kind typically having certain physical and mental characteristics and who lived a distinctive form of life, then how could we explain why so many prominent rights theorists have argued that certain human beings, e.g. fetuses, young children, the mentally limited, and the comatose, are not eligible for membership or in some cases full membership in the realm of moral rightholders? Obviously, it will not do to claim that these subjects are not human, anymore than it would do to claim that black slaves in the antebellum south or Jews in Nazi Germany (who were also denied the status of moral rightholders) were not human. Moreover, how can we explain why other prominent rights theorists have argued that certain nonhuman animals and other entities, real and imagined, e.g. animals, trees, ecosystems, rational aliens, works of art, and corporations, are or would be eligible for membership or in some cases partial membership in the realm of moral rightholders?

A defender of the humanity standard might claim that these two possibilities, namely that some humans do not count and that some

---

[6] For a discussion of this, see George E. Panichas, "The Rights-Ascription Problem," *Social Theory and Practice* 23 (1997), 365–98.

[7] For useful discussions of the connection between rights ascription and the humanity standard, see Douglas Husak, "Why There Are No Human Rights," *Social Theory and Practice* 10 (1984), 125–41, and Panichas, "The Rights-Ascription Problem."

nonhumans do count as moral rightholders, demonstrate the absurdity of relying upon a standard other than humanity to ground moral rights. Once we depart from this standard, so the objection goes, we will be stuck with properties that are either too narrow, thereby excluding some human beings from the realm of moral rightholders, or too broad, thereby including some nonhuman beings within the realm of moral rightholders. The first possibility is untenable because human beings are generally assumed to be the paradigm instances of moral rightholders and, therefore, cannot cease to be moral rightholders. It is also pernicious since it rules out a moral rights-based objection to certain kinds of treatment unbefitting human beings. For instance, if certain human beings cease to be moral rightholders, then we can no longer object to treating them unjustly or immorally on the grounds that it violates their prior moral rights. The second possibility is untenable because it attributes rights to beings that could not possibility benefit from having them. What significant purpose could possibly be served by ascribing moral rights to rabbits, elm trees, or works of art?

These objections are not decisive, however. For one, it is only a contingent fact that human beings are the paradigm instances of moral rightholders, and whether they are taken to be the paradigm instances will depend on whom you ask. Some members of PETA (People for the Ethical Treatment of Animals) will presumably have a different view of the matter. They might retort that the matter is decided not by asking whether something can reason but whether it can suffer; therefore, any animal that can suffer is a paradigm instance of a moral rightholder, whether it be a human animal in full possession of its rational capacities, a human animal with substantially diminished rational capacities, or a nonhuman animal with no rational capacity at all. Furthermore, there is considerable disagreement among rights theorists, who do take human beings to be the paradigm instances of moral rightholders, over which fact(s) about human beings are relevant. And as for the point about perniciousness, this is only a serious worry if presocial moral right-based arguments against treating human beings unjustly or immorally are the only or the best moral arguments we have at our disposal; but this remains to be shown.

Finally, whether a subject can benefit from the possession of moral rights will depend upon our underlying theory of the function or point of rights as well as the nature of the would-be moral rightholder. If, for instance, we assume that the function of rights is to protect or promote a subject's well-being or interests, then anything that has interests or well-being can benefit from the possession of rights. While it may be the case that this theory of the function of rights imposes restrictions on what can be a member of the class of moral rightholders, it is equally clear that on this theory the class of moral rightholders will not be limited to the class of human beings since some nonhuman entities can have interests or a well-being to be protected or promoted—unless of course one construes the intention of these concepts so narrowly as to rule this out. Hence, contrary to appearances, neither of these possibilities—that some humans do not count and that some nonhumans do count as moral rightholders—constitutes a *reductio ad absurdum* of the claim that moral rights can be grounded in properties other than the property of being human.

Two additional points are worth mentioning. First, rather than accounting for our practices of attributing rights to nonhumans and denying rights to certain humans in moral, legal, political, and fictional discourse, one might contend that insisting on the humanity standard forces us to interpret such practices as uniformly mistaken. But this is too presumptuous. A better strategy would be to explain these linguistic practices rather than to deny their reality. Second, if we embrace the humanity standard, then many of the most intractable moral problems that have occupied ethicists, such as the problems of abortion, euthanasia, the treatment of those with diminished capacity, animal and environmental matters, cease to be hard problems. If we choose to view the problems in terms of rights and decide in advance that only humans can have rights, and presume that rights claims generally trump other kinds of moral considerations, then the problems become much more manageable. Of course, proponents of the humanity standard might take this to be a virtue rather than a vice; however, it is more reasonable to view these hard cases as challenges to the humanity standard by showing that humanity as such cannot be the ultimate ground of rights, or moral status more generally, unless of course one is prepared to accept worrisome consequences.[8]

So despite the fact that many rights internalists use the humanity standard as an intuitive starting point for theorizing about what constitutes the relevant moral right-endowing nature, they clearly do not rest with it. For the real controversy pertains to how this standard should be unpacked. Attempts to offer a more fine-grained account have led them to

---

[8] Carl Wellman, one leading advocate of rights internalism, has embraced these worrisome consequences and has provided strong arguments for why we ought not to be so worried about denying rights to fetuses and other "alleged right-holders." See Wellman, *Real Rights*, ch. 5.

propose more nuanced views about the kind of thing something must be to possess moral rights, championing such properties as agency, sentience, autonomy, personhood, project pursuit, and many others.

Perhaps one might suggest that in advancing these properties internalists are merely working out their views on which properties are essential to humanity as such, a project that has occupied many great philosophers of the past including, most notably, Immanuel Kant, who held that having a rational nature, broadly understood as the capacity to act on principles and to set ends, was the defining characteristic of humanity. But even if we accept this interpretation of what internalists are doing, the initial problem of absence of consensus about what constitutes the relevant right-endowing property still remains. At first blush, appealing to humanity appears to settle the matter; however, since there is no consensus among internalists about which properties are most essential to humanity as different properties are defended, the appeal to the concept of humanity turns out to be nothing more than a placeholder for many would-be candidates for the title of relevant rights-endowing property. As further evidence for the claim that humanity is not the relevant property, we need only reflect on the common practices of including within the realm of rightholders whatever possesses this essential property (even if it is not human in the biological sense) and excluding from the realm of right-holders whatever does not possess this essential property (even if it is human in the biological sense). My consideration of the connections between race and rights in chapter 4 will make full use of this point.

SELECTING THE RELEVANT PROPERTY

It might be objected that although there is no consensus in practice among rights internalists about what constitutes the relevant moral right-endowing nature, and despite the fact that humanity is not the obvious choice, the possibility that there could be consensus in principle has not yet been ruled out. If internalists could agree in principle on what constitutes the relevant nature, then what initially appears to be a serious shortcoming of the ontological approach will cease to be so. But to see why the prospect of consensus in principle is very unlikely we must reflect on how the choice of moral right-endowing properties is made.

My conjecture is that the selection of properties is part of an effort to find the correct fit between pretheoretical judgments about who or what is a moral rightholder and general theoretical outlooks regarding the ground of moral rights. In other words, the selection of properties is part of an effort to reach reflective equilibrium between pretheoretical judgments regarding who or what is a moral rightholder and theoretical views regarding the criteria for moral rights possession.[9] This Rawlsian method, which assigns our pretheoretical moral beliefs a prominent justificatory role, affords us a way of deciding between conflicting moral theories (or theories of distributive justice).[10] Here is a simplified version of how it goes.[11] After identifying a class of moral judgments that we think are intuitively correct, we look for a set of general principles that would lead us to make these same judgments independently of our pretheoretical moral beliefs. We then proceed both to modify our principles and to revise our judgments, working back and forth until we reach a state of equilibrium in which we are no longer inclined to modify our principles or revise our judgments but are prepared to accept the principles selected and the judgments they support.

Similarly, when theorizing about what constitutes the relevant moral right-endowing property, rights internalists begin with their pretheoretical views about which things have moral rights (e.g. babies, fetuses, animals, and trees), and then look for a common property which they then deem to be the relevant one and appeal to in their subsequent theorizing (e.g. sentience, interests, life). When their pretheoretical and theoretical views do not line up they are revised as needed until they square their theoretical view about what counts as the relevant moral right-endowing property with their pretheoretical views about which things are moral rightholders. For example, upon realizing that taking rationality to be the relevant moral right-endowing property rules out fetuses, children, and the severely mentally limited from being moral rightholders, which does

---

[9] I am not claiming that this is what people ought to do when attempting to select the relevant property. In this regard my reference to Rawls's notion of reflective equilibrium may be misleading, since he employs it in making out a case for how we ought to arrive at the correct principles of distributive justice. My conjecture speaks to what philosophers in fact do when selecting the relevant moral right-conferring properties. Thus I am making a descriptive, not a normative, claim.

[10] For Rawls's views on reflective equilibrium, see "Outline of a Decision Procedure for Ethics," *Philosophical Review* 60 (1951), 177–97; *A Theory of Justice*, §9; and "The Independence of Moral Theory," *Proceedings and Addresses of the American Philosophical Association* 47 (1974–5), 5–22.

[11] A more complex account would need to be formulated in terms of wide reflective equilibrium, which attempts to produce coherence in an ordered triple of sets of beliefs held by a particular person, namely (a) a set of considered pretheoretical judgments, (b) a set of moral principles, and (c) a set of relevant background theories. But this level of complexity is not necessary for present purposes. For a discussion of the significance of the distinction between wide and narrow reflective equilibrium, see Norman Daniels, "Wide Reflective Equilibrium and Theory Acceptance in Ethics," *Journal of Philosophy* 76 (1979), 256–82. And for a more recent discussion of the significance of our pretheoretical beliefs in the justification of moral theories, see Thomas Scanlon, "The Aims and Authority of Moral Theory," *Oxford Journal of Legal Studies* 12 (1992), 1–23.

not conform to their pretheoretical beliefs, they search for another attribute and take it to be the relevant one to secure a tighter fit between their pretheoretical and theoretical views. The final objective is to achieve coherence between their views regarding which things are moral rightholders and what it takes to be one.

Internalists get into trouble, however, when they take the property that emerges from this epistemic process to be the objective foundation of moral rights, i.e. the property that all rational parties must take to be necessary for the possession of moral rights. The nature of the process by which properties are selected helps us to see why this is a mistake. Our views about which things are (and not simply should be) moral rightholders will turn on which things we want to reap the benefits of being a moral rightholder. If, for example, we want animals to be treated with respect, and we believe that only moral rightholders can elicit this kind of treatment, then we may take animals to be moral rightholders. The same goes for fetuses, babies, the mentally limited, animals, and trees: if we want them to be treated in certain ways and not in others, we may take them to be moral rightholders as well. Thus the content of our pretheoretical judgments will be determined by practical considerations, i.e. desires, wants, political agendas, and so on.

Hence from this perspective our views about what it takes to be a moral rightholder, that is, our views regarding the ontological foundation of moral rights, will also be determined by such considerations. For instance, given their different practical commitments, defenders of animal rights or environmental rights may embrace radically different views about the relevant moral right-endowing property than individuals who believe that the class of human beings and moral rightholders is coextensive. Admittedly, these parties need not have radically different views about the relevant moral right-endowing property. They may simply disagree about whether a particular property that is agreed to be relevant (e.g. rationality) is in fact possessed by certain entities.

But if they do have radically different views about the relevant property, then clearly the properties that emerge upon reflection are obviously unfit to serve as objective or public grounds of rights. At best, they can serve as the grounds suited for individuals who share certain practical commitments. One could of course claim that these properties constituted the normative foundation of rights, the grounds that all rational parties should take to be necessary for the possession of rights. Yet it behooves one to offer reasons for why this conclusion should be drawn. While rights internalists may also endorse this normative thesis, I think that they endorse the objective thesis as well: they take their preferred property to be necessary not just sufficient for the possession of rights.

To complete this argument it would have to be argued that these practical commitments were irreconcilable and that the resulting properties were mutually exclusive. If the practical commitments were not irreconcilable, then perhaps it would be reasonable to think that we could all begin with the same pretheoretical judgments about which things were moral rightholders, and thus increase the likelihood of our arriving at a consensus regarding the ground of moral rights. And if the properties were not mutually exclusive, then there might be more common ground between animal rights, environmental rights, and human rights proponents than I am willing to allow. Though I think that these arguments can be given, I shall not try to give them here.

It is now apparent why consensus in principle about what constitutes the relevant moral right-endowing property appears unlikely: given the range of possible subjects a proponent of rights may want to protect or to secure some measure of respect for, different persons reasoning from different pretheoretical judgments informed by different practical considerations will arrive at different properties none of which will be universally endorsed. While I realize that this is a controversial conjecture about what guides the selection of properties, it is certainly not far-fetched. The practice of moral rights ascription has always proceeded on the assumption that possessing moral rights serves the well-being or interests of the things that possess them. Moreover, it is usually assumed that moral rights possession constitutes a supreme form of protection, if not for any other reason than that people think that it does. Hence it is obvious that if you really want to afford some subject the highest measure of protection against being violated in certain ways or protection against being left without the things that it needs to promote its well-being, then you must show that our obligations to leave it alone or to assist it are grounded by moral rights that it possesses against us, in which case our duty to respect it is not one that we merely owe to God, to the sovereign, to other persons, to society, or to future generations, but first and foremost a duty that we owe to the subject itself insofar as it possesses moral rights.

Of course, we need to know whether the goal of protecting the well-being of these would-be moral rightholders can be promoted without expanding the realm of moral rightholders to include them. If it can, then it may be best to refrain from doing so to minimize the possibility of rights conflicts and the subsequent devaluing of rights associated with such conflicts. This is the familiar argument made against extending the realm of moral rightholders beyond the class of human beings to include nonhuman animals, trees, and other entities. It is argued that we need not view these subjects as moral rightholders to promote their well-being and, moreover, that we should refrain from doing so to safeguard the moral rights of human beings which would be threatened by these competing moral rights. But despite this objection some parties will insist on expanding the realm of moral rightholders, even when it is unclear whether this is necessary to protect the well-being of the subjects at issue. And this is because they realize that the best way to guarantee that concern for the moral rights of human beings does not result in the demise of nonhuman animals, trees, and other valued entities is to view them as members (though not necessarily equal members) of the realm of moral rightholders.[12] An obvious way to address this concern is to select the moral right-endowing property that enables one to achieve the practical end of putting the things that one values on the same moral playing field as the things valued by others. But this strategy is precisely what my conjecture regarding what guides the selection of properties captures.

PROPERTY SELECTION AND THE FUNCTION OF RIGHTS

Even if we grant the plausibility of the foregoing conjecture regarding what guides the selection of properties, we may wonder whether a better one is available. Perhaps there is another explanation which has the additional virtue of showing that consensus in principle about the relevant moral right-endowing property is possible. In particular, it may be thought that a better way to determine what constitutes the relevant moral right-endowing property would be to begin with a theory about the function of rights, since this bears directly on the question of rights possession.

There are two predominant views concerning the function of rights in the philosophical literature: the interest and the will theories. While both theories assume that there is a class of rights that correlates with duties,[13] and that possessing rights is in some sense advantageous to their possessors, they disagree about the nature of the advantage gained by possessing

---

[12] Compare this argument to Mary Ann Warren's argument for extending moral status to all living things, *Moral Status* (Oxford: Clarendon Press, 1997), p. 150.

[13] Readers familiar with Wesley Hohfeld's influential classification of rights, *Fundamental Legal Conceptions* (Yale University Press, 1919), know that there are classes of rights that do not have duties as their correlatives; however, for the sake of simplicity I will ignore these classes and focus exclusively on rights in the "strict" sense—claim-rights—which do indeed correlate with duties. And although most expositions of the interest and will theories focus narrowly on so called claim-rights, which have duties as their correlative, both theories can be developed to take into account liberty-rights, power-rights, and disability-rights as well. For example, see Carl Wellman, *A Theory of Rights* (Totowa: Rowman & Allanheld, 1985).

rights, which ultimately leads them to support different properties as the grounds of rights. The interest theory construes the advantage gained by having rights broadly to involve having one's interests or well-being protected by the performance of dutiful conduct. On this view, then, rightholders are the intended beneficiaries of the performance of dutiful conduct. In passing I should add that the qualification that a possible rightholder is the "intended" beneficiary, and not simply standing to benefit or likely to benefit, is important. It rules out the possibility of coincidental beneficiaries being rightholders. Without this qualification a subject that lacks a relevant right but stands to benefit from dutiful conduct will count coincidentally as having a right. Suppose, for example, that *A* wants to buy a gift for *C* but can only afford the gift if *B* repays the loan *A* made to *B*. While *C* certainly stands to benefit from *B*'s repayment of the loan, it would be a mistake to say that *C* has a right against *B* that *B* repay the loan to *A*. This mistake cannot be avoided if we accepted the unqualified version of the benefit theory.[14]

According to the interest theory, it follows that having interests is the relevant right-endowing property, since being the intended beneficiary of dutiful conduct is roughly a matter of possessing interests that serve as the justification for imposing duties of forbearance and assistance on others.[15] Consequently, the realm of moral rightholders will be populated by all and only beings that can have interests. On the other hand, the will theory construes the advantage gained by having rights narrowly as affording rightholders freedom or dominion over the performance of another person's duty in a confrontation of wills. The requisite control demonstrated by a rightholder involves, among other things, being able to insist upon the performance of a correlative duty or to release others from its performance. From this it follows that being an agent (in the sense of having control or dominion over the surrounding normative relations) is the relevant right-endowing property because only agents are capable of exercising dominion. Consequently, the realm of moral rightholders will be populated by all and only beings that have agency.

Although interest and agency are not the only properties that have been forwarded to ground rights, they constitute distinct properties that have

---

[14] For the qualified version of the benefit theory, see David Lyons, "Rights, Claimants, and Beneficiaries," *American Philosophical Quarterly* 6 (1969), 173–85. The unqualified version is associated with Bentham. Hart's *Essays on Bentham* contains a useful analysis of Bentham's view.

[15] Joseph Raz develops the benefit theory of rights in this form. See his "On the Nature of Rights," *Mind* 93 (1984), 194–214, and "Legal Rights," *Oxford Journal of Legal Studies* 4 (1984), 1–21.

had widespread appeal and, moreover, each gains support from the interest and will theory of rights respectively. One may wonder whether these properties—interests and agency—are sufficiently distinct groundings for rights, especially because we can stipulate that the relevant interests which ground duties are higher-order interests in freedom and autonomy. In some cases, interest and will theorists will certainly agree about whether a subject counts as a rightholder. For example, suppose that I promise you that I will take out your trash for a year in return for your assistance with solving a philosophical problem that has been troubling me. In this case you are the intended beneficiary of the duty, as well as the one with the freedom and control over my performance of the duty. You can insist upon its performance or graciously release me. In cases like this, where one and the same subject is both the beneficiary and the controller of the duty, the interest and will theorist will agree that this subject is a real rightholder. But in cases involving third-party beneficiaries who do not have control over the performance of duties, as well as cases involving the unborn, babies, animals, and anything else that does not and could not have such control, they will disagree.

Suppose that I promise to take care of your senile mother while you are away on holiday. While it is true that your mother will benefit from my discharging the resulting duty, I owe it to you to look after her and my negligence would be a wrong done to you, though your mother may certainly be wronged as a result. Moreover, it is you and not your mother who has the freedom and authority to insist upon my performance of the duty or release me. In this case the interest theory will assign your mother a right on the assumption that she has interests which are promoted and protected by the performance of the duty. The will theory, on the other hand, rejecting the interest criterion, will not assign your mother a right since she does not have dominion over the performance of my duty.[16]

So even if we can determine the relevant moral right-endowing property by beginning with a theory of the function of rights, we would still find ourselves with at least two distinct moral right-endowing properties. An obvious yet somewhat unsatisfying conclusion to draw here is that one's view about what constitutes the relevant moral right-endowing property will depend upon one's preferred theory concerning the function of rights. Not only will this conclusion be unsatisfying to those who believe that there is some one property (or sets of properties) which

---

[16] This example is an adaptation of Hart's example in "Are There Any Natural Rights?" in Jeremy Waldron (ed.), *Theories of Rights* (Oxford University Press, 1984), p. 81.

grounds moral rights, it shows that this detour through the function of rights points to the same conclusion reached above—namely, that there will not be consensus regarding what constitutes the relevant moral right-endowing property.

Perhaps one might try to show that only one of these theories is the "true" theory. Though this would be a significant result, some rights theorists, myself included, are skeptical about the prospects for narrowing down the field. There is no reason to think that rights cannot have both of these functions, in which case it appears to be somewhat arbitrary to single out one and give it definitional priority.[17] Pending this case being made, the foregoing conclusion must stand: there is no reason to think that appealing to the function of rights will enable rights internalists to reach consensus in practice or in principle regarding the relevant moral right-endowing property. It is reasonable to construe rights as having multiple functions, and to highlight them leaves one with properties that enable one to draw the line between moral rightholders and nonrightholders wherever one chooses.

Let us now briefly consider an important way in which this lack of consensus in practice and in principle undermines the attractiveness of the ontological approach to the source of moral rights.

THE PROLIFERATION PROBLEM

Concerns about moral rights proliferation can pertain to the alleged subjects of moral rights or their alleged content. In the former case, the criticism is that it is a mistake to expand the realm of moral rightholders beyond the class of normal adult human beings, as when it is held that fetuses, infants, animals, trees, corporations, nations, or cultural groups can possess moral rights. In the latter case the criticism is that it is a mistake to suppose that moral rightholders can possess positive moral rights to assistance, such as moral rights to political asylum, to health care, to government subsidized food and housing, or to a minimum wage. For present purposes I am interested in the former case. I believe that the ontological approach does not constitute a sufficiently demanding standard for regulating entry into the realm of moral rightholders, and hence does not afford us a promising solution to the moral rights proliferation problem.

---

[17] Rex Martin and James Nickel, "Recent Work on the Concept of Rights," *American Philosophical Quarterly* 17 (1980), 171.

Imposing a more demanding admission standard on entry into the realm of moral rightholders would be a virtue insofar as this would more effectively undermine a source of skepticism about moral rights. Prior to these right-dominated times when the realm of alleged moral rightholders seems to be expanding exponentially, moral rights were believed to afford their possessors significant protection against being treated in harmful ways, against being neglected, or, more generally, against having their interests ignored or trumped. In practice this meant, among other things, that human beings would come out ahead whenever their interests conflicted with the interests of nonhumans, and that normal adult human beings would come out ahead whenever their interests conflicted with the interests of children, fetuses, or mentally impaired persons. But things are not so simple anymore. Citing a moral right now is merely the first move in a series of appeals to moral rights, which usually ends in a stalemate with opposing sides of the debate asserting moral rights or having them asserted on their behalf. Hence it has been argued that the proliferation of moral rightholders has compromised the rhetorical authority of moral rights and consequently has diminished their protective power, which has provoked some observers to question the wisdom of dealing with normative issues in terms of moral rights and other observers to deny their existence altogether.[18]

A systematic way of responding to these concerns is to articulate the possession conditions for moral rights.[19] Addressing this second-order conceptual problem enables us to readily sort genuine moral rightholders from alleged moral rightholders and thereby ascertain which first-order rights claims are to be taken seriously. We might wonder whether there are other ways of mollifying skeptical doubts about moral rights stemming from moral rightholder proliferation short of having to provide and defend an account of moral rights possession. If so, we could adopt a more straightforward solution to the problem. For instance, if someone ascribes moral rights to an octopus, a California redwood tree, or a human corpse, we can simply dismiss such ascriptions as erroneous, since these things could not possibly be bearers of moral rights, and spend our time

---

[18] For cases in favor of the dispensability of moral rights, see Robert Young, "Dispensing with Moral Rights," *Political Theory* 6 (1978), 63–74, and Raymond Frey, *Interests and Rights: The Case against Animals* (Oxford: Clarendon Press, 1980). For a case against the existence of moral rights, see MacIntyre, *After Virtue*, ch. 6.

[19] For recent work in the philosophy of rights that addresses the proliferation problem by systematically attending to the possession conditions for rights, see Lomasky, *Persons, Rights, and the Moral Community*, Sumner, *The Moral Foundation of Rights*, and Wellman, *Real Rights*.

more productively by searching for an explanation for why some people mistakenly ascribe moral rights to these entities. This is certainly an option. However, this abrupt dismissal implicitly presupposes a conception of what it takes to possess moral rights, according to which it is not possible for the above entities to be moral rightholders. I suspect that any seemingly "straightforward" attempt to mollify skeptical doubts will have the same result, in which case the search for a more systematic solution will be inevitable.

To be sure, providing an account of the possession conditions for moral rights will not guarantee that the realm of moral rightholders will be limited to normal adult human beings (in fact an account which guaranteed this would be highly implausible); it should at the very least provide an admission standard demanding enough to guarantee that entry into the realm of moral rightholders does not become a free for all. And this is probably the best outcome we can hope for.

The conclusion drawn in the previous section makes it apparent why the ontological approach offers little effective control over moral rights inflation; it makes it relatively easy to expand the realm of moral rightholders. Recall that on this view one can expand the realm of moral rightholders either by showing that a subject possesses the property deemed relevant by those whom one is trying to convince or by showing that a subject has some other property and arguing that this property is at least sufficient if not necessary for possessing moral rights. So, for instance, to make a case for including great apes in the realm of moral rightholders one needs to show either that great apes are rational agents (if "rationality" is the property deemed relevant by those whom one is trying to convince), or that great apes are sentient and that being sentient is at least sufficient for possessing moral rights. The ontological approach would offer more effective control if there were consensus regarding what constituted the relevant moral right-endowing property. But, as I argued above, there is no consensus in practice as rights internalists have proposed different properties, and consensus in principle seems unlikely if my conjecture regarding how the selection of properties is determined is correct. In the absence of consensus, whenever one cannot show that a subject possesses the property deemed relevant by those whom one is trying to convince, one can always introduce another property and argue that this property is sufficient for possessing moral rights. Thus, if we embrace internalism, not only should we expect to see moral rights being ascribed to everything from human beings to works of art, we should expect to see this done with relative ease.

Even if there were consensus in practice or in principle about which property was relevant, there would still be the problem of gaining consensus about whether particular subjects possessed this property. Though the prospects for solving this problem are somewhat greater, in some cases intractable disagreements will persist. For example, there can be serious disagreement about whether certain animals are sentient or whether they are rational. I suspect that this disagreement is also connected with my conjecture linking property selection to practical concerns and political agendas. One may be more open to accepting the case for the claim that certain animals are rational if one assigns high priority to protecting them and, moreover, one believes that demonstrating that they are moral rightholders by the prevailing criterion will go further toward protecting them than demonstrating that they are moral rightholders according to an unorthodox criterion. On the other hand, one may be less open to accepting this case if one assigns a lower priority to protecting them, or if one believes that they can be protected adequately without ascribing moral rights to them at all by simply arguing that we have duties to protect them that are not grounded by their correlative rights.

Hence although rights internalism provides a standard for entry into the realm of moral rightholders, it is not demanding enough and thus concerns about moral rightholder proliferation will continue to fuel skeptical doubts about the existence of moral rights. It is important to note that I have taken issue with rights internalism as a self-standing solution to the moral rights ascription problem. But, as will become clear later, I am not averse to assigning ontological considerations a role in my alternative account of the source of moral rights, though this role will be quite different. On my account we will not be able to infer directly or indirectly from the fact that a subject is constituted in a certain way that it possesses moral rights. Instead, we will be able to appeal to these considerations as reasons for or against affording a particular subject the social recognition necessary for possessing a moral right.[20]

RIGHTS AND MORALLY VALID CLAIMS

As noted earlier, the prevailing conception of moral rights affirms the existence of presocial rights in a theologically neutral sense, that is, it takes these rights to be possessed prior to and independent of both human and

---

[20] For criticism of the argument I present in this section, see David Lyons, "Rights and Recognition," *Social Theory and Practice* 32 (2006), 10–11.

divine agency and authority. Hence the main challenge for proponents of this conception is to account for how individuals come to possess these prior prepolitical and presocial moral rights without making recourse to human or divine agency. Thus far I have critically assessed the shortcomings of one dominant philosophical way of accounting for the existence of these rights, one that takes human nature or some aspect of it to be the source of these rights. In what remains of this chapter I shall critically assess another dominant approach to grounding moral rights before presenting my alternative in the next chapter.

One might object that replacing a theological with an ontological explanation of the source of prepolitical and presocial moral rights is not a dramatic improvement precisely because it will also be vulnerable to the metaphysical and epistemological concerns I raise above, and so offers us an equally mystifying conception of moral rights. Alternatively, some rights theorists have proposed to demystify these rights by accounting for their naturalness or their presocial character not by appealing to ontology but by appeal to the notion of a morally valid claim. What I shall call the morally valid claims (or the valid claims) approach to explaining the source of these so-called presocial moral rights takes a semantic conception of what a right is as a conceptual point of departure.

Wesley Hohfeld's seminal classification of fundamental legal conceptions, which underscores the centrality of the idea of a claim-right, is the beginning of wisdom for current philosophical analyses of what a right is. Hohfeld observed that in legal reasoning the term "right" is used indiscriminately to refer to claims, privileges, powers, and immunities. His main complaint was that this lack of precision in legal reasoning was a great hindrance to stating, understanding, and solving legal problems. To remedy this situation he distinguished these four fundamental legal conceptions by defining them in terms of their respective jural correlatives. This yielded the following analyses. Party X has a *claim* against another party Y that Y does some action when Y has a *duty* to X to do the action. Party X has a *privilege* in the face of party Y to do some action when Y has *no-right* against X that obliges X not to act. Party X has a *power* over party Y with respect to some relation when Y is *liable* to having this relation changed by X. Party X has *immunity* from party Y with respect to some relation when Y has the *disability* of not being able to change this relation.

These four fundamental conceptions and their respective correlatives—claims (rights) and duties, privileges (liberties) and no-rights, powers and liabilities, immunities and disabilities—constitute what Hohfeld characterized as "the lowest common denominators of the law." But because Hohfeld was critical of the broad and indiscriminate use of the term "right" to cover privileges, powers, and immunities, he sought to define the term more narrowly and, to his mind, more appropriately. Consequently, he proposed to reserve the term "right" to designate the invariable correlative of a duty and used the term "claim" to designate a right in this limited sense. His hope was that conceptual clarification of the various uses of the term "right" in judicial reasoning, and restricting the term "right" to designate the correlative of a duty, would ultimately improve judicial reasoning. Many contemporary philosophers have followed Hohfeld's lead in analyzing rights as claims with correlative duties and in taking this to be the default position by holding that only claim-rights are rights strictly speaking.[21]

According to the best-known contemporary proponent of this approach: "A man has a moral right when he has a claim the recognition of which is called for—not (necessarily) by legal rules—but by moral principles, or the principles of an enlightened conscience."[22] A reasonable interpretation of this point is that subjects possess moral rights if they possess claims that can be morally justified by some substantive moral theory. Hence the difference between moral and legal rights possession is that one possesses a moral right if one has a claim that is justified by moral principles, and one possesses a legal right if one has claim that is justified by legal rules.

Apart from telling us that the difference between moral and legal rights is that the former are claims validated by moral principles and the latter are claims validated by governing legal rules, this general analysis of moral rights leaves some important philosophical questions unanswered. What is the metaethical status of the justifying moral principles, and does this matter? In other words, does it matter whether these principles are given a

---

[21] Wellman takes issue with this restrictive use of the term. While he welcomes and embraces Hohfeld's classificatory scheme, Wellman contests the thesis that only claims-rights are rights strictly speaking. He contends that not only is it a waste of scarce conceptual resources to use the terms "right" and "claim" to designate one and the same relation; it begs the question against those who would identify rights with the other fundamental legal conceptions (see *A Theory of Rights*, p. 56). Wellman sees no problem in using the term "right" to designate each of these elements provided that we understand that they constitute distinct elements, and provided that we say something about what claim-rights, liberty-rights, power-rights, and immunity-rights have in common to make them species of a single genus. Addressing this second issue has special importance for Wellman because it is the key to understanding his complex model of rights, which is, in turn, instrumental for understanding his account of the connection between rights and protection.

[22] Feinberg, *Rights, Justice, and the Bounds of Liberty*, p. 154.

subjectivist, intersubjectivist, or objectivist construal?[23] At first blush, it would seem that they must be given an objectivist construal if they are to yield rights that can serve as universal standards of moral criticism, say, in global politics. Presumably, defenders of unrecognized moral rights want to say that they are binding on all governments and override local customs and moralities in cases of conflict. Secondly, as it stands, this analysis gives no indication about what specific general moral principles are relevant. Will any moral principle suffice to morally validate a claim? For instance, can the relevant validating principle be goal-based, duty-based, virtue-based, contractarian, or rights-based?

It seems clear that on pain of circularity a proponent of this view cannot have a rights-based moral theory (one which assumes that non-conventional rights are morally basic first principles) in mind. Insofar as the overarching goal is to account for what possessing unrecognized moral rights amounts to, and the idea of claims justified by moral principles is utilized to develop this account, one is precluded from presupposing the existence of the very rights one is trying to account for. To be sure, defenders of the valid claims approach appear to be well aware of the risk of circularity that arises when they connect the issue of what rights are with the issue of what possessing a right amounts to:

It will not help to attempt a formal definition of rights in terms of claims, for the idea of a right is already included in that of a claim, and we would fall into a circle. Nevertheless, certain facts about rights, more easily, if not solely, express-ible in the language of claims and claiming, are necessary to a full understanding of what rights are and why they are so vitally important.[24]

But they ultimately fail to avoid this problem by using the idea of a claim to elucidate of the idea of a right insofar as they take the morally valid claim condition to be sufficient for establishing the existence of moral rights.

Indeed, this constitutes a crucial difference between this approach and the one that I shall propose: while valid claims theorists take such justification to be sufficient for possessing moral rights, I shall maintain that it is necessary but not sufficient. In other words, while they assign moral justification of claims an exclusive role in accounting for the source of moral rights, I shall assign it a supporting role. It seems clear, however,

---

[23] For a discussion of these classifications, see Geoffrey Sayre-McCord, "The Many Moral Realisms," *The Southern Journal of Philosophy* 24 (1986), 1–22.
[24] Feinberg, *Rights, Justice and the Bounds of Liberty*, pp. 139 and 149.

that although valid claims theorists are generally silent about which moral principles can or must supply the requisite moral justification, presumably they cannot allow that the most basic moral principles are right-based insofar as they are attempting to elucidate the very idea of having moral rights. It would be circular to reintroduce basic moral rights to specify the shape of the justification conferring moral principles. In the final analysis, morally valid claims will have to be validated by some sort of non-rights-based general moral principles. There is a sense, then, in which valid claims theorists and myself occupy important common ground: we both want to appeal to moral justification to establish the existence of moral rights and none of us regards moral rights as being morally basic insofar as they cannot supply the requisite moral justification.

Another concern raised by the valid claims approach is that major defenders fail to elaborate on whether the argument from the general moral principles to the moral validity of the claim must be a sound argument, or whether it simply needs to be reasonable, relatively persuasive, or something else. If it must be a sound argument, does this mean that we must reason from "true" moral principles? If so, are there any true moral principles and how do we establish their truth? What happens if there is more that one true moral principle? And, moreover, what happens if their application in the same cases yields different results regarding the validity of the claim? Could it turn out that one and the same person possessed a moral right reasoning from one set of true moral principles and did not possess the very same moral right reasoning from another set of true moral principles?

While these important questions need to be addressed to add more substance to the valid claims approach (or any conception that contains a moral justification component), the crucial point for present purposes is that according to this conception the justification of a claim by general moral principles is alone sufficient for possessing moral rights. To be sure, proponents of this approach will add that moral rights conceived of as morally valid claims can be institutionalized in national and international legal systems, and can be included in political declarations of independence and bills of rights, but they will insist that moral rights—understood as moral valid claims—are possessed by human beings prior to and independently of whether these claims are afforded any sort of social, legal, or international recognition, and regardless of whether they are promoted by social or governmental action.

To avoid the suspicion and hostility directed against the traditional conception of natural rights due to questionable metaphysical assumptions, one can certainly follow contemporary proponents of the valid claims approach to account for the source of moral rights using the construct of a morally valid claim. But even if we grant this formulation and concede that it avoids the metaphysical and epistemological difficulties of traditional natural rights discourse, there still remains a significant philosophical issue—namely, whether the possession of a morally valid claim is sufficient for possessing a moral right. An often cited reason why some valid claims theorists prefer their account, which does not require that a practice be legally ratified or otherwise socially recognized, is because it allegedly "has the added advantage of preserving the direct and indicative character of rights claims, which is assumed, at least in our time and in our culture, by moral common sense."[25]

But there are several problems with this justification. First, valid claims theorists generally appeal to common sense without defending the interpretation of common sense that is being proffered. Certainly there will be some people in our culture who do not take this view to be moral common sense. Furthermore, they wrongly assume that rights theorists who impose a social constraint on moral rights possession are attempting to describe common sense. Revisionary analyses of concepts are revisionary precisely because they challenge our common sense beliefs. While proponents of unrecognized moral rights begin with the thought that certain rights exist independently of human activity or prior to any form of social recognition, other rights theorists begin with the thought that the only actual rights are those that are operative, and from here they argue that moral rights must be products of social recognition to be operative, thereby rejecting "our common sense." And, lastly, although squaring with common sense is a criterion of adequacy for a theory, it is certainly not the only one or even the most important one. In this case, I think that common sense (if it is *common* sense) leaves us with an account that does not take a wide enough view of the historical facts. And to save moral rights from certain skeptics may require that we rethink their source in a way that makes them less likely to be dismissed on these grounds.

One might contend that the valid claims approach to grounding moral rights was a more formidable target since it does not forge a connection between rights possession and ontology. In other words, it does not

---

[25] Feinberg, "In Defence of Moral Rights," p. 169.

attempt to represent moral rights possession as a fact about how subjects are constituted, or as a matter of subjects possessing certain right-endowing properties or characteristics. While this approach avoids directly linking the possession of moral rights with ontological consider-ations, once we ask "What is required for a subject to possess a claim?" facts about the nature of subjects become relevant. Indeed, Feinberg, the greatest champion of the valid claims view, defends the connection between rightholder status and ontology more directly by arguing that "having interests" is the relevant claim-endowing and hence right-endowing property. Therefore, the morally valid claims approach does appear to rest upon a connection, albeit an indirect one, between rights possession and ontology.[26]

It is clear, therefore, that while the valid claims approach avoids theology, it does not avoid appealing to ontological considerations to ground moral rights. It merely delays this appeal. Advocates of the valid claims approach cannot forestall addressing the question of what kinds of subject can have claims and hence be the proper subject of rights. To be sure, there is a sharp difference of opinion on this matter. Some propon-ents claim that only beings capable of claiming their own rights, under-standing their rights, waiving their rights, or otherwise making use of the power of rights can in fact possess them, while others argue that a subject only needs to have interests to be a proper subject of rights since it is interests that are protected by legal and moral rules. But in either case the question of what subjects can have claims and hence rights is resolved, in the end, by identifying some property the possession of which is taken to endow the subject with rights.

Thus the semantic approach to the source of moral rights, which analyzes having moral rights in terms of having morally valid claims and thereby masquerades as a better alternative to the ontological approach, does not manage to escape assigning ontology a role—albeit a less direct one—in explaining the source of moral rights. Furthermore, defenders of this approach have yet to make a convincing case for why we must assume that merely possessing a morally valid claim is sufficient for possessing a moral right.

---

[26] For the valid claims approach to rights and a defense of the interest criterion of rights possession, see Feinberg, "The Nature and Value of Rights" and "The Rights of Animals and Unborn Generations," in *Rights, Justice, and the Bounds of Liberty.*

THE MORAL IMPOVERISHMENT THESIS

The strongest and most frequent case made for this sufficiency thesis attempts to demonstrate the dire moral consequences that would follow were we to reject it. The basis of this case is to argue that our world would be morally impoverished in various respects were we to reject the view that possessing a morally valid claim was sufficient for possessing a moral right. Among the claims that have been made is that we would not be able to justify complaining when wronged, that we could not capture the distinction between acting wrongly and wronging someone, that we would have no basis for respect for self or others, and, perhaps most damning, that we could not argue effectively against social practices such as slavery. I will not attempt to take on all of these claims here.[27] Instead I will address only two in what remains of this chapter: the claim that individuals could not justify complaining and the claim they would not have a basis for self-respect or respect for others in a world devoid of presocial rights. In chapter 5 I will show that we can indeed argue effectively against slavery without relying on presocial natural rights to do so.

According to Feinberg the most conspicuous deficiency of worlds without natural rights has to do with the activity of claiming. Individuals who have been treated wrongly, either interfered with or left without the things they need, cannot "leap to their feet" and demand righteously to be left alone or to be assisted, nor can they make claims to what is owed to them, since they have no notion of rights, and hence, no notion of what is due to them.[28] At most, they may demand that others fulfill their duties under a code of *noblesse oblige* or to God. Of course when Feinberg says that individuals lacking natural rights cannot make claims to what is their due, he does not mean that when they open their mouths no sound comes out. Obviously individuals lacking natural rights can complain and demand that others not treat them cruelly. Rather his point is about what they may be or are entitled to do, as he makes quite clear:

If A has a duty to treat his slave B decently, but B being a mere slave, has no right that A do his duty (or any other right against A for that matter), and A proceeds to violate his own duty by treating B cruelly, then B will be "able to demand"

---

[27] I take up the moral impoverishment thesis at greater length in my article "Are Worlds without Natural Rights Morally Impoverished?" *The Southern Journal of Philosophy* 37 (1999), 397–417. Much of what I say about the valid claims approach in this chapter draws from this article.

[28] Feinberg, *Rights, Justice, and the Bounds of Liberty*, p. 148.

that A do his duty in the sense that if he opens his mouth to utter words of complaint, the intended sounds *will* come out, or if he merely speaks to remind his master, with the utmost tact, of his duties, (say) under a code of *noblesse oblige*, those sounds *will* come out . . . But it isn't a question of B's physical abilities, his being able to utter certain sounds; it is a question not of what he *can* do, but of what he *may* do under the accepted rules that govern his conduct and A's, and under those rules any claim he may make will be infirm; he will have no legal or moral *power* to affect his master's duties or his own; he will be *able* to complain but not *entitled* to complain; he will in a sense "have a complaint" but he will not have a genuine moral *grievance*. . ."[29]

But when exactly does someone—enslaved or free—have a basis to complain? Surely it will not be enough to say that one has a basis to complain when one has a "genuine moral grievance?" For then we shall want to know when someone has such a grievance. And on pain of circularity this cannot be accounted for by saying that one has a genuine moral grievance when one is entitled to and not merely able to complain, nor can it be accounted for by saying that one has a genuine moral grievance only when one has a natural or presocial moral right. For one, this is clearly question begging, since we can take the issue that divides proponents of natural rights and their critics to be whether we need to invoke these rights to explain when someone has a genuine moral griev-ance. Secondly, it is circular: since Feinberg takes a right to be a valid or justified claim, it amounts to saying that one has a genuine moral grievance when one has a right and one has a right when one has a genuine moral grievance. We obviously need to dig deeper to understand when someone has a basis to complain.

Let us consider two plausible proposals on Feinberg's behalf.

Sanction proposal (SP):   an individual has a basis to complain when and only when others cannot ignore him without risking external sanctions.[30]

According to SP, if I have a basis to complain that you have mistreated me, then by turning a deaf ear to my complaint you risk receiving a sanction, whether physical, monetary, or moral, whether proceeding from

---

[29] Feinberg, "The Social Importance of Moral Rights," *Philosophical Perspectives* 6 (1992), 181.
[30] This proposal is taken from William Nelson, "On the Alleged Importance of Moral Rights," *Ratio* 18 (1976), 153–4. Though Nelson takes this proposal to be inadequate, he does not explain why it is. I agree with Nelson's conclusion that the proposal is inadequate; however, I make an effort to explain why.

God, the state, or the community of fellow men and women in which you live. But what about complaints that do not have the force of divine, formal, or informal law backing them and thus can be ignored without risk of external sanctions? Proponents of natural or presocial moral rights will want to say that individuals can have such rights even when not backed by the force of law. Indeed, they take this to be the main difference between moral and conventional rights. However, if natural rights do not have the force of law behind them, then there will be no external sanctions associated with violating them and by hypothesis individuals will not have a basis for complaining about these violations.

For example, if we suppose that the slave has a natural right not to be treated cruelly, then proponents of natural rights will certainly want to say not merely that the slave is able to complain that he not be treated cruelly but, moreover, that he has a basis to complain that he not be treated cruelly. But what if the slave's natural right not to be treated cruelly does not have the backing of law? What if neither God nor the state has laid down laws against being cruel to one's slaves, and there are no informal laws against slave cruelty in the slaveholder's community? If the slave's natural right to not be treated cruelly does not have the backing of law, whether divine or man made, then there will be no external sanctions associated with turning a deaf ear to the slave's claim. But I take it that Feinberg and other proponents of natural rights will still want to say that the slave has a basis to complain and is not merely able to complain.

It appears, then, that SP does not give us a necessary condition for when one has a basis to complain, because some of the rights that proponents of natural rights are prepared to recognize will not have the backing of law and hence will not be backed by external sanctions; nevertheless, individuals having these rights will, on their view, still have a basis to complain. Nor is it obvious that it gives us a sufficient condition for when one has a basis to complain. One may risk being sanctioned for ignoring the bus driver's demand that you relinquish your seat on the bus to the wealthier man that just boarded. I suspect, however, that proponents of natural rights will deny that the bus driver (or anyone else) is entitled to demand that you give up your seat even if federal, state, and local laws require that wealthy people be given priority seating on the bus. Thus having a complaint that is backed by the force of law may not suffice, in their view, to afford one a basis to complain.

One may be tempted to salvage SP by modifying it to take internal as well as external sanctions into account. Recall that Mill characterizes an internal sanction as "a feeling in our own minds; a pain, more or less intense, attendant on violation of a duty [or valid claim], which in properly cultivated moral natures rises . . . This feeling . . . is the essence of conscience."[31] Modifying SP to take internal sanctions into account yields:

Internal sanction proposal: an individual has a basis to complain when and only when others cannot ignore him without risking internal sanctions.

Hence in cases where claims are not backed by law or by informal public sanctions, ignoring them will be sanctioned by this subjective feeling of pain in the guilty parties. But is this always true? And more importantly is it true in the cases that matter most? Let us return to the slave example to test this hypothesis.

While internal sanctions may affect individuals who have properly cultivated moral natures, i.e. individuals who have been raised and educated to believe that cruelty to slaves is morally wrong and should not be tolerated or condoned, this will not be the case with individuals who do not have properly cultivated moral natures. It is highly unlikely, for instance, that slaveholders will experience pain upon turning a deaf ear to their slave's complaint of being treated cruelly. One might try to defend Feinberg by holding that SP applies only to those cases where natural rights are either backed by law or conscience. Obviously, the scope of SP can be restricted in this way, but not without costs. For one, it leaves proponents of natural rights without a convincing account of the sense in which having a natural right protects rightholders. If the protection only kicks in when the right is backed by sanctions, why should we care so much about having natural rights as such? Why can we not simply be content with conventional rights, which come backed by sanctions to begin with? In short, the problem is that if SP is restricted in this way, then natural rights as such do not appear to afford rightholders any real protection.

What is more, embracing this restriction reduces SP to explaining when individuals have a basis to complain in cases where it is unlikely that they will have much need or cause to complain. For instance, the slave does not

---

[31] John Stuart Mill, in George Sher (ed.), *Utilitarianism* (Indianapolis: Hackett Publishing Company, 1979), pp. 27–8.

have cause to complain about being treated cruelly by God-fearing and law-abiding individuals with properly cultivated moral natures. He does not, for example, have cause to complain about a truly virtuous man treating him cruelly. Indeed, in all likelihood individuals with properly cultivated moral natures would not even own slaves—even if the laws of the land said that it was okay to do so. These individuals are clearly not targets of the slave's complaint. On the other hand, the slave would have cause to complain about being treated cruelly by individuals who were not really God-fearing and law-abiding individuals with properly cultivated moral natures. To wit, the slave will have to worry about being treated cruelly by the slaveholder. Surely the slaveholder is the real target of the slave's complaint. Accordingly, it is reasonable to expect any proposal of when someone has a basis to complain to explain when individuals have such a basis in cases in which they will actually have cause to complain. But restricting the scope of SP along the lines considered here is to ignore such cases altogether. Thus this salvage effort fails. We are still owed an account of when the slave has a basis to complain and is not merely able to complain.

Let us consider a second proposal, which some critics of my attack may allege is arguably closer in spirit to what Feinberg actually intended.

Moral proposal (MP):   an individual has a basis to complain when and only when recognition of her claim is called for by moral principles or "the principles of an enlightened conscience."[32]

But what exactly does this mean? Since Feinberg does not elaborate on this proposal, let us consider two plausible interpretations.

MP1:   an individual has a basis to complain when and only when others cannot ignore him without committing a moral wrong.
MP2:   an individual has a basis to complain when and only when he would be morally justified in complaining.

Given MP1, to establish that worlds without natural rights are impoverished in the respect under consideration, Feinberg must show that what makes it morally wrong for others to ignore an individual who has a basis to complain is that doing so violates some natural or presocial moral right.

---

[32] Feinberg, *Rights, Justice, and the Bounds of Liberty*, p. 154.

But on pain of question begging he cannot simply assume this. For the issue that divides proponents of such rights and their critics is over whether these rights need to be invoked to account for what makes it morally wrong for others to ignore an individual having a basis to complain. Critics will contend that other moral concepts (e.g. duty, utility, virtue, solidarity, etc.) can do this work as well. Feinberg has several options. He could take on each of these moral alternatives and show that they cannot do the work. He could show that each of these moral concepts can be reduced to natural rights. Or he could concede that each of these concepts can do the work but argue that natural rights do it best. I doubt that any of these burdens can be discharged successfully. If my assessment is correct, Feinberg is at best justified in concluding that in worlds without natural rights individuals cannot account for why it is morally wrong to ignore other individuals having a basis to complain by appealing to presocial natural rights. But of course this will not be problematic if inhabitants have a host of other moral concepts to which they can appeal.

Given MP2, to establish that worlds without natural rights are morally impoverished in the respect under consideration, Feinberg must show that individuals are morally justified in complaining only when their natural rights have been violated. But he cannot simply assume this either on pain of question begging. Critics of natural rights will contend that other moral concepts can be invoked here as well. And failing to discharge the burdens mentioned above, the most that Feinberg is permitted to conclude is that inhabitants of worlds without natural rights cannot appeal to such rights to explain when an individual is morally justified in complaining. But, again, this is unproblematic if other moral concepts can do the work.[33]

We began with Feinberg's claim that worlds lacking natural rights would be morally impoverished because inhabitants of such worlds would not have a basis to complain when they were treated wrongly. We then noticed that Feinberg did not address adequately the question of when

---

[33] Here I am merely developing Nelson's point:

> I suspect that there are a number of different conditions which we regard as sufficient to justify complaining. Infringement of a right may be one of them, but there are probably others. That someone's action causes me physical harm or involved the neglect of a duty that affected me adversely would, I suspect, be generally regarded as sufficient to justify my complaining. Thus, it seems to be false that only possessors of rights may complain.

See Nelson, "On the Alleged Importance of Moral Rights," p. 154.

exactly someone has a basis to complain. Two proposals were considered on his behalf, the sanction proposal and the moral proposal, both of which were found lacking. Pending further defense, then, the most reasonable conclusion to draw is this. Inhabitants of worlds without natural rights would certainly be unable to invoke such rights to ground their complaints, but they would not be any worse off so long as they could invoke other moral considerations to do so. Simply stipulating that they would be worse off, as Feinberg appears to do, is argumentatively unfair. We have yet to be convinced that there is a necessary conceptual connection between natural rights and claiming one's due.

RIGHTS AND RESPECT

Another alleged deficiency is that in a world devoid of natural rights there can be no respect for persons. And to understand why we must begin with the idea that natural rightholders are entitled to make claims against others. It has been argued that the activity of claiming is the basis of respect for persons. Individuals who are not prospective makers of claims (i.e. individuals lacking natural rights) cannot secure the respect of others. They are completely at the mercy of others to perform their duties or to act in accordance with the common good. Individuals without rights are like beggars who must secure their needs by begging and pleading with others. And insofar as this basis of respect is absent in worlds without natural rights such worlds are morally impoverished.[34]

To adequately assess this thesis we must reflect upon the nature of respect. Only then can we determine whether there is a necessary conceptual connection between being a rightholder or a prospective claim-maker and being entitled to respect. After developing a familiar way of understanding the nature of respect, I shall argue that it undermines this tight connection between claiming and respect. More specifically, I shall utilize the conception of recognition respect to explain why being a prospective claim-maker (or rightholder) is not a necessary condition of being an object of respect.

Roughly speaking, a subject (S) is the object of recognition respect if we assign importance to some fact about S, and give it appropriate

---

[34] Feinberg, "The Social Importance of Moral Rights," p. 180; also see Feinberg, *Rights, Justice, and the Bounds of Liberty*, p. 151, and Feinberg, "In Defence of Moral Rights," p. 155.

consideration or recognition in our deliberations about how to act.[35] So, for example, I am the object of recognition respect if my students assign importance to my being their philosophy professor and give this appropriate consideration in their deliberations about whether to challenge my arguments in class without adequate preparation. By the same token, male infants are objects of such respect if we assign importance to the fact that they are sentient and give this appropriate consideration in our deliberations about whether to circumcise them without anesthetic. Though we can debate whether the appropriate recognition requires a specific type of action or simply placing a certain fact among the relevant considerations to be weighed in deciding how to act, the crucial point here is that recognizing certain facts about a subject in thought and action is one way of respecting it.

Arguably, persons are the paradigm objects of recognition respect. They are objects of such respect insofar as we assign significance to the fact that S is a person and give this appropriate consideration in our deliberations about how to act. Of course what constitutes the proper treatment of persons ultimately depends upon what our duties to persons turn out to be; but this is open to debate and need not be settled here. The crucial point is that persons are not the only objects of respect. Many things can be objects of recognition respect.

In particular, nonpersons can also be objects of respect if we assign significance to some fact about them and give it appropriate consideration in our practical deliberations. Thus, animals, fetuses, trees, corporations, the dead, aliens, and other entities are all potential objects of respect. They go from being potential to actual objects of respect by our assigning importance to some fact about them and giving it appropriate consideration in our practical deliberations. For instance, trees are objects of respect if we assign importance to the fact that they are living things and give this appropriate consideration in our deliberations about whether to cut them down to make paper products. Likewise, fetuses are objects of respect if we assign importance to the fact that they have the potential for rational agency and give this appropriate consideration in our deliberations about whether to outlaw abortions.

We may of course display our respect for nonpersons in diverse ways, in ways similar to and different from our ways of respecting persons. Some people would say that we display our respect for nonhuman animals by

---

[35] My discussion of the nature of respect draws on Stephen Darwall, "Two Kinds of Respect," *Ethics* 88 (1977), 34–49.

not eating them, by not using them to test cosmetics, and by not treating them cruelly. We display our respect for fetuses by not aborting them (unless it is necessary to save the mother's life), and by not using drugs and alcohol while they are in the womb or while they are being nursed. We display our respect for works of art by not vandalizing them or otherwise defiling them, and by displaying them proudly in our museums, galleries, and in our homes. To be sure, some philosophers will object to talk of our respecting nonpersons; however, the idea of recognition respect, which amounts to assigning worth to some aspect of a subject's being and giving it due consideration in thought and action, clearly supports such talk.

Because we endow personhood with importance and assign it due consideration in our practical deliberations, subjects that are persons count as objects of recognition respect. However, if we were to endow sentience, life, or agency with importance (as we in fact do) and assign it due consideration in our deliberations, then subjects that possessed these features must also count as objects of recognition respect, be they persons or nonpersons. Indeed, I suspect that there are no restrictions on what we can endow with importance, which of course entails that there are no restrictions on what can count as an object of recognition respect.[36] But even if I am wrong about this, it seems clear that whatever feature(s) we assign importance to will determine what entities turn out to be objects of respect. In general, all of those entities that possess this feature will be objects of recognition respect. Let us call the relevant respect-conferring feature the basis of respect.

If we take seriously the possibility that nonpersons can be objects of respect, then there is no necessary conceptual connection between being a

---

[36] If we assign consideration to the fact that something is rational in our thought and action, then many human beings will count as objects of respect in virtue of their rationality. But if we believe that sophisticated computers are also rational, then for the sake of consistency we must embrace the counterintuitive position that they too can be objects of respect. Of course, this does not commit us to the implausible view that humans and sophisticated computers have equal moral status. There is no reason to think that all objects of respect are on a par. After all, there may be more that we respect about some subjects than we do about others. So although the concept of recognition respect is meant to have broad implications, this is not a reason for rejecting it. This point notwithstanding, one way to limit the counterintuitiveness of the concept of recognition respect would be to restrict it by taking some interest of a subject or some aspect of its well-being as the relevant fact about it that must be taken into account in thought and action. It would then be a precondition of being an object of respect that a subject had interests or well-being. Though this precondition is arguably satisfied by some nonpersons, e.g. animals and perhaps plants and trees, it is, arguably, not satisfied by others, e.g. cars, lecterns, computer keyboards, and other inanimate objects. Of course, we would still have to deal with the intuitions of those who think that it is counterintuitive to hold that we can respect animals and nature.

prospective claim-maker and respect, since nonpersons certainly do not share this basis of respect with persons, i.e. nonpersons are not prospective claim-makers. Of course, one could insist that subjects lacking this feature could not be objects of respect, but then one must either reject the conception of recognition respect altogether, which renders talk of respecting nonpersons sensible, or show that being a prospective claim-maker is the only possible basis of respect. But the conception of recognition respect is much too sensible to be rejected outright without serious justification, and proving that being a prospective claim-maker is the sole basis of respect is hopeless. For even if we do not take seriously the possibility that nonpersons can be the objects of respect and instead focus solely on persons, it is quite clear that other facts about persons, aside from their being prospective claim-makers, serve as possible bases of respect. For example, their humanity, their rationality, their intelligence, and their consciousness are facts about them that are also given due consideration in our deliberations about how to act and, consequently, all of these features are possible bases of respect.

Still, one might object that this merely shows that there are other necessary conceptual connections to be found, not that there is no such connection between being a prospective claim-maker and respect. But this just forces us back to the case of nonpersons, or even to the case of diminished persons, e.g. infants, young children, and mentally retarded adults, who are not prospective claim-makers yet are clearly objects of recognition respect insofar as other facts about them weigh in our deliberations about how to act. Hence the most reasonable conclusion to draw is that being a prospective claim-maker is neither the sole nor a necessary basis of respect for persons, though it is arguably a sufficient one. But this obviously undermines the moral impoverishment thesis, which postulates a much tighter connection between being a prospective claim-maker and respect.

Perhaps this tighter connection can be salvaged. One might distinguish between two kinds of recognition respect, moral and nonmoral recognition respect, and contend that the connection holds up in the case of moral recognition respect. What distinguishes moral from nonmoral recognition respect is that a failure to give certain features due consideration in thought and action will result in moral wrongdoing. For example, not giving consideration to the fact that S is a person in our deliberations about how to act will result in a moral wrong, whereas not giving consideration to the fact that S is 6 feet tall or the fact that S is a police officer or the fact that S is a philosophy professor will not result in a moral wrong. We can thus say that respect for prospective claim-makers is a moral requirement.

Failure to recognize the fact that *S* is a prospective claim-maker in one's deliberations about how to act would result in behavior that was morally wrong. But this does not save the moral impoverishment thesis from defeat. For we can also claim that respect for sentient beings, living beings, beings with interests, and so on, are also moral requirements. Failure to recognize the fact that *S* is sentient in one's practical deliberations would also result in moral wrongdoing, whether *S* was a person or a nonperson. It appears, therefore, that the tighter conceptual connection between being a prospective claim-maker and respect cannot be sustained even if we have moral recognition respect in mind.

These conclusions extend to the attempt to posit a strong connection between claim-making and self-respect as well. It has been argued that being able to make claims against others and demand one's due gives an individual a sense of self-worth: "being in a position to make claims and afterward to voice grievances, are the grounds of the greater dignity and self-respect that are associated with the role of right-holder."[37] The question, however, is whether worlds without natural rightholders, i.e. individuals in a position to make claims in virtue of their natural or presocial moral rights, would have other grounds for self-respect. To see that they would let us begin with the widely held view that having self-respect is a matter of having a favorable attitude toward oneself, and then ask what could ground this favorable attitude. Clearly, the fact that one is in a position to make claims (for whatever reason) can ground this attitude and, consequently, can ground self-respect. But is it equally clear that this is not the only fact about oneself that can ground this attitude. It could, for example, be grounded by the fact that one has a certain social status, the fact that one is a human being, or the fact that one is a person (however this is defined), or even the fact that one can act for reasons, or that one lives in accordance with personal or moral standards of conduct. My point, then, is that one's sense of worth can be grounded in numerous ways, which means, of course, that there would still be ample grounds for self-respect in worlds without natural rights. As best, being able to make claims is sufficient, not necessary, for self-respect.[38]

[37] Feinberg, "The Social Importance of Moral Rights," p. 189.

[38] For more on the grounding of self-respect, see Thomas Hill, "Self-Respect Reconsidered," Diane T. Meyers, "Self-Respect and Autonomy," and Robin S. Dillon, "Toward a Feminist Conception of Self-Respect," in Robin S. Dillon (ed.), *Dignity, Character, and Self-Respect* (New York: Routledge, 1995), pp. 117–24, 218–48, 290–310.

I have focused on two alleged deficiencies of worlds devoid of natural rights: that the inhabitants of such worlds would have no basis to complain when wronged and they could not respect themselves and others as persons. To be sure, I have not considered all of the alleged moral deficiencies of worlds without natural rights that have been advanced. But I have done enough to cast serious doubt on the moral impoverishment thesis. I have shown that it cannot be taken for granted that worlds without natural rights would be morally impoverished and that anyone wishing to defend this view has a much greater burden than has been realized by proponents of the prevailing view. Having undermined the prevailing view by exposing the shortcomings of the two predominant ways of accounting for the source of moral rights, the way is clear for considering my social recognition-based conception of how we come to possess moral rights.

CHAPTER 3

Rights and recognition

> I was in bondage in Missouri, too. I can't say that my treatment was
> bad. In one respect I say it was not bad, but in another I consider it
> was as bad as could be. I was a slave. That covers it all. I had not the
> rights of a man.
>
> —Benjamin Miller, *Slave Testimony*[1]

For many people it is comforting to believe that we have natural rights,
ones that come to us by the hand of our creator or by the hand of human
nature. But I believe that there are no rights that exist prior to and
independent of some form of formal or informal social recognition of
ways of acting and being treated by a community of persons. Hence
insofar as natural rights, human rights, and presocial moral rights are
typically understood as having such prior and independent existence,
I believe that there simply are no such rights. All rights—moral ones
included—are a species of unnatural rights. So contrary to the prevailing
view—the dominant versions of which I critically assessed in the previous
chapter—whatever rights we do have (if any at all) are bestowed on us by
a community of persons.

While possible shortcomings of this view come readily to hand, its
virtues are more elusive for readers steadfastly devoted to the prevailing
view. I proceed therefore by advancing a political justification for imposing a social constraint on what having moral rights amounts to. Although
this is certainly not the only way to justify doing so, it is the one that
I champion in this book, given my methodological orientation to taking
race and racism seriously. Furthermore, insofar as I take this to be the most
widespread justification for embracing the prevailing view itself, the
general point will be that if combating oppression and subordination
has historically been used to justify embracing natural or presocial moral

---

[1] Benjamin Miller, an ex-slave in a Freedman's Inquiry Commission interview, cited in John
W. Blassingame (ed.), *Slave Testimony* (Baton Rouge: Louisiana State University Press, 1977), p. 439.

rights, then the same general considerations also justify eschewing belief in such rights. Of course, some readers may conclude that this is so much the worse for political justification, and more reason to pursue other means of defending a philosophical conception of rights. Nevertheless, I will proceed in this fashion.[2]

A POLITICAL JUSTIFICATION

From the earliest defenders of natural rights during the American War of Independence with Great Britain, to those who appropriated natural rights to criticize chattel slavery and the subordination of women in the United States of America, and, most recently, to those who have mar-shaled them to protect animals and the natural environment, as well as those who have used them to justify intervention into the domestic affairs of other sovereign nations, natural rights (and their modern progeny) have been used to condemn various forms of oppression. They have served this function by providing social actors with a powerful standard for criticizing the conduct of governments and individuals as morally wrong or unjust. Hence a general justification, and arguably the primary justification, for postulating a class of rights that exist prior to or independently of human invention has been a political one, namely that doing so is politically instrumental for condemning oppressive social practices and institutions as immoral or unjust. Although embracing a theory of rights for a political purpose may not be the best reason for doing so, and should not be our only reason for doing so, it has been and continues to be a primary reason for allegiance to the doctrine of natural or presocial moral rights.

Rather than taking issue with the adequacy of embracing a conceptual analysis for political reasons, in what follows I shall offer a political justification for imposing a social constraint on moral rights possession. To develop this justification I will begin with a brief summary of a general critique of rights discourse championed most recently by some critical legal studies scholars. The basis of this critique, which I shall refer to as the legitimation critique of rights, is that rights discourse is ideological insofar as appeals to rights often serve to legitimize oppressive social arrangements

---

[2] I am grateful to George Rainbolt for pressing this objection, though I continue to believe that he does not sufficiently appreciate the extent to which leading philosophical advocates of the prevailing view have utilized a political justification in its defense.

and institutions.[3] Drawing inspiration from critical social theory these critical legal studies scholars presume that by making agents aware of both the fact and causes of their oppression, critical theories endeavor to free agents from the grip of self-imposed oppression and place them in a position to positively transform social or legal arrangements. While all oppression is backed by coercion, the most devastating forms of oppression are supported by both external and self-imposed coercion. The former is when external force or the threat of external force is used to sustain oppressive social or legal arrangements. Though critical theories are clearly concerned with external coercion, they take self-imposed coercion to be more pernicious. For one, as a form of mental bondage, self-imposed coercion usually goes undetected and it is more difficult to free oneself from chains that one cannot see. Secondly, although we can imagine brute force being sufficient to maintain systems of domination, because external coercion is arguably easier to sustain if self-imposed coercion is widespread and effective, freedom from mental bondage is crucial to gaining freedom from physical bondage. Thus critical theories are especially concerned with emancipating agents by making them aware of the way in which they actively participate in their own oppression by accepting forms of consciousness that legitimate existing social or legal arrangements which favor the dominant classes.

According to critical theorists, exposing forms of consciousness as ideological is a crucial step in the direction of enlightenment and emancipation since progressive social or legal transformation of society and ideological critique go hand and hand. Suppose that a form of consciousness is narrowly understood as a particular constellation of beliefs having certain distinctive properties: (1) they are widely shared; (2) they are systematically connected; (3) they strongly influence agents' behavior; and (4) their content is usually about central human issues, for example human nature, society, politics, law, economics, ethics, and religion. Although forms of consciousness are not inherently problematic, to call a form of consciousness ideological in a pejorative sense is to disparage it, to indicate that it is something to be exposed, rejected, and overcome. One of the ways in which a form of consciousness can be ideological in a pejorative sense is by legitimizing reprehensible social or legal

---

[3] For well-developed versions of this critique, see Karl Klare, "Labor Law as Ideology: Toward a New Historiography of Collective Bargaining Law," *Industrial Relations Law Journal* 4 (1981), 450–82, and Peter Gabel, "The Phenomenology of Rights-Consciousness and the Pact of the Withdrawn Selves," *Texas Law Review* 62 (1984), 1563–99.

arrangements, institutions, or practices. For purposes of this discussion I shall use the term "ideology" to refer to forms of consciousness that serve this very specific function.[4]

Some critical legal studies scholars claim that rights consciousness is ideological in a pejorative sense. Very roughly, this is to say that rights consciousness is part of a particular constellation of beliefs about law, rights, and the nature and limits of interactions between individuals, and between individuals and the state, that is widely shared, systematically connected, action-guiding, and that functions to legitimize reprehensible social and legal practices. They contend that rights consciousness has legitimized oppressive social and legal arrangements in at least two ways: first, by moralizing them, in other words, by representing them as just, fair, or moral, and thereby suggesting that agents should accept the existing status quo out of a sense of justice or out of respect for morality. Hence one way to encourage people to consent to their own oppression, or to discourage them from resisting oppression, is to appeal to their moral sensibilities. Rights consciousness, which presents the appearance that things are as they are as a matter of right or justice, is taken to be well suited for this task. Second, rights consciousness legitimizes oppressive social and legal arrangements by reification, for instance by representing them as natural and inevitable.[5] Rights consciousness can accomplish this by convincing agents that their subordination is the result of their natural "inferiority" or their "defective" character.

To be sure, the notion of reification must be used with care. It can mean seeing certain relations or (more to the point for present purposes) certain statuses (erroneously) as natural and immutable and not the product of social selection. But it can also mean solidifying existing oppressive social relations. These are not the same thing, however, since one can reify many things and many sorts of things in the first sense, but not all such reifications are oppressive. The natural rights thesis, as I have articulated it, reifies rights possession in the first sense, namely by

---

[4] Here I follow Guess, *The Idea of a Critical Theory.*
[5] Gabel, "The Phenomenology of Rights-Consciousness and the Pact of the Withdrawn Selves," p. 1581; Diane Polan, "Toward a Theory of Law and Patriarchy," in David Kairys (ed.), *The Politics of Law: A Progressive Critique* (New York: Pantheon Books, 1982), pp. 298–9; Robert W. Gordon, "New Developments in Legal Theory," in Kairys (ed.), *The Politics of Law: A Progressive Critique,* rev. edn. (New York: Pantheon Books, 1990), pp. 422–3; Cheryl Harris, "Whiteness as Property," in Kimberlé Crenshaw, Neil Gotanda, Gary Peller, and Kendall Thomas (eds.), *Critical Race Theory: The Key Writings that Formed the Movement* (New York: The New Press, 1995), pp. 283, 286–7.

representing the status of being a moral rightholder as natural and not the product of social construction. While this particular sort of reification need not be oppressive, it certainly can be, especially when a subject is believed not to be a rightholder on the grounds that it lacks the relevant nature or constitution. Bearing this clarification in mind, one way to flesh out this reification criticism is to claim that another way to encourage people to consent to their own oppression, or to discourage them from resisting oppression, is to dupe them into thinking that their situation is not the result of human agency or convention, but the result of facts that they have no control over. So, for example, an ideological use of rights would encourage a slave and others to think that his lacking moral rights was either because he had not been endowed with a certain nature, for instance a rational nature, or perhaps because his rational nature was not fully developed. Furthermore, it would encourage the slave and others to think that the master and other members of the dominant race possessed moral rights precisely because they had been endowed with rational natures or because their rational natures were fully developed.

As a result of this particular ideological function of rights in legitimizing oppressive social and legal relations, some critical theorists have concluded that rights cannot be reliable conceptual instruments to aid social struggles aimed at the radical transformation of society and have proposed that we reject them altogether and search for alternative political discourses. Although the reification critique of rights is not without merit, an outright rejection of rights is premature, unnecessary, and quite possibly counterproductive. The representation of moral rightholder status as something natural can be effectively addressed without rejecting moral rights altogether. Alternatively, it can be addressed by rethinking the source of rights so that certain social practices are taken to be an essential component in the possession of all rights, not just conventional or legal ones. In addition to enabling critical theorists to undermine attempts to represent exclusion from (and inclusion within) the realm of moral rightholders as a matter of natural as opposed to social selection, rethinking the source of moral rights instead of rejecting them outright will not foreclose the possibility of using moral rights for critical purposes (though we will certainly have to rethink what this amounts to if social practices are taken to play an essential role in grounding moral rights). Therefore, if it is an important goal of a critical theory to enlighten agents by making them aware of the fact and causes of oppression so that they can be better situated to combat it, then we can accomplish this goal within a rights framework by embracing rights externalism or the thesis that moral rights are partly the product of recognition, which conceives of moral rights possession as a social not an ontological fact.

Consider one pay-off of adopting rights externalism. One difference between rights internalism and rights externalism is that the former represents inclusion into (and exclusion from) the realm of moral rightholders as beyond the power of human authority to change. Whether a subject makes the cut is simply a matter of what kind of being it is—for instance, if it can reason, think, suffer, pursue projects, or act for moral reasons, then it counts, but if it cannot do these things then it does not count. For those subjects whose status as natural or moral rightholders has never been challenged or in doubt (for example, kings, nobles, and masters) this is a welcomed result, since it renders their enjoyment of the alleged benefits of moral rightholdership relatively secure. But for those whose status as natural or moral rightholders has been challenged or doubted (for example, peasants, Native Americans, slaves, and women) this is not such a welcomed result, since it represents their exclusion from the realm of moral rightholders (and the associated benefits) as an ontological shortcoming—an unfortunate result of failing to be endowed with the relevant nature or failing to be a certain kind of being. But the rights externalist contends that this is a misdiagnosis of the situation of kings and masters and slaves and women, one that misdirects our attention away from the social conditions that create and sustain existing social relations of domination and subordination, which can indeed be altered through social struggle and resistance.

I am not suggesting that a natural rights theorist will necessarily be, or will tend to be, less alert than a rights externalist in recognizing the need for social activism in making rights real and effective. While it could be the case that if you think of rights as natural, you will think of them as something people already have, and so you will be less alert to the possibility that their having them is not effective because of lack of social recognition, this need not be the case. A rights internalist can believe that people have presocial natural rights and that societies and governments have not respected them. And that person could be very militant in arguing for the need to persuade societies and governments to respect these rights. My main concern is simply to show that rights externalists can also give a political justification for their position. It would clearly take much more work to show that one side has a clear-cut political advantage over the other.

Hence by reconceptualizing moral rights possession as a social fact, that is, by adopting rights externalism, the practical aim of combating oppression through enlightenment can still proceed even within a rights framework. Rethinking the source of rights along social as opposed to ontological lines affords us a pragmatic account of the situation of those who are excluded from the realm of moral rightholders, what is at stake in their exclusion, and what is needed to overcome it. A pragmatic theory of moral rights possession tells us that their predicament is not the result of failing to be endowed with a certain nature. Rather it is the result of failing to be afforded a certain kind of treatment or respect. For peasants, slaves, women, animals, and other subjects whose status as moral right-holders has been challenged, emancipation is not about getting others to recognize, maintain, and enforce natural rights that these subjects possess prior to or independently of whether certain ways in which they may act or be treated have been socially recognized, maintained, and enforced. Rather it is about the establishment of social conditions in which these ways of acting and being treated are socially recognized, maintained, and enforced. Hence by adopting this general approach to rights possession one can claim that social activism on the part of subjects and their advocates is necessary to create the social conditions whose instantiation is an essential ingredient in the very possession of moral rights, since their exclusion from the realm of moral rightholders is the result of social forces, and thus well within their power and that of others to change.

Earlier I conceded that embracing a conceptual analysis of moral rights possession for a political reason may not be the best reason, and should not be our only reason, for doing so. But insofar as this has been and continues to be a primary reason for allegiance to the doctrine of natural rights, my concern in this section has been to supply a political justification for imposing a social constraint on moral rights possession. To be sure, the political justification for embracing natural rights differs in content from the justification for embracing rights externalism, though both are equally concerned with conceptualizing moral rights possession in a way that enables us to combat oppression. Of course, once we see that both approaches can stake a claim to being able to combat oppression, one may wonder whether one or the other concep-tualization of moral rights possession affords us a better way to combat oppression. But even if it turns out that one view does provide better resources for combating oppression, this does not undermine the main point of this section, namely that we can justify embracing both of these conceptions of moral rights possession on political grounds.[6]

THE SLAVE CASE

It is not surprising that slavery is often utilized in efforts to defend the utility of believing in natural rights. Typically it is argued that the reason why chattel slavery was morally wrong, and had to be abolished, was that it constituted a violation of the natural rights of enslaved blacks, rights that slaves possessed even though they were not socially recognized and enforced in the antebellum United States. This is not surprising because such arguments are an obvious extension of earlier natural rights-based arguments against arguably immoral or unjust government practices. Yet we must pause before concluding that the utility and popularity of these arguments settle once and for all the question of how the source of moral rights should be understood. The proclaimed political utility of natural rights in arguments against slavery (and other immoral or otherwise unjust government and societal practices) does not oblige us to accept the view that there is a class of rights that exist prior to and independently of all forms of social recognition. Of course, if we believe that such arguments afford us the only or the best way to argue for the immorality of slavery, then we will be committed to believing in natural rights come what may. I will take issue with these assumptions in due course. But for now I will show that on closer reflection the case of slavery also illuminates the political utility of imposing a social constraint on moral rights possession. Furthermore, this reflection will allow me to underscore some important differences between the prevailing conception of the source of moral rights and my alternative.

Suppose that Dred is a slave. He is chattel that can be bought and sold and used as his owner sees fit. Dred's life is completely at the disposal of his master. He cannot go and come as he pleases; he cannot eat and sleep when he chooses; he cannot marry and raise children; he cannot sell his labor

---

[6] There are two other recent attempts in the philosophy of rights to systematically develop and defend a conception of moral rights possession that satisfies a social constraint. See Sumner, *The Moral Foundation of Rights*, and Martin, *A System of Rights*. While I have benefited greatly from their work, my account differs from theirs in important respects. One very important difference is that we are led to this approach for different reasons. Neither Sumner nor Martin offers a political justification for imposing a social constraint on moral rights possession. Yet collectively our work builds a very powerful case for a conceptual position regarding the source of moral rights that has not been taken seriously enough.

for a wage to the highest bidder or enter into any other contractual arrangements, nor can he own property, speak his mind to his master, learn to read and write, or even worship God. It is important to underscore the distinction between being able to do these things and being able to do them with impunity. For example, although Dred can indeed run away, if successful he will live in constant fear of being captured and returned to his master and possibly even killed to set an example for other slaves. Furthermore, those who object to Dred's enslavement and who aid his escape will also live in constant fear of being discovered and subsequently sanctioned for assisting a runaway slave. In stark contrast, Dred's master and others who uphold and practice slavery do so with impunity. Even the most abominable offense against one's slaves, killing them, meets with either mild or negligible punishment, while other offenses such as rape, whipping, and depriving them of adequate nourishment, shelter, and rest meet with no punishment at all. Thus the relevant sense in which Dred "cannot" do these things is that he is not able to do them with impunity.

Suppose further that Dred is a human being and possesses all of the traits typically possessed by human beings: he can think, reason, select and pursue projects, distinguish right from wrong, and can experience both higher and lower pleasures and pains. Furthermore, suppose that the immorality of slavery is not in doubt. It is fitting to criticize the practice of slavery as immoral or unjust, to accuse slaveholders of committing a moral wrong or an injustice by holding slaves, to cite the immorality or injustice of slavery as a reason for abolishing it and for punishing those who participate in it, and it is even fitting to cite the immorality or injustice of slavery as a reason for its eventual demise. Now consider the following questions. Does Dred have a right to go and come as he pleases? Does he have a right to marry and raise children? Does he have a right to sell his labor for a wage to the highest bidder or to enter into any other contractual arrangements? Does he have a right to own property, to speak his mind, to learn to read and write, or even to worship God?

Both defenders of natural rights and rights externalists can agree that Dred does not have any of the foregoing rights under slavery if the rights at issue are merely conventional or legal rights. Yet the former will quickly add that although Dred may not have a legal right to go and come as he pleases under slavery, or a legal right to marry and raise children, or a legal right to sell his labor, or any other legal rights for that matter, he does have a natural or presocial moral right to go and come as he pleases, to marry and raise children, and to sell his labor. Moreover, they will add that having such natural rights benefits Dred by enabling us to criticize the institution of slavery as a violation of these natural rights. Indeed, this is a political pay-off we gain by embracing the natural rights thesis.

Obviously natural rights theorists would reject Bentham's view that all bona fide rights are products of positive law. They contend that natural rights are bona fide rights even though these rights are not products of positive law. Consequently, it would be fruitless to take the choice between the natural rights approach and rights externalism to turn on the issue of what constitutes a bona fide right. By taking a version of Bentham's definition as my point of departure I am not begging any questions against natural rights theorists since I am not arguing from this definition to rights externalism or from this definition against a natural rights conception. Rather I am advancing this definition, offering a conception of moral rights that squares with it, providing some positive justification for embracing it, and showing that certain objections to this conception can be answered.

Of course, insofar as proponents of the natural rights thesis hold that these rights are not products of social conventions or positive law, they owe us an alternative account of their source and we considered two leading approaches in the previous chapter. It is clear how internalists can respond to the Dred case. They can say, for instance, that Dred has a natural right to go and come as he pleases, even under slavery, merely in virtue of his humanity, or in virtue of his rational capacity, or in virtue of possessing some other relevant right-endowing property. A salient aspect of this approach is that the possession of such rights need not be manifested in the overt behavior of either the rightholder or those who are bound by these rights. In other words, a subject can have such a right even though the right is not exercisable with impunity, or even though others can disregard it with impunity. This must be so if these rights are to provide the political pay-off of supplying a moral standard for criticizing Dred's enslavement.

Alternatively, I contend that under conditions of chattel slavery Dred has neither a legal right to go and come as he pleases, to marry and raise children, to sell his labor, nor a moral right to do these things if he cannot do them with impunity, or if others can prevent him doing them with impunity.[7]

---

[7] This example could be made more precise (as well as more complex) by formulating it using the Hohfeldian classificatory scheme for rights. For example, to say that Dred does not have a right to go and come as he pleases is to say that others do not have a duty to assist him or to refrain from interfering with him. Thus this would be to deny that Dred has a claim-right to go and come as he pleases. And to take just one more example, to deny that Dred can sell his labor for a wage is to say that someone has a claim-right that Dred would be violating by doing so. But for the sake of simplicity I will not develop my analysis using the Hohfeldian classificatory scheme.

And, as is the case with possessing legal and other conventional rights, for these circumstances to materialize certain social practices having to do with the social recognition, maintenance, and enforcement of certain ways of acting and being treated must obtain. Rights externalism takes the instantiation of these social practice conditions to be necessary for the very possession of moral rights. To wit, the obtaining of these conditions renders moral rights possession a social as opposed to an ideal reality.

For example, my having a moral right to enjoy a meal at a fine restaurant covers the social reality of being able to do so without fear of being hauled away by local law enforcement officials. Of course, I may have a moral right to enjoy the meal yet still have some fear of being hauled away by the local police, since it is possible that these individual law enforcement authorities may not recognize my right to enjoy a meal at this particular restaurant. But so long as I can count on the backing of a higher positive authority to enforce my being able to eat in this restaurant—backing which might be offered by sending federal troops to escort me into the restaurant or by imposing stiff sanctions on the proprietors and the local police, for instance—then my right remains a social reality. But it is quite possible that a higher positive authority, and perhaps even the highest political authority, might refuse to recognize my right to dine in the restaurant. In this case my alleged right would not be a social reality. For it would not have any practical efficacy: I would not be able to eat at the restaurant without fear of being hauled off to prison, nor would I have the assurance of knowing that those responsible for hauling me off to prison would be legally sanctioned for doing so.

Obviously this same reasoning applies in Dred's case. Dred's having a moral right to go and come as he pleases covers the social reality of being able to do so without fear of being tracked down by fugitive slave catchers and hauled back to the plantation for punishment. So from the perspective of rights externalism, Dred's having a moral right to go and come as he pleases covers the social reality of his being able to go and come as he pleases without fear of being sanctioned and with the assurance that those who interfere or prevent him from doing so will be sanctioned or at least threatened with sanctions.

Thus the most striking difference between the prevailing conception and my own is that the latter forges a necessary connection between moral rights possession and the existence of certain social practice conditions and the former does not. Reading this case in the initial way brings out the political value of embracing the prevailing conception. However, reading this case in the second way brings out the political value of rights externalism. This conception offers us a more pragmatic account of the situation of those who are excluded from the realm of moral rightholders, what is at stake in their exclusion, and what is needed to overcome it. For someone like Dred, whose status as a moral rightholder has been withheld, this enables us to overcome ideological attempts to appropriate rights to legitimize his oppression by suggesting that his predicament is the result of failing to be endowed with a certain nature rather than the result of failing to be afforded a certain kind of treatment or respect.

Hence by embracing rights externalism the political aim of combating oppression through enlightenment can still proceed even within a rights framework. From this vantage point emancipation will involve the establishment of social conditions in which certain ways in which Dred may act, and ways in which he may be treated, are socially recognized, maintained, and enforced, which are all well within the power of social actors to change. Another very important difference between these approaches, which I will return to later, regards the resources that they have at their disposal for moral argument. Defenders of both approaches agree that slavery is morally objectionable; however, a rights externalist cannot offer the same explanation as advocates of the prevailing conception as to why it is morally objectionable. The latter can appeal to natural rights but the former cannot. In chapter 5 I shall show that this outcome is not as troubling as it initially appears. For now I turn to the development of rights externalism in more detail.

THE SOCIAL DIMENSION OF MORAL RIGHTS

In what follows I shall elucidate the social dimension of rights possession using the idea of institutional respect. I will assume that affording a subject legal rights is a paradigm case of affording it institutional respect. We can gain a clear statement of what being afforded institutional respect amounts to by specifying the conditions for legal rights possession.[8] But it does not follow from this that we must develop the idea of institutional respect using a legal model. If we wish to impose a social constraint on moral rights possession, we need not suppose that only formal legal practices as opposed to more informal social practices can suffice for this constraint. Although I do think that there are reasons for grounding moral rights possession in more formal social practices, mainly having to do with

---

[8] My presentation of this model borrows from Hart, *The Concept of Law.*

my belief that this is a very strong form of protection for rightholders, the argument of this book does not require ruling out the possibility that the respect necessary for grounding moral rights could be imparted by less formal social practices. In fact, I will develop this less formal grounding when I reconstruct Green's argument against slavery in chapter 5. This will supplement what I have to say here. For now I use the legal model simply for ease of exposition. But it is important to keep in mind that I believe that informal and nonlegal forms of recognition can also give rise to moral rights.

So I shall assume that all rights are established ways of acting or being treated.[9] Furthermore, I shall assume that the social establishment of ways of acting or being treated by certain authorities is required to convert a mere way of acting or being treated into a right. The point is not merely that these authorities agree that the relevant ways of acting and being treated constitute rights. Rather the point is much stronger, namely that they can do things that have the effect of turning them into rights in much the same way that an umpire can turn a pitch into a strike or a queen can make a man a knight. To be sure, which authorities are empowered to turn them into rights, and which of their activities are relevant, can vary from society to society and even within the same society, depending upon the kind of right at issue. Finally, if we assume that a legal system is operative when it is generally efficacious, and that it is generally efficacious when the rules regulating the conduct of individuals under its jurisdiction are generally complied with, and the rules conferring legislative and adjudicative powers on public officials are endorsed by these officials, the possession conditions for legal rights can be understood as follows:

S possesses legal rights if and only if S's acting in a certain way or being treated in a certain way is legally established within an operative legal system.

The legal establishment of practices involves at least two kinds of activities: officially recognizing a practice as a right and maintaining and enforcing the right-designated practice. If the recognition requirement is satisfied we can say of some practice that it has been officially recognized by some source of valid law as specified by the rule of recognition for a particular legal system. This source is empowered to convert a mere practice into a right by engaging in some kind of legislative activity.

---

[9] Here I follow Martin, *A System of Rights*.

The relevant activity can vary. For instance, it might amount to a practice being laid down in a formal document like a constitution that was upheld by the sovereign authority, or it might amount to its being laid down via the rulings of a judiciary body whose rulings counted as law unless overturned by a higher body. The maintenance requirement tells us that any practices officially recognized as rights must also be maintained and enforced by whatever authorities are charged with this duty. Maintaining and enforcing a practice involves, among other things, identifying publicly (or at least making publicly available) the officially recognized practices, backing them up with the threat of force, and, when necessary, imposing sanctions for noncompliance.

So, for example, suppose that voting in public elections is a practice. For this practice to be a legal right it must be legally ratified. But voting in public elections will not constitute a legal right if the source empowered to convert mere practices into rights simply stipulates that voting in public elections is okay. This body (or some other designated body) must also back up this practice. It must, as a matter of course, be prepared to do whatever it takes to gain compliance. This might require merely threatening sanctions for interfering with those who attempt to vote in public elections; but it might also require sending federal troops to escort would-be voters to the polls under the watchful eye of disgruntled onlookers. The maintenance requirement acknowledges that words or pronouncements are not enough to establish rights; deeds aimed at backing up these pronouncements are also required.

Therefore, given this connection between institutional respect and legal rights, it follows that a sufficient condition of a subject's being afforded institutional respect, which itself is a necessary condition of it possessing moral rights, is that a way of treating the subject (or a way in which the subject might act) be legally ratified within an operative legal system. Hence, on this view, the social practices relevant to affording a subject institutional respect, and ultimately moral rights, are those formal practices involved in making it the case that the subject possesses legal rights.

A distinctive feature of the foregoing conception of rights possession is that it forges a connection between rights possession and practical efficacy by grounding rights socially and thereby rendering them social realities whenever they exist. In addition, this analysis applies to all rights, not just legal or nonlegal conventional ones. While my suggestion that the possession of rights requires an institutional framework which guarantees that they will be practically efficacious whenever they exist is controversial, the general connection between practical efficacy and rights is not meant to be so. Even Locke, perhaps the most famous proponent of natural rights, acknowledges the importance of some kind of social framework for rendering natural rights valuable. Locke's doctrine of executive power makes this quite clear. He argued that the natural rights of man as given by the law of nature would be in vain if there was nobody in the state of nature to enforce these rights. Thus to prevent the law of nature from being a law in name only, and natural rights from being mere nominal rights, Locke argued that every person in the state of nature (minus children and madmen) had the power to enforce the law of nature. Of course, this could only be a temporary arrangement, since individuals could not be trusted to enforce the law of nature impartially; they would be too easy on themselves and their associates and too harsh on their enemies, competitors, and strangers. Thus the establishment of a civil government with institutions and officers assigned to interpret the law, adjudicate disputes, and enforce the law would remedy this and other inconveniences of the state of nature.[10]

For present purposes, however, the relevant point is that Locke thought that it was important to make sure that natural rights would be more than mere nominal rights by assigning individuals in the state of nature the power to enforce these rights. Locke and I agree that rights must be backed up or enforced in some way if they are to be practically efficacious; however, I differ from Locke in that I take the supporting social framework, which renders rights practically efficacious, to be necessary for the very possession of moral rights. Whereas Locke would say that although they would be in vain we could have natural rights even if they were not efficacious, I would say that the only rights we actually possess are those that are efficacious.

Having ascertained the possession conditions for legal rights, we now have a working model of institutional respect and a more detailed understanding of the social dimension of rights possession. One question raised by this analysis is how we can distinguish between moral and legal rights possession if both contain the same social dimension. As noted in the previous chapter, some rights theorists have relied on the idea of moral justification to elucidate the difference between moral and legal rights possession. On this view subjects possess moral rights if they possess claims that can be morally justified by some substantive moral theory. Hence the difference between moral and legal rights possession is that one

---

[10] Locke, *Two Treatises of Government*, pp. 271–3.

possesses a moral right if one has a claim that is justified by moral principles, and one possesses a legal right if one has a claim that is justified by legal rules. Yet a significant difference between valid claims theorists and rights externalists, however, is that while the former take such justification to be sufficient for possessing moral rights, externalists maintain that this is necessary but not sufficient. In other words, valid claims theorists assign moral justification an exclusive role while externalists assign it a supporting role.

Feinberg in particular is silent about which moral principles can or must supply the requisite moral justification, as I argued in chapter 2. Presumably he cannot allow that the most basic moral principles are right-based ones since he is attempting to elucidate the very idea of having moral rights. It would be circular to reintroduce basic moral rights to specify the shape of the justification conferring moral principles. The moral justification requirement, whatever it is for Feinberg, cannot make recourse to basic moral rights on pain of circularity. So in the final analysis morally valid claims will have to be validated by some sort of nonrights-based general moral principles. There is a sense, then, in which Feinberg and I occupy important common ground: we both want to appeal to moral justification to establish the existence of moral rights and neither of us regards moral rights as being morally basic insofar as they cannot supply the requisite moral justification.

Philosopher L. Wayne Sumner also appeals to moral justification to ground moral rights. But *contra* Feinberg he does not believe that the existence of a moral right follows directly from the fact that a particular claim is morally justified. Instead, like me, Sumner imposes a social practice constraint on the possession of moral rights. Thus, on his view, moral justification will only be necessary, not sufficient, for the possession of moral rights. But one significant difference between our accounts is that I am neutral about the kind of moral justification needed to ground moral rights, while Sumner defends a consequentialist moral justification in extensive detail.[11] For Sumner the substantive moral theory that lends justification to corresponding legally established practices is a consequentialist one. Even though Sumner's defense of consequentialism is comprehensive and penetrating, he is well aware that one might try to give an alternative moral justification of a given social practice. For instance, one might give a contractarian one, which takes the social recognition of the

---

[11] Sumner, *The Moral Foundation of Rights*, ch. 6.

right to be justified if it is the product of the appropriate collective choice procedure or deliberative procedure. Or one might give a Kantian justification, a theistic justification, or some other moral justification. Insofar as no substantive moral theory has been proven to be the one true moral theory, each having its defenders and detractors, I think that it is premature to commit oneself to one particular normative theory—at least for purposes of developing a conception of what having moral rights amounts to. Not only does this impose a heavy burden to defend the selected moral theory, it ultimately requires the undermining of every plausible alternative moral theory—a rather daunting task.

Accordingly, I favor a strategy that falls between these two. Following Sumner, my strategy assigns moral justification a supporting role and not an exclusive one, but following Feinberg my strategy does not defend a substantive moral theory to play the justifying role. Instead it enables us to avoid prejudging this issue of which moral theory should play the justifying role, while at the same time allowing us to set a constraint on any possible contender. Though I wish to remain neutral about which substantive moral theory can supply the requisite justification, in part because I do not wish to take on the large project of defending a general moral theory in this book, insofar as we are attempting to theorize about the nature of moral rights possession this is a reasonable criterion of adequacy that any proposed moral theory should satisfy. Yet I should add that although I take neutrality to be a virtue of my conceptual analysis, this is not to claim that we can avoid selecting a substantive moral theory. My concern is not so much to avoid this, but to avoid building a commitment to a particular substantive moral theory into the conceptual analysis of moral rights possession. Nevertheless, I shall make my particular normative commitments explicit in the final chapter when I mount my argument against slavery.

TRUTH

By now an obvious yet important contrast between moral rights externalists and advocates of the prevailing conception (whether they adopt the valid claims or ontological approach) is that the former appeal to social practices in specifying the truth conditions for moral rights assertions and the latter do not. Both are cognitivists about rights assertions insofar as they both take rights assertions to have a truth value. However, some moral rights foundationalists, in particular ones who ground rights ontologically, hold that whether a subject possesses rights is a fact about the subject's nature, e.g. how it is constituted or what abilities it has. They are objectivists in that they make no essential reference to conventions or social practices in specifying the truth conditions for moral rights assertions. On the other hand, moral rights externalists are intersubjectivists in that they do make essential reference to social practices.[12] They hold that for any claim of the form "*S* possesses a right" to be true certain social practices conditions must obtain, e.g. a certain way of acting toward *S* must be socially ratified or *S* must be afforded institutional respect.

For instance, if I say that Dred, a chattel slave, has a right to the fruits of his labor, whether this claim is true or not will depend upon whether certain social practice conditions obtain. One might respond that this point is uncontroversial since it is obviously true of legal or conventional rights. But according to the rights externalist this is a point about legal and conventional rights as well as moral ones. Hence if I say that Dred has a moral right to the fruits of his labor, the truth of this claim will also depend upon whether certain social practice conditions obtain. If the relevant social practice conditions do not obtain, e.g. if Dred has not been afforded institutional respect, then my assertion is false insofar as a necessary condition of possessing moral rights has not been satisfied.

Let us consider what appears to be a problem case for this position.[13] Consider the case of the vegetarian who asserts that all animals have a moral right to life and thus cannot under any circumstances be justifiably killed for food, medical research, clothing, or for any other reason. Moreover, suppose that no social practices establish this moral right, that is, suppose that animals have not been afforded institutional respect. Were we to ask the vegetarian how he could assert a moral right in the absence of certain social practice conditions being satisfied, he would say that his complaint is precisely that certain practices do not exist but ought to exist, because as things stand now animals really do possess a moral right to life independently of whether this right has been socially or legally recognized and implemented.[14] But if we embrace moral rights externalism, then the vegetarian cannot make this argument, since it rests on the contentious claim that animals can possess a moral right to life even though they have

---

[12] For a detailed discussion of the distinctions between cognitivism and noncognitivism, and objectivism and intersubjectivism, see Sayre-McCord, "The Many Moral Realisms."

[13] The arguments that follow here, and in the next section, are drawn from my essay "Grounding Rights in Social Practices: A Defence," *Res Publica* 9 (2003), 1–18.

[14] For a development of this criticism directed at a practice theory of rules, see Joseph Raz, *Practical Reason and Norms* (Oxford University Press, 1999), p. 53.

not been afforded institutional respect, i.e. even though the relevant social practice conditions do not obtain.

It is easy to see why some people find this case compelling. These presocial moral rights-based moral arguments are very familiar to us and we make them all the time. Indeed, these arguments are a central part of the Western liberal political tradition in which natural rights and their various descendants have been the main normative category. Thus it is tempting to think that any account of moral rights possession that precludes us from making these arguments must be rejected outright. Of course, I grant that if we are fully invested in these kinds of moral and political arguments, then we will be reluctant to embrace an account of moral rights possession that forces us to give them up. Yet it certainly does not follow that such an account is false simply because it has this consequence. Indeed, one of the main points at issue between moral rights externalists and moral rights foundationalists is whether one can make the kind of argument the vegetarian wants to make. One way to frame the issue that divides them is over whether such arguments are permissible. Moral rights externalists think that they are not, while the moral rights foundationalists think that they are. The vegetarian case does nothing more than draw attention to a fundamental difference between moral rights externalists and proponents of the prevailing view, namely a difference regarding the truth conditions for moral rights assertions. This case does nothing to undermine the thesis that social practices figure into an account of the truth conditions for moral rights assertions; in other words, it does not show that an intersubjectivist construal of the truth conditions for moral rights assertions that makes essential reference to facts about a subject's social milieu in grounding moral rights is false or inconceivable.

SEMANTICS

According to moral rights externalism the vegetarian's claim that animals possess a moral right to life will be false unless certain social practice conditions obtain. But if the vegetarian's claim that animals possess a moral right to life in cases where such practices do not obtain is false, what exactly is the vegetarian claiming when she uses rights critically? Presumably moral rights externalists do not want to deny that rights assertions can be used critically. But then they must offer a semantic interpretation of critical rights assertions (especially in cases where the relevant social practices conditions have not been satisfied) that does not require the positing of presocial moral rights.

In response one could claim that in these cases the moral rights assertion is not really an assertion about what rights a subject actually has, but instead is an assertion about what rights they ought to have, or, more generally, about what social practices ought to be recognized socially or legally.[15] I shall refer to this as the "there ought to be a publicly recognized right" interpretation, or the "there ought to be a right" interpretation for short. According to this interpretation, the vegetarian must be understood really to be saying not that animals presently have a right to life, but that current social practices ought to be arranged so that such a right is socially or legally recognized and maintained. In other words, the vegetarian's claim is not really about what rights there are but about what rights there ought to be.

But it may be objected that this semantic interpretation grossly misrepresents the claim that rights asserters sometimes intend to make in cases where certain social practice conditions do not obtain. In these cases rights claimants really are citing the existence of a presocial moral right; moreover, they take the existence of this right to be the moral reason for why social practices ought to be rearranged in more desirable ways. For instance, the vegetarian is claiming that animals have a presocial moral right to life which at present imposes duties on us not to use them for food, medical research, clothing, or for any other reason. Indeed, the vegetarian wants to insist that this right is the basis for claiming that the appropriate practice conditions be established, which would suffice to turn this presocial moral right into a conventionally recognized moral right. Hence the problem with moral rights externalism is not only that it prevents us from making presocial rights-based moral arguments, but that it offers a semantic interpretation of rights assertions which grossly misrepresents what rights claimants are saying in certain cases.[16]

It is correct to point out that moral rights externalists cannot accept an interpretation of rights assertions that countenances presocial moral rights. Moreover, it is correct to point out that the "there ought to be a right" interpretation of what rights claimants are really saying is misleading. Nevertheless, moral rights externalists must give an alternative semantic interpretation, and this interpretation will have something to do with a

---

[15] Dworkin, *Taking Rights Seriously*, p. 52. Both Sumner and Martin endorse this interpretation: Sumner, *The Moral Foundation of Rights*, pp. 142ff.; Martin, *A System of Rights*, pp. 93ff. For another formidable challenge to the "there ought to be a right" interpretation, see Feinberg, "In Defence of Moral Rights."

[16] For a similar criticism directed at a practice theory of rules, see Raz, *Practical Reason and Norms*, p. 55.

speaker's moral commitments. The crucial issue is this. How can moral rights externalists explain critical uses of rights if they ground the possession of all rights in social practices and, consequently, are unable to explain such uses by invoking presocial moral rights for critical purposes? As we shall see shortly, H. L. A. Hart offers moral rights externalists an important conceptual resource for addressing this issue.

Recall that for some critics the main difference between noncritical and critical uses of rights is that the former are purely descriptive and the latter are evaluative. When a sociologist says that individuals possess rights in a particular community, he means only to describe or report that this community has certain social practices that it takes to create rights. But when a member of the community asserts a right he is not simply describing or recording that certain practice conditions have been met. Rather he believes that there is such a right and is appealing to it to criticize or to evaluate existing practices, or perhaps to justify the establishment of different practices. On this interpretation the sociologist is asserting some kind of social right, but the member of the community is asserting some kind of presocial moral right. The sociologist's assertion will be true only if a certain factual state of affairs obtains, namely only if the relevant social practice conditions for possessing social rights obtain. But the latter assertion will be true only if a very different factual state of affairs obtains, e.g. the subject in question possesses some property p (humanity or rational agency) the possession of which suffices to endow S with the right, or S's claim to act or be treated in a certain way is justified by moral principles. The two parties are appealing to different kinds of rights.

For the sake of argument let us grant that critical uses of right do have an evaluative dimension. The question is whether we need to capture this fact by positing presocial moral rights that have their source in ontology or moral justification alone. Hart offers a different way to distinguish between noncritical and critical uses of rights, one that enables us to account for the critical uses of rights without positing the existence of a distinct class of presocial moral rights. He distinguishes between the existence of a practice (right) and the acceptance of a practice (right) by individual members of the community. With this distinction in hand we can say that the real difference between the sociologist and the member of the community is the attitude each displays toward the practice. When the former asserts the existence of a right he only says that certain practice conditions have been met. When the latter asserts the existence of right he is committed to certain practice conditions having been met, but in addition he displays his acceptance or endorsement of the right as a standard for guiding and judging conduct. Thus he identifies a social practice and indicates his disposition to conform his behavior to it or his acceptance of it. But in both cases the truth conditions of the respective assertions are determined by whether the relevant social practice conditions obtain. Thus on Hart's view the critical use of rights involves an endorsement dimension, as well as an existential commitment to the existence of the practice conditions.

The difference, then, between noncritical and critical assertions of rights is not a difference in the kinds of right at issue, as some critics have suggested—social rights on the one hand and presocial rights on the other—but rather a difference in attitude toward the practices conferring the right. When the vegetarian claims that animals have a right to life, whether what he says is true partly depends upon whether the relevant practice conditions have been met, but he goes beyond these conditions by indicating his moral endorsement of instituting such practice conditions. However, this response suggests that when the vegetarian asserts this right he is presupposing that the relevant practice conditions have in fact been met. But this need not be so. Indeed, the issue may be whether these conditions should be established, and, in this context, the vegetarian may be appealing to this right to argue that they should. According to rights externalism, however, what the vegetarian takes himself to be claiming is somewhat beside the point; regardless of what he takes himself to be claiming, the truth of his rights assertion will partly turn on whether certain social practice conditions have in fact been met. Therefore, when the vegetarian asserts the existence of this right, it is not that he is committed to certain practice conditions having been met—he may or may not be committed: rather it is that the truth of this assertion partly depends upon whether they have been met.

The more serious problem for the moral rights externalist, then, is that the "there ought to be a right" interpretation of what the vegetarian is really saying is misleading, though not in the way that some critics have suggested. The problem is not in taking social practices to determine the truth conditions of moral rights claims. The problem is with the overly strong way of cashing out the moral endorsement dimension, namely as a specific moral commitment to there being certain publicly recognized rights. Though this is certainly one way to cash out the moral endorsement dimension of critical assertions of rights, it is not the only way and, in my view, it is much too strong. The problem with the "there ought to be a right" interpretation is that it commits a person who asserts a moral right to a view about how things ought to stand legally or socially. But this is too strong. Although some morally justified practices, or practices that we would morally endorse, ought to be legally recognized, not all of them ought to be, nor do we always intend to take a stand on this issue when we use rights critically.

For example, one may believe that sodomy between consenting adults is morally justified, or that same-sex marriages are morally justified, or that physician-assisted suicide is morally justified, or that capital punishment is morally justified, without also believing that these practices should be afforded legal recognition or should be afforded continued legal recognition if they are already publicly recognized. Indeed, it is fairly common for us to distinguish between something being morally justified and something being entitled to legal recognition. Furthermore, a person who asserts a moral right need not have a view about whether a practice should be legally recognized. Perhaps he has not thought the matter through and chooses to be agnostic. And even if a person does have a view about the matter, he certainly need not intend to make this view explicit. Hence the most serious problem with the "there ought to be a right" semantic interpretation of critical uses of moral rights is that it commits the speaker to a view about how things ought to be legally or socially, and requires us to interpret the moral rights assertion as expressing a considered view about the matter.

Fortunately, the moral rights externalist can adopt a much weaker semantic interpretation that is not vulnerable to the objection under consideration. According to this interpretation, a person who uses a right critically is never presupposing the existence of practice conditions that establish the truth of the rights assertion; rather the person is indicating a moral endorsement of these conditions were they to be met; in other words, indicating a readiness to supply moral reasons in favor of the practice if need be. But it does not follow from this that the person must be invoking a right whose existence does not turn on the existence of a social practice. Intersubjectivism about the truth conditions for rights assertions has not been ruled out: whenever anyone asserts a right the truth of this assertion (no matter what the speaker thinks) partly depends upon whether certain social practice conditions have been met. Yet whenever S asserts a right critically S need not be presupposing that practice conditions have been met; rather S is merely recording his preparedness to endorse these conditions if they had been, or were to be, met. Let us call this the weak semantic thesis, or the weak thesis for short.

This weak thesis is more attractive because it does not run roughshod over the distinction between a practice being morally justified and a practice being entitled to social or legal recognition. Now let us reconsider the vegetarian case to see how it can be better handled by assuming the weak thesis. The crucial question is how moral rights externalists can explain critical uses of rights if they ground the possession of all rights in social practices and, consequently, are unable to explain such uses by invoking presocial moral rights for critical purposes and, moreover, if the "there ought to be a right" interpretation is unacceptable. According to the weak thesis, when the vegetarian asserts that animals have a right to life (whether or not certain social practice conditions obtain), he is merely recording his preparedness to morally endorse these conditions were they to obtain. Or perhaps, even more generally, he is merely announcing the availability of a moral justification of certain social practices. While he could be making the stronger claim that certain social practices with regard to animals ought to exist as a matter of convention or law, he certainly need not be saying this. Perhaps he thinks that this is one of those rare moral matters about which law should be silent. But even if he does believe that certain publicly recognized practices regarding animals should exist, this belief should not be built into the very meaning of his moral rights assertion, and the weak thesis guarantees that it is not.

If we assume that animals have a moral right to life only if they have been afforded the relevant kind of institutional respect within an operative legal or conventional system, then there are two possibilities: either that system affords animals institutional respect or it does not. If it does and the practices at issue are also morally justified, then we can say that animals possess a moral right to life. But if animals are not afforded institutional respect, then nothing follows about what ought to be the case as a matter of social or legal practice. All that follows is that, were certain practices to eventually be recognized, we would have created a moral right, so long as a moral justification of the relevant practice could be given. Of course, it may be morally justified to afford animals institutional respect, or to sustain it once it has been given, but this needs to be established by a separate argument (and this argument need not be a moral argument or only a moral argument insofar as nonmoral considerations can be brought to bear as well). So, then, the vegetarian who asserts that animals have a moral right to life in a critical sense is, at most, simply announcing that he morally endorses treating them in certain ways.

Whether animals actually have a moral right depends in part upon whether the institutional respect has been afforded.

We might suggest that moral rights externalists drop the social practice constraint on the truth of moral rights assertions and simply retain the endorsement dimension. The resulting view would be much closer in spirit to the morally valid claims approach. But to do this would be to give up what is most distinctive about moral rights externalism, namely the view that social practices play an essential role in grounding all rights, moral ones included. While there may be compelling reasons for dropping the social practice constraint, and for embracing the morally valid claims approach, or some version of moral rights foundationalism, I have shown that the foregoing fails to supply reasons for either of these options.

To be sure, this line of criticism does show that moral rights externalists should not misrepresent rights assertions by committing speakers to claims that they clearly do not hold. However, it does not give us reason to think that social practices cannot play an essential part in accounting for the truth conditions for rights assertions. And so long as this possibility stands moral rights externalism remains a viable alternative. This line of criticism also forces defenders of moral rights externalism to acknowledge that, if we are going to adopt a social practice conception of moral rights possession, then we must give up critical uses of presocial moral rights altogether. This is clearly a casualty of any such program. But, as I will argue in more detail later, moral rights externalists can live with this outcome since such natural rights do not exhaust the realm of critical morality.

MORAL RIGHTHOLDERS

In this section I elaborate on an additional aspect of rights externalism, namely how it accounts for which subjects fall within the realm of moral rightholders. In so doing I will suggest that it does a better job than rights internalism of regulating the flow of subjects into the realm of moral rightholders. According moral rights externalism, two conditions must be met for a subject to be admitted into the realm of moral rightholders: (1) it must be afforded institutional respect, which may amount to a way of treating the subject being legally ratified within an operative legal system; and (2) the way of treating it must be morally justified. At first blush, it appears that this conception offers us very little control, if any, over rights inflation. If a subject must be afforded institutional respect to be a moral rightholder and this amounts to its being afforded legal rights, then, as is the case with legal rights, it appears that just about anything can gain admission into the realm of moral rightholders including but not limited to fetuses, animals, trees, corporations, the dead, and even works of art.

Let us take a closer look at the reasoning supporting this claim. Whether a subject possesses legal rights is essentially a matter of whether it has these rights conferred upon it by the activities of legal right-conferring bodies, which can of course vary across legal systems, but which usually amounts to enacting a statute or reaching a judicial decision. To say that a subject's status as a legal rightholder is conferred is to deny that it is a function of the subject's nature. But if this status is not grounded in the nature of subjects, and is instead conferred upon them, then there appear to be no fixed limits on the kinds of beings that could possess legal rights. Presumably legal right-conferring bodies can confer rights on whatever kind of thing they choose. Indeed, this reasoning has led some to defend the granting of legal rights to trees, forests, oceans, rivers, and other natural objects,[17] others to emphasize that the class of legal rightholders and human beings is not coextensive, and still others to emphasize that there are no ontological limitations on granting legal rights to these and other "nonstandard" objects:

We have assumed that to be a legal person is to be [a subject of rights], and have seen that the sovereign can, and, if it suits its purposes, does, confer legal personality upon subjects that are not human beings . . . But if the sovereign power confers legal personality upon a ship, or an idol . . . such ship or idol . . . ipso facto is a party to legal relations.[18]

Thus it should be clear that if we take three statements such as "Smith is a legal person," "Krupps is a legal person for the purposes of the law of Massachusetts," and "Corporations are legal persons," there is little profit in taking "Smith," "Krupps," and "Corporations," to search them for the common essence which will identify them as legal persons. The only common factor may be that they are all, within some existing legal system, treated in accordance with the rules of that system as [persons] for that system's method.[19]

Because the status of legal rightholder is within the gift of authority, whether a subject has this status is solely a matter of whether it has been granted the status by the relevant authority, and since this status is not tied to the nature of things, right-conferring authorities can extend this status to whom or whatever they choose, be it a fetus, a great ape, a tree, a

---

[17] Christopher Stone, "Should Trees Have Standing? Toward Legal Rights for Natural Objects," *Southern California Law Review* 45 (1972), 450–501.

[18] Bryant Smith, "Legal Personality," *Yale Law Journal* 37 (1928), 295.

[19] G. W. Paton, *A Textbook of Jurisprudence*, 4th edn. (Oxford: Clarendon Press, 1972), pp. 409–10.

corporation, the American flag, or a sacred Indian burial ground. But if, as I have argued, possessing legal rights is a necessary condition of possessing moral rights, then there appear to be no fixed limits on the kinds of beings who could be moral rightholders either. The realm of moral rightholder will be at least as broad as the realm of legal right-holders. However, if this is the case, then moral rights externalism does not offer any real control over the problem of rights inflation—indeed it may even exacerbate the problem. In either case, the alleged virtue it has over an ontological approach to the source of moral rights possession cannot be made out.

One way to resist this conclusion is to concede that the granting of legal rights is within the gift of authority but to deny that the ability of legislators and judges to confer legal rights is unlimited. But what limits their abilities to confer legal rights? Here it is tempting to follow Carl Wellman, who maintains that: "What limits the ability of lawmakers to confer rights on some kinds of beings is not any decree of Nature, but the nature of those kinds of beings *together with* some presupposed conception of a legal right or a legal right-holder."[20] According to Wellman, the essential function of a right is to confer freedom and control, or agency, on the rightholder. He argues that the ascription of rights to any being incapable of exercising freedom and control is idle because no purpose is served by granting freedom and control to subjects incapable of taking advantage of these things, and it is inappropriate because it misleads us into thinking that freedom and control belong to subjects incapable of acting freely or exercising control. Since only an agent can act freely or exercise control, an agent alone can be a possible rightholder.[21] So, then, the power to confer legal rights is not unlimited because the will theory of rights (which Wellman and other rights theorists defend) entails that a would-be rightholder must be an agent to possess rights. Wellman extends this conclusion to moral rights by maintaining that only beings that are capable of moral agency could be possible moral rightholders.

But this solution is obviously off limits to the rights externalist since it reintroduces nature as the ground of rights. Although Wellman's selection of agency is backed by extensive and subtle philosophical argument, in the end he is committed to the ontological approach—a subject must possess a certain nature, or some property *p*, the possession of which confers rights upon the subject. For Wellman, agency is the relevant

[20] Wellman, *Real Rights*, p. 134.
[21] *Ibid.*, p. 107.

right-conferring property. Internalists who adopt a conservative approach will be attracted to Wellman's view since it limits entry into the realm of moral rightholders to agents. However, as I argued earlier in chapter 2, there is no consensus in practice or in principle among internalists regarding what constitutes the relevant moral right-conferring property, which means that internalists who adopt a more liberal approach will opt for properties that admit agents as well as nonagents into the realm of moral rightholders. Indeed, extreme liberals will be able to expand the realm of moral rightholders to include fetuses, great apes, trees, corporations, and even works of art, by simply choosing a property that these things possess and elevating it to the status of moral right-conferring property.

Therefore, although the realm of moral rightholders could be quite broad on an externalist conception, it is certainly no broader than it would be if we embraced rights internalism. Nevertheless, I agree with Wellman that there are limitations on what can be an object of institutional respect—not just anything can be a legal rightholder. However, contrary to Wellman, these limits are not set by the nature of beings. Rather they are set by practical considerations. We cannot grant institutional respect to subjects that we cannot protect against being interfered with or being deprived of something due to them. The basic idea is that we must be able to maintain and enforce a way of acting toward some subject for it to be capable of having legal rights. For example, it seems clear that ghosts, quarks, and aliens could not be legal rightholders on this view. But this is not because they fail to possess some right-conferring property (for all we know ghosts and aliens could be agents); instead, it is because a way of acting toward them could not be maintained and enforced in practice, for what I take to be obvious reasons. Thus, satisfying the maintenance requirement, which is one of the conditions for possessing legal rights and for being afforded institutional respect, would be a practical impossibility with these subjects. However, this requirement can certainly be satisfied where the subject is a human being, a fetus, a natural land reserve, a spotted owl, a sacred burial ground, or the American flag, which means that these subjects are certainly capable of being afforded institutional respect and, consequently, of being legal rightholders.

But even if I am incorrect about this, the issue of just how broad the realm of rightholders could be is beside the point. It does not follow that, if *S* is a possible legal rightholder, *S* is an actual legal rightholder or *S* should be an actual legal rightholder, nor, more importantly, does it follow that if S is a legal rightholder, S is a moral rightholder. Whether S is an actual legal rightholder will, on this view, depend upon whether it has in fact been afforded institutional respect. And whether it should be will depend on what reasons, moral or otherwise, could be given in support of making it a legal rightholder. Whether a legal rightholder is also a moral rightholder will depend on whether the practices that are legally ratified within an operative legal system can be morally justified by a reasonably adequate substantive moral theory. But this is obviously a much higher admission standard for the realm of moral rightholders than the one used by internalists. According to the externalists, a subject can possess sentience or agency but not be afforded institutional respect or, alternatively, it could be afforded institutional respect but the practices that were legally ratified might not be morally justified. In either case, the subject would fail to be an actual moral rightholder.

For instance, a great ape could be both sentient and capable of agency but not be afforded institutional respect, in which case it would fail to be a moral rightholder even if legally ratifying a way of so treating it could be morally justified. Alternatively, a great ape could be afforded institutional respect and still fail to be a moral rightholder if the legally ratified way of treating it could not be morally justified. The same thing can be said of fetuses, young children, mentally handicapped human beings, and even normal adult human beings. However, since the ontological approach advocates grounding moral rightholder status in nature, and there is no consensus in practice or in principle about what nature is relevant, gaining admission is rather easy on this view; one simply needs to elevate a property possessed by the would-be moral rightholder to the status of moral right-conferring property to secure it admission into the realm of moral rightholders.

Hence the externalist conception clearly regulates the flow of subjects into the realm of moral rightholders more effectively than does an ontological approach. Consequently, it is a more attractive standard for this reason as well. Since it does a better job at controlling rights inflation it more successfully undermines skepticism about moral rights stemming from concerns about moral rightholder proliferation. Indeed, some may argue that the standard is too stringent rather than too permissive. The realm of moral rightholders may turn out to be significantly smaller in practice than is usually supposed, assuming that fewer of the things that we ascribe moral rights to have actually been afforded institutional respect, or assuming that we cannot give a moral justification of the appropriate sort for the right-conferring practice. This is not that troublesome, however, since, as externalism brings to light, the power to increase or decrease the class of moral rightholders is more firmly within our control that is usually thought. It is not some natural fact of the matter to be discovered. On the contrary, it can be fought for and it can be won or lost. We can extend and withhold institutional respect, perhaps guided by our practical concerns and political agendas; in addition, we can supply moral justifications and argue against them. Thus, the possession of this status is more within our control than it would be if we believed that we either have to be lucky enough to have the relevant moral right-conferring property, or hoped that others could convince the mainstream that they were mistaken about which property was relevant, and that we could defend the relevance of some other property. So in addition to imposing a much higher standard on admission, and thereby providing more effective control, externalism makes clear that we are firmly in charge of who gets admitted.

ONTOLOGY

By advocating the thesis that moral rights are a species of unnatural rights I have rejected the view that subjects possess moral rights merely in virtue of their natures. In other words, I have denied that the status of being a moral rightholder is grounded by ontological considerations, having to do with what kind of subject one is. But this dismissal of ontology (as the ground of moral rights) appears to raise at least three problems, two of which I shall address below, while the third will be addressed in the next chapter.

The first problem arises insofar as I assign justification by a substantive moral theory an essential role in my account of moral rights possession. Even though I have not settled upon a specific moral theory to play the justifying role, the problem is that so-called ontological considerations will factor into the application of moral principles underlying any substantive moral theory. For any theory that we choose presumptions will be made about the nature of subjects that fall under the protection of its basic moral principles. A moral theory will demarcate the population of subjects according to their possessing or failing to possess some property deemed morally crucial, such as the minimum rationality requisite to be an autonomous being (Kantianism), or the ability to feel pain (utilitarianism), and assign moral status to those subjects that possess this property and refrain from assigning moral status to those subjects that do not possess this property. Thus it appears that insofar as I assign normative theories a role in grounding moral rights possession I cannot eschew ontological considerations. So not only is the contrast between grounding moral rights in the very nature of the subjects that possess them and grounding them in general moral principles misleading—as if the latter approach eschewed ontological considerations whereas the former did not—it might be objected that insofar as rights externalism also makes recourse to ontological considerations any shortcomings of rights internalism will also carry over to rights externalism.

This objection is simply an invitation to say something about the role that ontological considerations will play on an externalist account. But first let me redirect this objection to a rival account. There are two dominant ways of developing the prevailing view. Following moral validity theorists one could say that a subject possessed such a right if and only if it possessed a claim validated by a substantive moral theory. Following rights internalists one could say that a subject possessed such a right if and only if it possessed a particular right-endowing property. If the foregoing objection has force, then it will obviously apply to moral validity theorists as well. In response to this objection, however, moral validity theorists might concede that ontological considerations played a role but distinguish between their playing a direct role and an indirect one. They could rightly point out that such considerations play a direct role for the rights internalist who holds that "if I have moral rights it is something about me; it is because I am constituted in a certain way." Yet these considerations play an indirect role on their account. According to moral validity theorists, "if I have moral rights it is because I have a claim that can be justified by general moral principles." To be sure, these principles will be applied in light of commitments about who or what fails within the scope of the principles. Whether one embraces consequentialism, contractarianism, theism, or Kantianism, presumptions will be made about who or what is included in the scope of these moral theories, and this will require appealing to ontological considerations. Nevertheless, moral validity theorists will insist that it is the fact that the claim can be rationally derived from the principles, not the fact that the subject possesses a particular property, that grounds the moral right on their view.

Following moral validity theorists, rights externalists also assign moral justification by general moral principles a role in accounting for what possessing moral rights amounts to. So if ontological considerations play any role at all in grounding moral rights, it will be an indirect one. A major difference between these approaches, however, is that rights externalists do not assign these principles an exclusive role in grounding moral rights. A social constraint must also be satisfied so that a subject cannot be taken to possess a right if this constraint is not met and cannot be taken to possess a moral right if the justification requirement is not met. But this does not entail that ontological considerations have no role at all to play. Rather it suggests that if they play any role at all it is not constitutive (they do not ground moral rights possession) but practical; they serve as considerations for or against instantiating the social constraint that is essential for the possession of a right. This is a more precise explanation of the indirect role of ontological considerations.

For example, the fact that a subject possesses the minimum rationality requisite to be an autonomous being or a sentient being does not logically entail that the subject possesses certain moral rights. Yet these considerations can be reasons in favor of affording it institutional respect, that is, for bringing it about that ways of treating subjects possessing these properties are socially recognized, maintained, and enforced. Of course, ontological considerations are not the only reasons that one could give, but they must certainly be included among the reasons that one could give. I hope that this gesture suffices to indicate the proper role of ontological considerations in my account.

The second problem is that one might contend that grounding rights in ontological considerations might ultimately be more attractive than I have acknowledged. So even if rights externalism were successful at eschewing ontological considerations altogether, this would arguably make it less attractive than an account that did not eschew such considerations. Earlier in my discussion of the political justification for imposing a social constraint on moral rights possession I underscored the fact that this leaves us with an account of moral rightholder status as something within our power to change. But does this presume that the prevailing view is less attractive insofar as it does not represent moral rightholder status as within our power to change? If so, internalists will certainly disagree. Indeed, they might argue that this was a virtue of their account. By grounding moral rights in ontology we ensure that this valuable status is not subject to the contingencies of changing and changeable social practices. In response to those who would withhold institutional respect from women because they are not men, or blacks because they are not white, rights internalists can simply respond that because women and blacks are certain kinds of beings (human, rational, project pursuers, or what have you) they are deserving of such respect. One might conclude that it is precisely because rights internalists ground rights in ontological considerations, something beyond our power to change, that they are able to make this argument.

Let me reply briefly by first noting that the issue is not about which beings are "deserving of respect." Rather it is an issue about which beings are objects of respect or moral rightholders, and the rights externalist proposes that there is an ineliminable social dimension involved in accounting for this. Secondly, a moral argument that takes moral rights to be basic is neither the only nor the best way to establish moral conclusions about how people ought to be treated or whether people ought to be respected. So while I grant that ontological considerations can play a role in arguments about how people deserve to be treated or arguments about whether people ought to be afforded institutional respect, I deny that the class of beings that deserve such respect is coextensive with the class of beings that have been afforded such respect. Perhaps a morally perfect world in which all and only those beings deserving of respect were respected would give us all that we could wish for, but in our morally imperfect world this is certainly more than we can reasonably expect.

Admittedly, the natural/unnatural rights dichotomy would not serve us well if facts about a subject's nature played a necessary though not sufficient role in grounding moral rights. It is certainly plausible to think that facts such as whether a subject can reason, think, or suffer will play some role in grounding these rights. While I concede that these ontological considerations do indeed have a role to play, I have proposed that they do not play a constitutive role in grounding moral rights. More precisely, the mere fact that a subject has these traits does not justify concluding that the subject possesses moral rights. Alternatively, I have proposed that these traits play a practical role in grounding moral rights. They serve as considerations for (or against) affording a subject the social standing or respect that is necessary for making it a moral rightholder. For instance, the mere fact that a subject can reason or suffer could indeed justify concluding that it ought to possess a moral right to be left alone or assisted in some way. In this case the fact that the subject can reason or suffer would be a consideration for affording it the social standing that is necessary for making it a rightholder. From this vantage point these ontological traits (facts about how the subject is constituted) play a practical and not a constitutive role in grounding moral rights. Hence insofar as I deny that facts about a subject's nature play a constitutive role in grounding moral rights the natural/unnatural rights dichotomy is quite apt.

CONCLUSION

Beginning with the assumption that all bona fide rights are products of certain social practices, I have advanced an account of the source of moral rights with two main components: a social component that takes being afforded institutional respect to be a necessary condition for moral rights possession, and a moral component that takes the moral justification of socially established ways of acting or being treated by a substantive moral theory to mark the difference between legal and moral rights possession. The upshot of this account is that moral rights possession is both a social and a moral fact, not merely an ontological or moral one. The social constraint renders the possession of moral rights a social reality. The moral justification constraint enables us to ground moral rights in social practices without losing the title of being "moral" rights.

It is fitting to conclude this discussion by reconsidering the testimony with which this chapter began. In taking himself to be without the rights of man while he was a slave, Benjamin Miller was not failing to recognize that he had certain rights in virtue of his nature as a man, a human being, a rational agent, a project pursuer, a child of God, or whatever. Instead, he was accurately summing up the harsh social reality of his predicament as a slave, namely the reality of not being able to go and come as he pleased with impunity, the reality of not being free to eat and sleep when he wished, the reality of not being able to marry and raise children, the reality of not being able to sell his labor for a wage, the reality of not being able to set and pursue ends or projects, the reality of not being able to own property, to speak his mind, to learn to read and write, or to worship God. In sum, Benjamin Miller was urging us to see that from his vantage point, the point of view of the oppressed, the reality of possessing rights did not cover any other reality except the social reality of being able to act in certain ways with relative impunity. The reality of possessing moral rights, in particular, covers this reality as well as the moral reality that being able to act in certain ways with relative impunity is justified by moral principles, ones that I would say promote individual freedom in the fullest sense.[22] Seeing the matter from this critical perspective reveals that social activism and struggle are not only essential to securing and maintaining our status as legal rightholders but as moral rightholders as well.

Undoubtedly, some critics, particularly those who are firmly within the grip of the prevailing conception of moral rights, will be loath to give up natural rights. In particular, they will resist giving up natural rights because of their normative utility. With respect to the slave case, for instance, they will want to say that Benjamin Miller and other slaves did indeed have rights and they were wronged precisely because these

---

[22] What I mean by this will become clear in ch. 5.

unrecognized rights were violated under chattel slavery in the antebellum United States. But this reply fails to take proper account of the dual legacy of natural rights as instruments of both emancipation as well as subordination, as is so clearly illustrated when we consider the relationship between race and rights in the United States. More specifically, it overlooks the fact that the political utility of rights ascribed on the basis of humanity does not apply to those whose status as human beings is either denied or significantly diminished, in which case this way of conceptualizing the source of rights is rendered considerably less attractive from the vantage point of Benjamin Miller and those who still suffer from a diminishment of their humanity. I shall develop these observations in the next chapter by calling into question the assumption that presocial moral rights constitute an irreproachable ideal for combating black subordination, particularly when we embrace an ontological approach to grounding these rights.

CHAPTER 4

Race and rights

[Negroes] had . . . been regarded as beings of an inferior order, and altogether unfit to associate with the white race, either in social or political relations; and so far inferior, that they had no rights which the white man was bound to respect . . . This opinion was at that time fixed and universal in the civilized portion of the white race. It was regarded as an axiom in morals as well as in politics, which no one thought of disputing . . .

United States Supreme Court, *Dred Scott* v. *Sandford* (1857)

Though appropriate, the easy assertion by mainstream philosophers that all normal adult human beings are paradigm rightholders rings hollow against the background of American history, in which the opposite proposition has been quietly believed and loudly defended in the courts and legislatures to the detriment of nonwhites, women, and the unpropertied poor.

—Anita L. Allen[1]

The experience of black people in the United States of America during slavery and subsequently provides a fruitful point of departure for assessing the normative adequacy of the prevailing philosophical conception of the source and value of rights—a conception that posits the existence of a class of rights that individuals are taken to possess prior to and independently of any form of social recognition.[2] Few philosophers have attended to this general connection between the black experience and philosophical conceptions of rights. Philosopher and law professor Anita Allen is a notable exception. Drawing on the experience of the black underclass in particular, she maintains that prevailing conceptions of legal rights have joined with racism, politics, and economics in contributing

---

[1] Anita L. Allen, "Legal Rights for Poor Blacks," in Bill Lawson (ed.), *The Underclass Question* (Philadelphia: Temple University Press, 1992), p. 124.
[2] This chapter is a revised version of my essay, "Blacks and Rights: A Bittersweet Legacy," *Law, Culture, and the Humanities* 2 (2006), 420–39.

to the creation and persistence of the ghetto poor.[3] She argues that a study of American history—particularly as it pertains to the treatment of poor blacks in the law—illuminates the conceptual barriers to achieving equality and social justice for underclass blacks imposed by the ways in which American courts and influential rights theorists have generally conceived of what it means to have legal rights, who may have them, and what legal rights it is possible to have. This is a provocative thesis worthy of serious attention. What I find of special interest, however, is the general suggestion that philosophical theory and social practice can mingle in ways that have a measurable impact on how individuals are treated within a social milieu. Although Allen expresses hope that a more black-friendly conception of rights can be advanced that does not impose certain conceptual barriers to racial uplift and racial justice, the overall tone of her essay is one of skepticism toward the prevailing conceptions of what possessing legal rights amounts to as well as the utility of such rights as a means to achieving racial uplift and racial justice.

A similar sort of skepticism has been expressed about the prevailing philosophical conception of rights. The positive assessment of these non-legal rights—particularly as they are deployed within classical rights-based liberalism—and their normative potential for combating black oppression and subordination has come under fire within political philosophy as well. Some have suggested that rights-based liberalism is useless for blacks. It has been argued that when we take the legacy of slavery and black oppression into account, and when we also take into account that the United States was from its inception a polity premised on white supremacy and black subordination, we discover that rights-based liberalism's general principles of freedom and justice are not truly colorblind but are really racially encoded and were not meant to include blacks within their scope. Consequently, these principles cannot be recruited to expose and criticize past and present forms of black oppression as they themselves have served to legitimize this oppression. The upshot of this argument is that taking race and racism seriously in political philosophy reveals that rights-based liberalism has been and continues to be useless for black emancipation and various social justice projects to the extent that race and racism color its core principles to the detriment of blacks. Under

---

[3] Allen, "Legal Rights for Poor Blacks," p. 124.

the spell of this argument it is tempting to trash rights-based liberalism altogether.[4]

Although I find many of the reasons for being skeptical about the prevailing conceptions of legal and nonlegal rights compelling, we must resist the temptation to eschew appeals to rights altogether, in view of the undeniable role that they have played in progressive social struggles and political reform. Progenitors of rights and rights-based liberalism frequently remind us that the liberal principles articulated in America's founding documents, most notably the Preamble to the Constitution and the Declaration of Independence, provided the American colonists with the normative resources both to criticize British injustice, tyranny, and oppression and ultimately to justify founding a new nation in which respect for these principles would mark the scope and limits of political authority and legitimacy. And this is widely taken to provide the paradigm example of the progressive potential of rights.

Of course, these individuals are keenly aware of the fact that we cannot contemplate America's glorious past without also observing that this great liberal nation was from its inception a slaveholding nation that legally promoted and protected slavery, the slave trade, and the return of fugitive slaves to their masters. Yet despite this infamous legacy of slavery and black subordination, many social progressives argue that rights have

---

[4] As political philosophers, political theorists, and other humanists actively consider which political traditions are best suited for addressing persisting forms of black oppression and subordination in post-civil rights America, the question of whether liberalism should be embraced or trashed is one of the debates at the center of discussion in black political thought. For a variety of illuminating contributions, see Mills, *Blackness Visible*, David Carroll Cochran, *The Color of Freedom: Race and Contemporary American Liberalism* (Albany: SUNY Press, 1999), Carol A. Horton, *Race and the Making of American Liberalism* (Oxford University Press, 2005), and Arthur Rise, *Race, Slavery and Liberalism in Nineteenth-Century American Literature* (Cambridge University Press, 2006). Within the history of black political thought, however, Frederick Douglass's political philosophy provides, in my view, the best point of departure for philosophically interrogating the normative significance of liberal principles in combating black oppression. In his great 1852 speech on the meaning of July 4 for the Negro Douglass poses the question: "Are the great principles of political freedom and of natural justice, embodied in that Declaration of Independence, extended to us?" If this question is answered affirmatively, then presumably liberalism is good for blacks and can be relied on for black emancipation. But if the question is answered negatively then presumably liberalism is useless for blacks and cannot advance the cause of black emancipation. I believe that Douglass's political philosophy can be used to defend the thesis that liberalism is neither good for blacks nor useless to them but entirely indifferent to blacks and the normative project of combating black oppression. When considered in their full generality and taken alone, the liberal principles of freedom and justice for all men, as they are declared in the Preamble to the Constitution, are colorblind and thus indifferent to whether blacks (or whites for that matter) are slaves or free. However, this being said, these general colorblind principles when joined with assumptions about black humanity or personhood have supplied the normative basis for ideological defenses of both black oppression and black emancipation.

served equally well for blacks to the extent that they have been instrumental in explaining the nature of black oppression, criticizing past and persisting forms of black oppression, and arguing for various social justice projects. Indeed, it is in this spirit that Cornel West contends:

Liberalism is not the possession of white, male elites in high places, but rather a dynamic and malleable tradition, the best of which has been made vital and potent by struggling victims of class exploitation, racist subjugation and patriarchal subordination.[5]

As such, liberalism constitutes "a diverse and complex tradition that can be mined in order to enlarge the scope of human freedom."[6]

So if we recount both the perils and promises of rights, we cannot presume that they are necessarily good or bad for combating black oppression and subordination. The primary goal of this chapter is to draw on the ontological conception of rights to illustrate more precisely how rights can be used both as vehicles for and against racial uplift. From this conceptual vantage point, rights are more like a two-edged sword. Once we see this we have further reason for rejecting rights internalism in favor of rights externalism, which does not impose the conceptual barriers to racial uplift and justice that have tempted Allen and other progressive thinkers to turn away from the discourse of rights altogether.

The upshot of this chapter will be that when considered from the internalist vantage point, rights do not afford us an irreproachable ideal for advancing the progressive cause of black emancipation so long as antiblack racial attitudes, or beliefs about black inferiority, persist. After pointing out reasons for thinking that these beliefs do indeed persist in contemporary American thought, I will conclude that my externalist alternative is a more "black-friendly" philosophical conception of moral rights to the extent that it does not impose the conceptual barriers to racial uplift imposed by rights internalism. Of course, this will require offering another sword with which to wage the normative battle for black uplift that compels social progressives like West to refrain from trashing rights altogether, despite the fact that they cut both ways. I will attend to this task in the next chapter.

AN AMERICAN DILEMMA

The United States has long faced an apparent contradiction between the persistence of racial oppression and its espousal of natural rights to life,

---

[5] Cornel West, *Keeping Faith: Philosophy and Race in America* (New York: Routledge, 1993), p. 223.
[6] *Ibid.*

liberty, and the pursuit of happiness for all "men." Frederick Douglass famously argued that the normative ideals articulated in the Declaration of Independence could not be squared with racial subordination. And the thesis that blacks possessed natural rights was a crucial element in this strategy. Douglass and other critics of the "blacks have no rights" thesis—infamously articulated in the *Dred Scott* decision—maintained that apologists for slavery and racial oppression failed to appreciate what I shall call the argument from humanity:

1. All human beings have natural rights to life, liberty, and the pursuit of happiness.
2. All blacks are human beings.
3. All blacks have natural rights to life, liberty, and the pursuit of happiness.

Many Americans would not challenge this argument today, yet this was not so in the eighteenth and nineteenth century. Those defending a polity premised on white supremacy and black subordination rejected the argument from humanity.[7] Some of them claimed that the argument was unsound on the grounds that blacks were not human beings but a separate species altogether. And others claimed that it was invalid on the grounds that being human was not sufficient for having rights to life, liberty, and the pursuit of happiness.

Antebellum social critics should be applauded for answering these challenges by reasserting the argument from humanity, contesting the separate species and inferior race hypotheses, and insisting that being human was indeed sufficient for having rights to life, liberty, and the pursuit of happiness. Yet a plausible explanation for why these responses had limited impact in many circles is that the background conception of the source of rights operative in antebellum America not only enabled abolitionists to utilize natural rights to challenge slavery and racial oppression, it simultaneously enabled defenders of slavery and racial oppression to undermine these efforts. We can gain a deeper appreciation of this dual

---

[7] For example, see J. H. Van Evrie, *White Supremacy and Negro Subordination or, Negroes A Subordinate Race, and (so-called) Slavery Its Normal Condition*, ch. 3, in John David Smith (ed.), *Anti-Black Thought: 1863–1925* (New York: Garland Publishing, 1993), vol. III and William A. Smith, *Lectures on the Philosophy and Practice of Slavery, as Exhibited in the Institution of Domestic Slavery in the United States* (New York: Negro Universities Press, 1969), chs. 4–5 and 7–9. For illuminating historical studies that address the role of natural rights theory in proslavery thought, see William Sumner Jenkins, *Pro-Slavery Thought in the Old South* (Chapel Hill: University of North Carolina Press, 1935), and Larry E. Tise, *Proslavery: A History of the Defense of Slavery in America, 1701–1840* (Athens: University of Georgia Press, 1987).

legacy of rights by considering it against the backdrop of internalism—the ontological version of the prevailing view.

With this background conception of rights in hand, let us consider the underlying logic of the antebellum arguments for and against the "blacks have no rights" thesis. Suppose that set ß represents the set of rightholders at time *t* as would be determined by applying the ontological conception of rights. Now consider the following formulation of this conception. For any subject *S* and for any property *p* the following biconditional holds true:

$$S \text{ is a member of ß at } t \text{ if and only if } S \text{ has } p.$$

A crucial task for an internalist is to specify what constitutes the relevant right-endowing property. As deployed by abolitionists, the argument from humanity utilized the following substitution instances for the ordered pair ‹*S*, *p*›:

Case 1: ‹black people, humanity›

In the hands of Douglass and other proponents of this argument, this conception of rights was used to make a case for black inclusion in the realm of rightholders. Their point was that if "black people" was substituted for *S* and "humanity" for *p*, then, assuming that internalism was the operative conception of rights, it followed straightaway that black people were rightholders and that the American dilemma had force. On a strong interpretation the point was that black people were in fact rightholders whether or not they were treated or recognized as such. They too possessed the essential characteristics required for having standing. Therefore, if slavery apologists took the argument from humanity to establish the standing of whites (as many of them did), consistency required that they took it to establish the standing of blacks as well.

The most extreme proslavery reply to this was to deny the humanity of blacks. Some apologists accepted "humanity" as a valid substitution instance for *p* but argued that blacks constituted a separate species and were not part of the genus *Homo sapiens*. Although there is no scholarly support for the claim that this separate species thesis was widely defended during the antebellum period, there is ample support for the claim that some Americans proposed and defended this thesis. And for them the following resolution of the American dilemma was a genuine option: proponents of the separate species thesis conceded that the ideals articulated in the Declaration of Independence were indeed meant to apply to all men; however, they quickly added that these ideals were not meant to apply to blacks since they were not "men" in the proper sense but a separate species altogether. Hence against the backdrop of internalism we see how slavery apologists were afforded this extreme response to the argument from humanity, which constituted an inauspicious resolution of the American dilemma for the racially oppressed.[8] If having standing was merely a matter of having certain essential characteristics such as humanity, then the standing of blacks was denied by calling their humanity into question. But this response was extreme and implausible, even for ardent defenders of black subordination.

A late eighteenth-century opponent of slavery posed the following challenge to defenders of slavery:

unless we can show that the African race are not *men*, words can hardly express the amazement which naturally arises on reflecting that the very people who [embrace these revolutionary ideals] tell us, that these blessings were only meant to be the *rights of white men*, not of all *men* . . .[9]

The defense of the separate species thesis was an attempt to answer this challenge; however, the implausibility of this thesis made it necessary for slavery apologists to come up with what they took to be a less extreme and more effective response to the argument from humanity. And the black inferiority thesis served this purpose. An early nineteenth-century defender of black subordination expressed the black inferiority thesis this way: "I do not say that blacks are a distinct race: but I have not the slightest doubt of their being an inferior variety of the human species and not capable of the same improvement as the whites."[10] No doubt many contemporary Americans would find this view offensive and absurd, but in eighteenth- and nineteenth-century America the black inferiority thesis was widely affirmed.[11] And because it was taken to be much less extreme

---

[8] For a similar criticism of the contradiction-exposing justification, see Mills, *Blackness Visible: Essays on Philosophy and Race*, ch. 8, where he criticizes Douglass's famous "What to the Slave Is the Fourth of July?" speech.

[9] Jenkins, *Pro-Slavery Thought in the Old South*, p. 34.

[10] *Ibid.*, p. 252.

[11] Jenkins contends: "[t]he inferiority of the Negro was almost universally accepted in the South by all groups of pro-slavery theorists as a great primary truth," p. 252. But staunch proslavery theorists were not the only ones who espoused the black inferiority thesis. Even the most influential defender of liberty, namely Thomas Jefferson, expressed this view in his *Notes on the State of Virginia*. For a critical commentary, see Paul Finkelman, *Slavery and the Founders: Race and Liberty in the Age of Jefferson* (Armonk: M. E. Sharpe, 1996), chs. 4 and 5. For a classic study of notions of black inferiority prevalent in early America, see Fredrickson, *The Black Image in the White Mind*. For an indispensable guide to the relationship between the black inferiority thesis and American jurisprudence from the seventeenth to the twentieth centuries, see A. Leon Higginbotham, Jr., *Shades of Freedom: Racial Politics and the Presumptions of the American Legal Process* (Oxford University Press, 1996).

than the separate species thesis, many apologists for slavery put consider-able intellectual effort into trying to substantiate the black inferiority thesis, as it promised a more effective way to resolve the American dilemma.

Abolitionists appropriated the argument from humanity to expose the American dilemma. The separate species thesis was utilized as part of a possible though highly implausible and ineffective attempt to counter this argument. In contrast, the black inferiority thesis was utilized by apologists for slavery to launch a more successful counterattack. The first step of this counterattack required slavery apologists to propose a modified version of the argument from humanity as their target:

1. All human beings with property *p* have rights to life, liberty, and the pursuit of happiness.
2. All blacks are human beings with property *p*.
3. All blacks have rights to life, liberty, and the pursuit of happiness.

This modified argument, unlike the original one, makes explicit that being human is necessary though not sufficient for possessing rights. According to apologists for slavery, would-be rightholders had to possess certain additional properties to be considered rightholders. Thus the second step of the counterattack was to consider various substitution instances for the ordered pair ‹*S*, *p*›:

> Case 2: ‹black people, autonomy›
> Case 3: ‹black people, intelligence›
> Case 4: ‹black people, imagination›
> Case 5: ‹black people, rationality›

The third and final step was to argue that premise (2) was false not because blacks were not human, but because blacks did not have *p* for any of the relevant substitution instances that might be proposed. Cases (2)–(5) identify several of the properties that were frequently cited to distinguish so-called inferior from so-called superior races of mankind.[12] All of the values substituted for *p* are additional properties that would-be rightholders had to possess to be considered rightholders, according to slavery apologists.

This response to the modified argument was taken to be more effective because slavery apologists did not have to defend the highly implausible thesis that blacks were not human beings. Instead it would suffice to defend the weaker claim that blacks were in some important respects

---

[12] Samuel Cartwright, "The Prognathous Species of Mankind," in Eric L. McKitrick (ed.), *Slavery Defended: The Views of the Old South* (Englewood Cliffs: Prentice-Hall, 1963), pp. 139–47.

different from and consequently "inferior" to whites. Even many white Americans who were opposed to slavery still embraced the black inferiority thesis and thought that at a minimum it justified viewing blacks as something less than full and equal rightholders. So to deny that blacks were human beings with property p was not to deny their humanity. Rather it was to deny that they possessed characteristics unique to the so-called superior races of mankind.

One might object that this is not a decisive problem for the ontological conception since proponents of slavery and black subordination could be viewed as simply refusing to accept the truth that blacks were human or that they possessed the property necessary for having rights. This reply suggests that the question of what constitutes humanity, or what constitutes the relevant right-endowing property, and the truth about who is human and who has this property, can be settled without much controversy. But, as I will suggest in the next section, this is not so. To be sure, this objection to rights internalism is not decisive; yet it does make clear that grounding rights in ontological considerations gives equal advantage (or disadvantage) to both sides of this antebellum debate.

Thus, for slavery apologists who embraced rights internalism and the black inferiority thesis, the following inauspicious resolution of the American dilemma was proposed: it was claimed that the ideals articulated in the Declaration of Independence were not meant to apply universally to all men; rather they were meant to apply exclusively to men who possessed additional properties (e.g. autonomy, intelligence, rationality, etc.) that distinguished them as members of a superior race. And given their views regarding the differences between the white and darker races, which represented blacks as lacking these properties, slavery apologists concluded that these ideals were not meant to apply to black people since they were an inferior race. This response was taken to be a much more effective proslavery resolution of the American dilemma in eighteenth- and nineteenth-century America where the black inferiority thesis had such widespread support.

ADDRESSING THE PROSLAVERY RESOLUTION

This section will contrast two ways of addressing the proslavery resolution, namely the one supplied by rights internalism and the one supplied by rights externalism. Analyzing this debate from an internalist perspective affords us one way of elucidating the logic underlying the cases for and against the "blacks have no rights" thesis. At stake conceptually was whether or not blacks had rightholder standing. According to this approach, ascertaining the relevant property and determining whether blacks possessed it settled the standing issue. But there is a serious drawback to settling the issue ontologically: if facts about a subject's nature ground standing and views about what constitutes the relevant nature vary, then standing cannot be settled decisively unless there is an uncontroversial vindication of a certain right-endowing property. While some theorists may hold out hope for such vindication there are good reasons for doubting that it will be forthcoming. Although there may be more agreement now about which subjects have and do not have rightholder standing than there has been historically, there is still considerable disagreement on this issue, as well as over what constitutes the relevant right-endowing property, and which subjects possess it. Current debates concerning the status of infants and children, the mentally limited, the unborn, animals, groups, and other subjects that are both taken and not taken to be rightholders reflect the range and intensity of disagreement on these issues. Failure to supply an uncontroversial vindication of a particular right-endowing characteristic is especially devastating for proponents of internalism, however, because this is tantamount to not settling who or what has rightholder standing.

One might object that the question does not remain open but admits of conflicting answers. For example, one might concede that standing is settled by appealing to right-endowing properties, but argue that since the selection of these properties can vary there will be variation in views about who has standing. But the antebellum debate exposes the shortcoming of this conclusion. If we embrace relativism about standing at this level, then we are forced to conclude as follows: according to abolitionists, slaves and subordinate free blacks had rightholder standing but according to apologists for slavery and black subordination they did not. On the one side, abolitionists moved from the claim that blacks had a certain nature to the conclusion that they actually had standing. And on the other side, apologists for slavery either denied that blacks possessed this nature or alleged that it was not sufficient to support the conclusion that blacks had standing. But conceding that the question admits of conflicting answers does not help matters. Pending an uncontroversial vindication of the relevant nature, the prevailing conception of rights either renders the question of who has standing unsettled, or worse, admits of conflicting answers.

Confronted with this diverging opinion on what constitutes the relevant right-endowing property and on whether blacks have it, let us imagine a slavery apologist responding to an abolitionist as follows:

You can believe what you want about the nature of blacks. Moreover, you can contend that their nature justifies concluding that they have rightholder standing. The fact remains, however, that they are in bondage and cannot go and come as they please, sell their labor for a wage, or do many other things with impunity, like those of us who really do *have* standing.

Now let us consider two ways of responding. We can either insist that being able to act in certain ways with impunity has nothing to do with having rightholder standing or we can concede that it does. Rights internalists opt for the former. They maintain that while being able to do all of the things that the racially oppressed cannot do with impunity is important, we are justified in concluding that the racially oppressed actually have rightholder standing insofar as they are human or possess more specific right-endowing characteristics. Of course, they need not deny that blacks' standing as legal rightholders may be in doubt; however, their point is that if blacks have the relevant nature, their standing as "natural" or "moral" rightholders cannot be in doubt.

What do proponents of this view hope to gain by insisting that the racially oppressed have moral rightholder standing even where they are not able to act in certain ways with impunity? Perhaps the most significant thing is the ability to make a certain kind of moral argument against racial oppression that goes roughly as follows: blacks are rightholders merely in virtue of possessing *p*. Slavery and other forms of racial oppression are violations of their standing as rightholders. Since such violations are morally objectionable, slavery and other forms of racial oppression are morally objectionable. Hence they conclude that we ought to embrace rights internalism because it allows us to make this argument.

Thus the main concern is to register that there is a moral problem with racial oppression. But if we could make this point without embracing internalism, then a central motivation for embracing it would be undermined. Clearly, we can argue for the claim that slavery and other forms of racial oppression are morally objectionable without doing so on the grounds that they are violations of presocial moral rights, as I will show in the next chapter. Hence embracing internalism is not indispensable for critical purposes. Perhaps one might propose that appealing to presocial moral rights provides the best argument against slavery and racial oppression, but this remains to be seen. One might contend that when we say that the racially oppressed have rights merely in virtue of their nature this is really shorthand for saying that they ought not be oppressed, or more generally, that they deserve a certain kind of treatment. Yet some proponents of internalism reject this interpretation and insist that moral rights are existing rights at the moment they are asserted, capable of being respected or violated, but nonetheless possessed independently of whether or not they are respected.[13]

Secondly, if we concede this interpretation, then making the point about what ought to be the case, or what is deserved, in terms of rights is grossly misleading, since there are nonrights-based ways of making this point. I suppose that one could amend the interpretation by saying that assertions of such rights is really shorthand not for what ought to be the case generally, but what ought to be the case based on moral considerations concerning the intrinsic value of individuals. The fact that this interpretation does not show that a rights-based theory is uniquely concerned with the intrinsic value of individuals notwithstanding, this interpretation does not preclude us from holding that social practices that facilitate being able to act in certain ways with impunity play a necessary role in settling whether subjects have rightholder standing. In other words, it does not rule out imposing a social constraint on rights possession, a point that I argued for at length in the previous chapter.

This brings us to an alternative way of responding to the apologist. Rather than insisting that being able to act in certain ways with impunity has nothing to do with having rightholder standing, one could concede that it does. I favor this strategy, as I hold that rightholder standing is established not by the fact that subjects have certain essential characteristics but by the establishment of social practices that recognize, maintain, and enforce certain ways of acting and being treated. Recalling Miller's observation that he lacked the rights of a man while enslaved, defenders of the prevailing view maintain that Miller was mistaken in claiming that he lacked the rights of a man. They contend that there are certain rights that all human beings possess in virtue of their humanity (or some other essential characteristic). Instead of saying that he lacked the rights of a man as a slave, it would have been more accurate for him to say that his natural or human rights were being violated. Rather than assuming that Miller's assessment of his predicament was mistaken, however, we can assume that it was correct and view him as making a deeper point about what being a rightholder amounts to. The deeper point is that having the right to go and come as one pleases, the right to own property, the right to sell one's labor for a wage, the right to practice religion, or having any

---

[13] Feinberg, "In Defence of Moral Rights," p. 164.

other so-called "natural" or "human" rights, does not cover any other reality except the reality of being able to do these things with impunity. Hence, on a more charitable interpretation, as I observed at the close of chapter 3, Miller is summing up the harsh social reality of his predicament as a slave, namely the reality of not being able to act in certain ways with impunity. In a society where certain ways of acting or being treated—whether morally justifiable or not—are not recognized and enforced by the highest political authority, individuals unable to act in these ways, or not protected from being treated in certain ways, are without rights.

One reason for embracing externalism is that it accords with this deeper point. On a plausible interpretation of internalism the possession of certain essential characteristics establishes not simply who merits standing but who actually has standing. But it is naïve to think that attaining standing is simply a matter of being constituted in a certain way. From the vantage point of those whose standing has never been denied or called into question (on account of doubts about whether they possess the relevant right-endowing nature) this may be easy to believe, but for those whose standing has been challenged this is dubious. Adopting the externalist perspective allows us to interpret Miller as accurately calling attention to the constitutive social dimension of having moral rights.

AN EXTERNALIST DILEMMA

If being a moral rightholder is, generally speaking, a matter of subjects being afforded social recognition (whether understood as above or in some other way), then one wonders whether we can appraise instances of extending or failing to extend social recognition as correct or incorrect. For instance, assuming that Dred was not afforded the relevant social recognition in antebellum American, can we judge that this was incorrect? In other words, can we say that antebellum American society made a mistake by not socially enforcing and maintaining Dred's morally valid claims to act and being treated in certain ways? Or, to take a more current example, if we assume that human fetuses have not been afforded the relevant social recognition that is essential for moral rights possession, can we say that contemporary American society is making a mistake in its failure to socially enforce and maintain their morally valid claims to not be aborted, for instance? The general worry is that internalism and externalism will merge together (or that the distinction between them will not be as sharp) insofar as it seems unavoidable when distinguishing between correct and incorrect recognition to say that a failure to extend recognition is incorrect precisely because S possesses property p (or to say that extending recognition is correct precisely because S possesses property p).

For instance, to account for why antebellum America's failure to afford Dred the relevant right-conferring social recognition was mistaken, it appears that we must ultimately say that it was mistaken or unjustified precisely because Dred (and other persons of African descent) possessed property p, where p is taken to be the relevant right-endowing property, such as humanity, autonomy, rationality, and so on. Consequently, it appears that externalists cannot altogether avoid appealing to how subjects are constituted ontologically. Insofar as considerations about how subjects are constituted appear to be essential for distinguishing between correct and incorrect recognition and insofar as externalists affirm that this distinction is possible, the main point of contrast between externalism and internalism is blurred since externalism purportedly differs from internalism on account of not grounding moral rights possession in ontology. Hence externalists appear to be confronted with a devastating dilemma: either the significance of ontological considerations is denied altogether, in which case there seems to be no way to distinguish correct from incorrect social recognition, or ontological considerations are embraced, in which case the contrast between externalism and internalism breaks down.

Before resolving this dilemma let me say that, even if it is conceded that appealing to ontological considerations is indispensable for distinguishing between correct and incorrect recognition, this concession would not undermine the core externalist thesis that moral rights possession is partly grounded in social recognition. One could still maintain that social recognition was an essential ingredient in settling the question of whether a subject actually possessed moral rights. What constitutes the standard for determining whether social recognition has been correctly or incorrectly conferred is clearly a further question that certainly could (though it need not) be settled by appealing to facts about how subjects are constituted. If internalists insist on a strong interpretation of their view, according to which ontological traits are instrumental in determining not simply who merits rightholder standing but who actually has standing, then there remains a sharp contrast between externalism and internalism. But then the appeal to ontology as a standard of correctness, or a standard for determining who deserves or merits standing, is a red herring. Externalists need not deny that ontological characteristics can supply a criterion for settling these normative issues. Yet they do deny that they settle the question of who actually has rightholder standing.

If internalists retreat to a weaker interpretation of their view, according to which ontological traits are taken to determine who ought to be afforded rightholder standing, then they are clearly not contesting the thesis that rights possession has a social dimension. While some externalists may follow in appealing to ontological considerations for this purpose, others may not. Of course, if internalists embrace this weaker interpretation, they will have to deal with some of the challenges I raised earlier; in particular they will have to make the case that ontology provides the only or best normative standard. From this perspective the main point of contrast between the two approaches would be that for the internalist ontology plays a necessary role in distinguishing between correct and incorrect recognition but for the externalist it need not play this role. It would be quite surprising if internalists ultimately settled upon the weaker interpretation and refrained from contesting the social dimension of rights possession. After all, they have proclaimed the existence of rights that individuals possess independent of whether or not they have been socially recognized or acknowledged, and this is precisely what externalism denies.

The first horn of the apparent dilemma can be dispatched with relative ease by denying that ontology provides the only basis for distinguishing between correct and incorrect recognition. When distinguishing between correct and incorrect recognition, we need not maintain that a failure to extend recognition is incorrect precisely because S possesses property p (or that extending recognition is correct precisely because S possesses property p). Alternatively, one could propose that the correctness or incorrectness of an instance of recognition was not settled by whether it squared with some metaphysical fact about how subjects are constituted, but rather it consisted simply in the rational acceptability of the social recognition from an impartial and ideal point of view. For instance, on this view, one can claim that a failure to extend social recognition (of the sort that is essential for rights possession) to Dred is incorrect if it is called for by norms chosen by rational contractors under suitably idealized conditions. The fact that the social order violates these norms is not simply evidence of its incorrectness; it is what makes it the case that the failure to extend Dred social recognition is incorrect. Hence the measure of correctness is how things would stand from an ideal social order rather than a real or imagined metaphysical or ontological order. This metaethical position on the standard of correctness does not appeal to ontology, that is, facts about whether subjects possess property p, but to norms agreed to by parties under idealized conditions. To be sure, this contractarian-inspired metaethical theory will meet with a host of worries including but not limited to concerns about its being too relativistic and concerns about how to define and specify the parties in the original choice position as well as the norms that they would select. Nevertheless, this stance-dependent standard is certainly a viable theoretical alternative.[14]

The second horn of the dilemma can be addressed by sharpening the contrast between these conceptions of rights possession by expanding on the different roles that ontological considerations play in the respective theories. I take this horn of the dilemma to be an invitation to say more rather than an undermining objection. To be sure, one may worry that the internalism/externalism dichotomy breaks down if it turns out (in the final analysis) that facts about a subject's nature play a necessary though not sufficient role in grounding moral rights. It is certainly plausible to think that facts about a subject's nature, such as whether it can reason, think, or suffer, will play some role in determining whether it is or is not afforded social recognition. While this has already been conceded, it has not been conceded that the mere fact that a subject has these properties justifies concluding that it does or does not possess moral rights. At best, these properties serve as considerations for (or against) affording a subject the social recognition that is necessary for making it a moral rightholder.

In other words, on the internalist view, it is having p that is sufficient to justify concluding that S has status, whereas on the externalist view it is not. At most, having p is sufficient to justify concluding that S ought to have status. Thus while the internalist makes the stronger claim, she is only really entitled to a weaker claim, namely, that S ought to have status because S has p and having p is a reason for conferring status. But then opponents could attack by denying that S has p, or denying that having p is sufficient for having rightholder status. Once the case for conferring status is put on an ontological level these are some of the ways the dialectic can advance.

Hence a significant difference between rights internalism and rights externalism is the different roles that they assign to properties. The former assigns property possession a constitutive role, while the latter assigns them a practical role. Recall the earlier formal characterization of internalism: S is a member of ß at t if and only if S has p. To say that internalism

---

[14] I would develop this metaethical position along the same lines that contractarian constructivism is developed by Ronald Milo, "Contractarian Constructivism," *The Journal of Philosophy* 92 (1995), 181–204. Milo credits John Rawls with suggesting this metaethical theory in his John Dewey lectures: "Kantian Constructivism in Moral Theory," *The Journal of Philosophy* 77 (1980), 515–72.

assigns property possession a constitutive role is to say that there is a direct connection between S having p and S being a member of ß. To say that externalism assigns rights possession a practical role is to say that there is an indirect connection between S having p and S being in μ. The standard abolitionist response was to deny that blacks lacked p for any of the substituted values and to conclude that blacks were rightholders. Yet the abolitionist could have responded by claiming that whether or not all blacks lacked p for any value of p, lacking p would not be sufficient to conclude that they were not rightholders. So after going back and forth with slavery apologists on the issue of whether the white race had certain properties that the black race did not, it could have been added that the outcome of this dispute did not settle whether blacks actually had right-holder status, since there was no direct connection between S having p and S being a rightholder. Indeed, S could lack p yet still be a rightholder insofar as S had been afforded social recognition.

Therefore, by rejecting internalism—with its link between nature and rightholder status—and by affirming externalism, which holds that being a rightholder is a matter of being afforded a certain sort of social recognition, abolitionists could have thwarted attempts to make a direct leap from blacks having (or lacking) a certain nature to conclusions about whether or not they, in fact, had rights. If blacks were without rights in antebellum America, then it could not have been claimed that this was because they lacked some important property that only rightholders possessed and that was necessary for having rights; rather it was because they were systematically denied a certain kind of social recognition. Hence adopting an externalist conception of rights possession would have had the conceptual benefit of undermining attempts to move from the black inferiority thesis to the conclusion that blacks had no rights. While blocking this move would not have eliminated the problem of racial oppression, it certainly would have made a certain ideological defense of the "blacks have no rights" thesis a non-starter.

Of course, defenders of the "blacks have no rights" thesis still have room to maneuver. They could argue instead that blacks should not be afforded social recognition. But this leaves in place the externalist thesis that social recognition is necessary for possessing rights, and that having rightholder standing is firmly rooted in certain social practices and that the merits or demerits of extending or withholding standing are a distinct matter of presenting certain kinds of arguments that are open to debate and refutation. While this is consistent with the claim that social recognition can be mistakenly conferred or withheld, the externalist insists that such recognition is necessary for possessing rights and, as I have demonstrated in this section, the externalist is quite capable of distinguishing between correct and incorrect instances of social recognition.

THE PERSISTENCE OF ANTIBLACK RACIAL ATTITUDES

At first look, changing our background conception from internalism to my externalist alternative appears to have no relevance for contemporary political thought. For one, it appears that there is neither widespread nor serious endorsement of the black inferiority thesis in contemporary thought; what is more, no one in contemporary American exploits rights internalism to infer that blacks have no rights on the grounds that blacks are a separate species or on the grounds that blacks are inferior to whites. So even if remnants of racial oppression persist in America, it appears that contemporary social critics do not need to embrace a theory of rights possession that secures the conceptual benefit of shortcircuiting these antiquated rationales for the "blacks have no rights" thesis. Hence insofar as modern social critics do not have to worry about inauspicious resolutions of the American dilemma of the sort that vexed Douglass and other antebellum social critics, they have no justification relating to these matters for grounding rights externally rather than ontologically.

There are two distinct yet closely related claims underlying this argument: (1) no one in contemporary America (especially within the academy) endorses the "blacks have no rights" thesis; and (2) anyone who did endorse it would not utilize the separate species or black inferiority thesis to defend it. Before challenging both of these claims, let me explain why contemporary social critics would still have a justification relating to these matters for embracing externalism in favor of internalism even if (1) and (2) were true. A significant reason for embracing a theory of rights possession that secures the conceptual benefit of shortcircuiting these antebellum rationales for the "blacks have no rights" thesis is that the black inferiority thesis could be resurrected in the future to infer this conclusion, or to justify overturning social reforms that have been instrumental in combating racial oppression.[15]

Consider this illuminating case. In 1907, after a medical journal, *American Medicine*, reported empirical research arguing that the brains of black people were "more animal in type and incapable of producing

---

[15] Since I am willing to concede that the separate species hypothesis cannot be resurrected to defend the "blacks have no rights" thesis, I will omit it from the remainder of this discussion.

those thoughts which have built up civilization," the editors found it "dreadful that we did not know these anatomical facts when we placed a vote in the possession of this brain which cannot comprehend its use" and hoped that it was not too late to deprive blacks of the franchise.[16] It is certainly not inconceivable that current and future so-called scientific evidence of black inferiority could be exploited in a similar fashion. Any number of conditions could contribute to the resurrection of these views, including but not limited to perceived threats posed by blacks to "white interests." Indeed, some recent social scientific studies suggest that white opposition to race-targeted social programs and traditional prejudice rises substantially with increases in the local black population.[17] It is conceivable that if there were explosive increases in local black populations in both affluent and working class white neighborhoods across America, perceived threats to white real estate property values or to job prospects could foster conditions in which the black inferiority thesis was once again utilized to defend the "blacks have no rights" thesis.

Therefore, embracing externalism would constitute a preemptive conceptual strike, as it were, that would effectively block attempts to make a direct leap from the claim that blacks have (or lack) a certain nature to the conclusion that they lack certain rights. And making a preemptive conceptual strike is certainly a very reasonable strategy. Although I agree that there is "little reason to predict that citizens of the United States would allow our nation to return to a Jim Crow system of segregation and degradation,"[18] it would be unwise not to do what we can now (without much cost) to prepare for the worst. To wit, embracing rights externalism is a relatively cost-free way to prepare for the dire forecast that the gains won during the civil rights movement "will produce no more than temporary 'peaks of progress,' short-lived victories that slide into irrelevance as racial patterns adapt in ways that maintain white dominance."[19]

The foregoing considerations suggest that embracing externalism is reasonable even if, at present, no one in contemporary America is making a direct leap from the claim that blacks lack a certain nature or property to

---

[16] Cited in William H. Tucker, *The Science and Politics of Racial Research* (Urbana: University of Illinois Press, 1994), p. 7.
[17] Marylee C. Taylor, "The Significance of Racial Context," in David O. Sears, Jim Sidanius, and Lawrence Bobo (eds.), *Racialized Politics: The Debate about Racism in America* (University of Chicago Press, 2000), pp. 118–36.
[18] Jennifer L. Hochschild, "Lumpers and Splitters, Individuals and Structures," in *Racialized Politics*, pp. 324–43, p. 339.
[19] Derrick Bell, *Faces at the Bottom of the Well: The Permanence of Racism* (New York: Basic Books, 1992).

the conclusion that they lack certain rights. Yet a plausible case can be made for the much stronger claim that embracing externalism is a matter of urgency. For not only are remnants of the black inferiority thesis operative in contemporary America, both scholars and members of the public at large have actually used these remnants to defend the claim that blacks lack certain rights.

Historically, the attempt to make science an accomplice in racial oppression was facilitated by studies into the purported genetic and physiological differences between races and the correlation between these differences and cognitive and moral differences between races. Biologist Carolus Linnaeus, physiologist Johann Friedrich Blumenbach, surgeon Charles White, and physician Samuel Morton were early pioneers in this research. The search for so-called scientific proof of black inferiority was a primary research goal for defenders of white supremacy.[20] If such differences could be established scientifically, the denial that blacks have rights would have scientific backing. While empirical studies into race differences have varied in focus over the years, and have changed in the light of methodological developments, they proliferate today.[21] What is more, within the academy, these empirical studies continue to influence the thinking of those who are critical of continued government sponsored support of race-targeted social policies aimed to benefit blacks. For example, just several years ago recent empirical studies on race differences were used to defend the general thesis that "by ordinary Caucasoid standards [e.g. intelligence, industriousness, patience, self-sufficiency, and development of one's talents], the average white is a better person than the average black," and that on account of these normative deficiencies blacks had no rights to assistance.[22]

To be sure, some scholars have expressed skepticism about whether ongoing empirical research into innate differences between blacks and whites, such as Herrnstein and Murray's bell curve study, will have any real impact in the public at large on white attitudes towards race-targeted social policies recognizing black "group" rights.[23] However, even if this is

[20] Tucker, *The Science and Politics of Racial Research*.
[21] Richard J. Herrnstein and Charles Murray, *The Bell Curve: Intelligence and Class Structure in American Life* (New York: Free Press, 1994); J. Phillippe Rushton, *Race, Evolution, and Behavior: A Life History Perspective* (New Brunswick: Transaction Books, 1995); and Seymour Itzkoff's, *The Decline of Intelligence in America* (Westport: Praeger Publishers, 1994).
[22] Michael Levin, *Why Race Matters: Race Differences and What They Mean* (Westport: Praeger Publishers, 1997).
[23] Howard Schuman, Charlotte Steech, Lawrence Bobo, and Maria Krysan, *Racial Attitudes in America: Trends and Interpretations* (Harvard University Press, 1997), p. 170.

correct, some proponents of modern versions of the black inferiority thesis stop short of assigning genes an explanatory role in accounting for what they take to be so-called black defects in character.[24] And although innate differences in ability between races is least likely to be cited in public surveys to explain the social predicament of blacks, or to justify opposition to race-targeted social policies, recent empirical studies suggest that so-called black defects in character (with lack of motivation or will power being the most popular) have a considerable impact on white attitudes in public surveys.[25]

In addition, the black inferiority thesis—understood as a thesis about black defects in character—plays an explanatory role in several influential social scientific models presently used to explain white opposition to race-targeted social policies aimed at benefiting blacks. During the antebellum era, and some would say up through the civil rights era, the alleged cognitive, moral, and character differences between whites and blacks were given a biological explanation. Today, however, few whites would support "biological racism"[26] and defend the innate inferiority of blacks. Moreover, few whites would cite a belief in innate black inferiority to explain their opposition to state-enforced racial policies designed to benefit blacks. However, proponents of the symbolic racism model propose that a new form of racism has replaced biological racism.[27]

They maintain that this new form of racism is popular among white Americans. And in its defense they cite studies showing that symbolic racism is a strong predicator of white political views, in particular white opposition to race-targeted social policies, over and above the effects of such alternative predictors as biological racism, political ideology, party identification, individualism, authoritarianism, or demographic variables.

[24] For examples, see Dinesh D'Souza, *The End of Racism* (New York: Free Press, 1995), and Thomas Sowell, *Race and Culture: A World View* (New York: Basic Books, 1994).

[25] Schuman *et al.*, *Racial Attitudes in America*, ch. 3.

[26] Donald R. Kinder and Tali Mendelberg, "Individualism Reconsidered: Principles and Prejudice in Contemporary American Opinion," in *Racialized Politics*, pp. 44–74, p. 73.

[27] For defenses of this model, see David O. Sears and Donald R. Kinder, "Racial Tensions and Voting in Los Angeles," in Werner Z. Hirsch (ed.), *Los Angeles: Viability and Prospects for Metropolitan Leadership* (New York: Praeger Publishers, 1971), pp. 51–88; Donald R. Kinder and David O. Sears, "Prejudice and Politics: Symbolic Racism versus Racial Threats to the Good Life," *Journal of Personality & Social Psychology* 40 (1981), 414–31; John B. McConahay, "Modern Racism, Ambivalence, and the Modern Racism Scale," in John F. Dovidio and Samuel L. Gaertner (eds.), *Prejudice, Discrimination, and Racism* (Orlando: Academic Press, 1986), pp. 91–125; David O. Sears, "Symbolic Racism," in Phyllis A. Katz and Dalmas A. Taylor (eds.), *Eliminating Racism: Profiles in Controversy* (New York: Plenum Press, 1988), pp. 53–84; and David O. Sears, Colette van Laar, Mary Carrillo, and Rick Kosterman, "Is it Really Racism? The Origins of White Americans' Opposition to Race-Targeted Policies," *Public Opinion Quarterly* 61 (1997), 16–53.

For present purposes, however, a salient aspect of this model is that it shows that the black inferiority thesis still has force in contemporary America. The fact that black inferiority is no longer explicitly grounded in biological differences between races notwithstanding, blacks are still taken to be inferior to whites insofar as they fail to possess certain properties (e.g. a strong will, self-discipline, obedience to authority) and this sense of black inferiority is indeed used to infer that blacks lack certain rights to positive assistance.

A second social scientific model, the sense of group position model, has also been used to explain white opposition to race-targeted social policies aimed at benefiting blacks. This model assigns a prominent role to whites' shared group interests in maintaining the racial status quo in which whites assume a dominant position and blacks assume a subordinate one.[28] In addition, it holds that those in dominant groups develop views about in-group member superiority and out-group member inferiority to justify the racial status quo. Consequently, as members of the dominant in-group, whites' opposition to race-targeted policies aimed at benefiting blacks, and beliefs in white superiority and black inferiority, flows principally from the process of protecting their own interests.

To support this model defenders cite studies showing that whites tend to oppose liberal racial policies more than blacks, and that whites perceiving greater conflict of interest between the races are the strongest opponents of liberal racial policies. They take these studies to show that many whites will oppose race-targeted social policies aimed to benefit blacks (e.g. affirmative action) not so much because they see a race-based policy as contravening normative values such as fairness and equality or because of antiblack animus, but rather because they perceive blacks as competitive threats for valued social resources, status, and privileges.[29] In short, white opposition springs from a desire to maintain a privileged position for whites in the American racial hierarchy.

[28] Herbert Blumer, "Race Prejudice as a Sense of Group Position," *Pacific Sociological Review* 1 (1958), 3–7; Lawrence Bobo and Vincent L. Hutchings, "Perceptions of Racial Group Competition: Extending Blumer's Theory of Group Position to a Multiracial Social Context," *American Sociological Review* 61 (1996), 951–72; Lawrence Bobo, James R. Kluegel, and Ryan A. Smith, "Laissez-faire Racism: The Crystallization of a Kinder, Gentler, Antiblack Ideology," in Steven A. Tuch and Jack K. Martin (eds.), *Racial Attitudes in the 1990s: Continuity and Change* (Westport: Praeger Publishers, 1997), pp. 15–41; Lawrence Bobo, "Race and Beliefs about Affirmative Action: Assessing the Effects of Interests, Group Threat, Ideology, and Racism," in *Racialized Politics*, pp. 137–64.
[29] Bobo, "Race and Beliefs about Affirmative Action," p. 142.

In contrast with the symbolic racism model, the sense of group position model assigns an explanatory role to interest to account for continued negative stereotyping of blacks and for white opposition to race-targeted social policies aimed at benefiting blacks. Yet both models agree that old-fashioned racism—biological racism—is not a strong predictor of racial policy preferences and cannot be used to explicate versions of the black inferiority thesis held by contemporary Americans. Some proponents of the sense of group position model use the term "*laissez-faire* racism" to describe racism in the post-civil rights era. Its two components are

the continued negative stereotyping of blacks and the placing of responsibility for the socioeconomic racial gap on blacks themselves. In this form, blacks' primary shortcoming is no longer some inherent inferiority, but their cultural resistance to the work ethic.[30]

Hence, despite the differences in terminology, the general point is the same: the black inferiority thesis still has force in contemporary America.

In reviewing the foregoing social scientific models for explaining contemporary American racism I am not interested in assessing their merits and demerits. For present purposes, what is interesting is that both models assign the black inferiority thesis a role in explaining white opposition in the public at large to race-targeted social policies. Insofar as these policies usually call for some form of positive social or government assistance, this opposition can be summed up as the denial that blacks have rights to certain forms of social or state-sponsored support to redress past inequalities. And, according to these models, which offer different explanations for why this is the case, this conclusion is licensed by modern versions of the black inferiority thesis.[31]

But in form this is no different from responses to the argument from humanity that vexed Douglass and other antebellum social critics. We have a theory of rights possession that takes possessing a right to be a matter of being constituted in a certain way, and we have a thesis that blacks are not constituted in the relevant way. For example, they are said to lack motivation, self-sufficiency, industriousness, and other right-endowing

---

[30] David O. Sears, John J. Hetts, Jim Sidanius, and Lawrence Bobo, "Race in American Politics: Framing the Debates," in *Racialized Politics*, pp. 1–43, p. 25.

[31] My concern is not to claim that all opposition to extending blacks rights is motivated by the presumption of black inferiority; there are other arguments for resistance to these social policies. Another familiar argument of opponents of such state measures is that they will only reinforce the subordination of blacks by making them dependent on state support, and that the real path to civil and social equality is a sink-or-swim approach that forces blacks to learn to thrive in a market economy. This argument is about consequences and not about black inferiority.

properties. Consequently, it is inferred that they do not have rights to various forms of state-sponsored support to redress past injustices. Reasserting the argument from rights and denying that blacks lack motivation, self-sufficiency, industriousness, and so forth is certainly one way to counter this response. Yet another way to do so is to reject the view that possessing rights, any rights, is a matter of being constituted in a certain way, and to embrace the view that being a rightholder is a matter of being afforded a certain sort of social recognition. This counter-response would effectively block attempts to move directly from allegations of black inferiority to the conclusion that blacks lack certain rights.

POSITIVE RIGHTS AND FREEDOM:
LESSONS FROM SOUTH AFRICA

Reflecting on the predicament of blacks under chattel slavery, and the role that the orthodox natural rights conception played in both justifying and challenging this infamous social practice, this chapter has supplied a concrete example of how philosophical theory and social practice can mingle in ways that have a measurable impact on how individuals are treated within a social milieu. In the same vein that Allen argues that prevailing conceptions of legal rights have imposed conceptual barriers to achieving equality and social justice for underclass blacks, I have illuminated the conceptual barrier to black emancipation and racial uplift imposed by taking rights to be possessed merely in virtue of how individuals are constituted, particularly under circumstances where views about black inferiority persist. I have argued that this conception of rights, when combined with contemporary views about black inferiority, can suffice to undermine the ascription of rights to blacks.

But one may wonder what sorts of rights are at issue. Presumably no one is seriously going to challenge the ascription of so-called negative rights to blacks using the strategy under discussion. For instance, no one is going to argue that blacks do not have a right to enjoy their property on the grounds that they are inferior to other property holders. Perhaps. Although I suspect that some philosophers who have examined the impact of environmental racism on black neighborhoods and black property rights might beg to differ.[32] Yet even if we suppose that this is so, there is still cause for concern.

---

[32] Laura Westra and Bill E. Lawson (eds.), *Faces of Environmental Racism: Confronting Issues of Global Justice*, 2nd edn. (Lanham: Rowman and Littlefield, 2001), see part 2, "Racism in North America."

Allen contends that one conceptual barrier to achieving equality and social justice for underclass blacks pertains to what rights it is thought possible to have. She suggests that at least part of the solution to the plight of the ghetto poor requires more government intervention and a progressive social policy that recognizes and maintains various socioeconomic rights. But to the extent that this presumes that it is possible to have such rights to such assistance, the prevailing legal conception of rights imposes a conceptual barrier to racial uplift by denying the existence of such positive rights. As she puts it, "[w]ith the problem of the black underclass squarely before them, philosophers have good reason seriously to examine the arguments of moral philosophy and constitutional jurisprudence respecting economic welfare rights."[33] This skepticism about the existence of socioeconomic rights is most detrimental to the ghetto poor in the hands of those who argue that in the post-civil rights era, where all formal barriers to black participation in American society have been removed, the explanation for why some blacks failed to follow those who took advantage of the ensuing opportunities must lie within these "underachieving" blacks themselves. And here we find in form, if not in name, appeals to various incarnations of the black inferiority thesis, ranging from the claim that blacks are deficient in skills, have impoverished values, have defective psychologies, to general claims about the poverty of black culture. These observations are especially disconcerting when defended by black conservatives.[34] Thus, as Frederick Douglass astutely observed more than a century ago, efforts to resist the ascription of rights to blacks, be they negative or positive rights, continue to be found within the nature of blacks themselves:

The story of our inferiority is an old dodge, as I have said; for wherever men oppress their fellows, wherever they enslave them, they will endeavor to find the needed apology for such enslavement and oppression in the character of the people oppressed and enslaved . . . So, too, the Negro, when he is to be robbed of any right which is justly his, is an "inferior man."[35]

Positing the existence of socioeconomic rights for blacks may appear to pose a special challenge for my thesis that all rights are products of social

---

[33] Allen, "Legal Rights for Poor Blacks," p. 129.

[34] For an illuminating critique of black conservatism, see Bernard Boxill, *Blacks and Social Justice*, rev. edn. (Lanham: Rowman and Littlefield, 1992), chs. 2 and 11. Also see the essays in Lawson, *The Underclass Question*.

[35] Frederick Douglass, "What the Black Man Wants," in Manning Marable and Leith Mullings (eds.), *Let Nobody Turn Us Around: Voices of Resistance, Reform, and Renewal* (Lanham: Rowman and Littlefield, 2000), p. 128.

recognition. It may be thought that the social recognition thesis itself imposes a conceptual barrier on the existence of positive rights. Although some critics may remain hopeful that civil and political rights and other negative rights may one day enjoy widespread domestic and international social recognition and enforcement, they may insist that such optimism is especially unwarranted in the case of socioeconomic rights (of which rights to food, shelter, health, education, and employment are generally taken to be examples) because the positive nature of such rights poses an insurmountable obstacle to their actual domestic social recognition and enforcement. For example, in singling out social rights for special concern, one critic contends that governments of those parts of Asia, Africa, and South America where industrialization has hardly begun cannot be reasonably expected to secure social rights for millions of citizens who multiply so swiftly.[36]

Part of what is at issue here is the cost of rights. Obviously this reasoning may be used to challenge the possibility of securing such rights for underclass citizens in relatively well off nations as well. However, this feasibility critique loses much of its force if we deny that social recognition and enforcement of rights is an all or nothing matter. There is no reason to think that countries with limited resources and large populations cannot make significant progress toward the greater realization of at least some positive claims. And there is certainly no reason to think that those with considerable resources, like the United States, cannot make even greater progress. Furthermore, this feasibility critique is overly strong to the extent that it undercuts the existence of nonsocial rights as well, as Amartya Sen observes:

If the current feasibility of guaranteeing complete and comprehensive fulfillment were made into a necessary condition for the cogency of every right, then not only economic and social rights, but also liberties, autonomies and even political rights may well fall far short of cogency.[37]

Hence selective skepticism about socioeconomic rights seems untenable. All rights have costs that require some form of government action, where resources are limited and populations are large.[38] The enforcement of civil

---

[36] Maurice Cranston, "Are There Any Human Rights?" *Daedalus* 112 (1983), 13.

[37] Amartya Sen, "Elements of a Theory of Human Rights," *Philosophy and Public Affairs* 32 (2004), 315–56, 348.

[38] Stephen Holmes and Cass Sunstein, *The Costs of Rights: Why Liberty Depends on Taxes* (New York: W. W. Norton, 1999); Cass Sunstein, "Social and Economic Rights? Lessons from South Africa," *Public Law and Legal Theory* Working Paper no. 12 (2001), 1–15; Craig Scott and Patrick Macklem, "Constitutional Ropes of Sand or Justiciable Guarantees? Social Rights in a New South African Constitution," *University of Pennsylvania Law Review* 141 (1992), 85.

and political rights such as freedoms to speech and to vote have economic implications. And to the extent that this is not a bar to their justiciability, it need not be a bar to the justiciability of socioeconomic rights. We may, of course, distinguish between a weaker and a stronger position concerning the use of government action regarding socioeconomic rights. The weak position is that these rights can be protected from interference by government action, and the stronger one is that positive government action is needed to aid in their realization.[39] Though this latter position generates the greatest cause for concern, it is clearly within the realm of possibility, as is most clearly illustrated by recent events in South Africa in the last decade.

In the aftermath of abolishing apartheid, and after a long process of negotiation to reach a broad consensus on the shape of post-apartheid South Africa, the country adopted a new Constitution in 1996. The normative principles articulated in this founding document, specifically in its Bill of Rights, embody a general normative vision of what counts as legitimate and illegitimate conduct toward all of its citizens, but especially those still suffering from the effects of years of neglect and abuse in post-apartheid democratic South Africa.[40] Of special noteworthiness is the inclusion of various social and economic rights in this Bill of Rights, including the rights to equality, human dignity, to a healthy environment, access to health care, food, water, and social security, as well as rights pertaining to language and culture. The incorporation of socioeconomic rights into the Constitution as justiciable rights marks an important departure from other great constitutional experiments, but one that was deemed necessary to render the Constitution a potent instrument for

---

[39] Prior to the adoption of the South African Constitution, the Constitutional Court made clear that it did not in principle distinguish between the enforcement of civil and of social rights, and it did not view compliance with social rights as necessarily requiring state action. For examples, see Pierre De Vos, "Pious Wishes or Directly Enforceable Human Rights? Social and Economic Rights in South Africa's 1996 Constitution," *South African Journal on Human Rights* 13 (1997), 70, and Marius Olivier, "Constitutional Perspectives on the Enforcement of Socio-economic Rights: Recent South African Experiences," *Victoria University of Wellington Law Review* 33 (2002), 135.

[40] We must take care, however, not to overstate this point. For example, Murray Weston suggests that the Constitutional Court's overriding aim is to protect the interests of vulnerable minorities. See his "Grootboom and Beyond: Reassessing the Socio-Economic Jurisprudence of the South African Constitutional Court," *South African Journal on Human Rights* 20 (2004), 284–308, 293–94. The Court does not purport to take sides but only to assign promotion of human dignity (which vulnerable minorities have been denied) equal weight in judicial review grounded in the reality that the constitution is firmly and positively committed to this important normative value.

effecting positive and progressive social change in a country where a vast majority of citizens were deprived of the content of these rights.

As a rights externalist, I construe this domestic recognition of social and economic claims in the South African Constitution as an indispensable step in establishing the existence of socioeconomic rights in South Africa. And I join those who contend that the domestic recognition and enforcement of these rights is both possible and necessary to readdress the legacy of apartheid and the persisting social and material deprivation of the majority of black South Africans. Obviously, a similar justification can be used to defend the establishment of such rights in the United States Constitution, but on the grounds that it is necessary to redress the legacy of slavery and years of segregation and neglect that partly account for the persisting social and material deprivation of blacks in post-civil rights America.

Some critics will object that, even if these positive claims can be socially recognized and enforced, they ought not be recognized to the extent that negative rights are deemed to have a privileged status, and the recognition and enforcement of social rights would contravene this status notwithstanding the fact that the state must actively promote nonsocial rights:

Even if the protection of negative rights requires active performance by the state, there is the prior normative point that the state's refraining from interfering with the negative right indicates of itself the state's respect for the (negative) freedom of the persons who have the negative right . . . if this respect by the state is not recognized, if the state's positive tutelage is alone emphasized in relation to negative rights, then the way is opened for an illiberal authoritarianism in which the state is assigned a kind of creative, supernumerary role with regard to the rights, in contrast to the normatively prior freedom that moderates and limits that role. A similar respect for freedom is not, as such, betokened by the state's active intervention for positive rights.[41]

This objection turns on linking negative rights with respect for freedom and positive rights with a lack of respect for or concern with freedom. But in so doing it totally ignores the distinction between freedom in a negative and a positive sense, a distinction made by some liberals to justify a more expansive role for state action that would require the recognition and enforcement of positive rights. From this vantage point we can view the South African constitutional experiment with socioeconomic rights as radically progressive to the extent that it aims to take freedom very

---

[41] Alan Gewirth, "Are All Rights Positive?" *Philosophy and Public Affairs* 30 (2002), 321–33, 328.

seriously by recognizing a schedule of rights that reflect a commitment to valuing freedom in both senses.

The Preamble to the Constitution of the Republic of South Africa Act makes clear that among the purposes for its adoption include improving the quality of life of all citizens and freeing the potential of each person. This embodies a substantial normative outlook involving deeper reflection on the underlying conception of personhood or humanity, and on the role that social rights in particular are taken to play in helping to free this potential in each person. A plausible interpretation of this normative outlook has been expressed as follows:

Perhaps the strongest reason for including a certain number of economic and social rights is that by constitutionalising half of the human rights equation, South Africans would be constitutionalising only part of what it is to be a full person. A constitution containing only civil and political rights projects an image of truncated humanity. Symbolically, but still brutally, it excludes those segments of society for whom autonomy means little without the necessities of life.[42]

This outlook rightly recognizes that the predominant outlook, which is coupled with assigning an elevated role to civil and political rights and a subordinate one to socioeconomic rights, is that taking individuals seriously, or taking individual freedom in particular seriously, merely demands leaving individuals free from state or societal interference to exercise their autonomy and thereby shape their own lives, unless of course they are harming others or failing to fulfill clear and assignable obligations.

One way, however, to take issue with this widely held yet narrow perspective of what taking individuals seriously amounts to is to argue that autonomy and life shaping cannot be realized at all, or fully realized, by those who are deprived of some or all of the more basic necessities of a human life, including food, water, shelter, sanitary living conditions, and education. Either way, proper regard for individuals can demand much more than viewing them as bearers of negative civil and political rights imposing duties of noninterference on others to afford their autonomy widest scope. Moreover, it can demand taking a broader perspective on what it is to be a person, or a human being, so that viewing individuals as bearers of socioeconomic rights imposing duties of positive action on others is needed to guarantee that they are capable of exercising their autonomy and thereby shaping their own lives. Hence we could say that the normative outlook expressed in the Preamble to the South African

---

[42] Scott and Maklem, "Constitutional Ropes of Sand or Justiciable Guarantees?" p. 29.

Constitution entails the highest law of the land pursuing the goal of freeing the potential for each person to be fully autonomous by recognizing and enforcing not only civil and political rights but also social ones which guarantee the necessities of life without which autonomy would remain for many an unrealized ideal.[43] So considering the South African case offers strong support for the view that positive socioeconomic rights can and ought to be recognized in practice, though a thorough development of this case is beyond the scope of my current objectives.

It would be remiss of us not to appreciate the connection between social rights in the South African Constitution and the attempt to redress the persisting social and economic inequalities stemming from the long legacy of apartheid in South Africa, where the civil and political claims as well as the social and economic claims of black South Africans went unrecognized and unenforced. To the extent that the legacy of slavery and black discrimination account for the social predicament of many black Americans—including many in New Orleans who were displaced by Hurricane Katrina—it may be high time for the United States of America to consider taking steps in the direction of recognizing and enforcing similar positive claims in the Constitution of the United States of America. Perhaps if it had done so prior to Katrina, the fate of the victims would not solely be left to charity and goodwill. By example, South Africa has undermined the perception that social rights are ill suited for domestic recognition and enforcement; moreover, it has, ironically, come closer to making social rights and the enjoyment of positive freedom a reality for its citizens than has the United States of America, which has yet to assign social and economic claims that same sort of constitutional status. And this certainly does not speak well for a country that professes to be the world's greatest advocate and defender of human rights and human freedom.

CONCLUSION

In this chapter I have argued that embracing rights externalism is not merely reasonable but a matter of urgency as well. It would be reasonable insofar as older versions of the black inferiority thesis could be resurrected

---

[43] There are others ways of making this point where, say, equality or democratic citizenship are invoked to defend the inclusion of socioeconomic rights on normative grounds. And another particularly noteworthy strategy is to argue that socioeconomic rights are necessary to realize human dignity more generally. See Sandra Liebenberg, "The Value of Human Dignity in Interpreting Socio-economic Rights," *South African Journal on Human Rights* 21 (2005), 1–31. She relies on the work of Martha Nussbaum to develop her argument, in particular Nussbaum's *Women and Human Development: The Capabilities Approach* (Cambridge University Press, 2000).

in the near or distant future to license the inference that blacks lack certain rights. Yet embracing externalism appears to be a matter of urgency since remnants of the black inferiority thesis are still alive in contemporary America, and continue to influence political attitudes both within the academy and in the general public. One social critic claims that we do not need "biological racism to facilitate the maintenance of white skin privilege and black disadvantage. Yet in the popular mind, racism is now narrowly equated with cross burnings, hooded Klansmen, and the Jim Crow ranting of the likes of George Wallace and Lester Maddox."[44] In a similar spirit I claim that the black inferiority thesis need not appear in the form of biological racism and be used to infer that blacks do not have any rights at all for contemporary social critics to have cause for concern. There is ample cause for concern insofar as remnants of this thesis persist in the form of symbolic or *laissez-faire* racism, and in this "rearticulated"[45] form are exploited to infer that blacks do not have rights to remedies instrumental to redressing past and current inequalities in the United States.

Admittedly, from the perspective of a certain historical narrative, which has been defended recently with great effort, the fact that remnants of the black inferiority thesis persist in modern America, and are being used to license the inference that blacks have no rights to certain forms of state-sponsored action, should not be that surprising. In fact, it is just what we should expect in a racial polity. According to this narrative, America's promises of liberty were never meant to cover everyone on its soil, nor did they actually extend to most members of the polity until very recently.[46] The promise of rights to life, liberty, and the pursuit of happiness was only gradually extended to certain groups and only after long struggles involving great loss of life, liberty, and happiness for many. These attempts to extend the promises of liberty were not only met with physical resistance; they were met with conceptual or ideological resistance as well. In particular, some agents who resisted attempts to extend the promises of liberty to certain groups undermined these extensions on a conceptual level by using rights discourse—the prevailing political ideology of the United States—as well as theses about the so-called inferiority of members

---

[44] Bobo, "Racial Beliefs about Affirmative Action," p. 159.

[45] I borrow this usage from Michael Omi and Howard Winant, *Racial Formation in the United States: From the 1960s to the 1990s*, 2nd edn. (New York: Routledge, 1994), p. 123.

[46] Smith, *Civic Ideals*; Eric Foner, *The Story of American Freedom* (New York: W. W. Norton & Company, 1998); and Larry E. Tise, *The American Counterrevolution: A Retreat from Liberty, 1783–1800* (Mechanicsburg: Stackpole Books, 1998).

of these groups that were taken to justify viewing them as lacking some or all rights.

It would be naïve to suppose that racial oppression must stem from the denial of the rights of the oppressed; oppressors can acknowledge that victims have rights and trample on them anyway. While I concede that the problem of racial oppression cannot be solved conceptually, and that racial oppression can survive changes in our background conception of rights, I have endeavored to show that an externalist conception of the source of rights offers us a more illuminating understanding of what was at stake conceptually in the historical debate between antislavery thinkers and apologists for slavery. I am not suggesting the problems of slavery and racial oppression can be reduced to a mere logical dispute over who counts as a rightholder, nor do I purport to add anything new to our understanding of how the minds of racists work.[47] While some critical theorists might use the historical resources pertaining to this debate to discuss what was at stake politically, I have drawn on them selectively to illuminate the underlying logic of arguments for and against the "blacks have no rights" thesis. To be sure, the debate has important political dimensions; however, it also has a definite logical dimension. And my modest hope is that elucidating the logic of arguments for and against the "blacks have no rights" thesis will contribute to a broader understanding of the bittersweet legacy of rights discourse in American political thought.

It should be quite clear that I am not oblivious to what philosopher Jürgen Habermas describes as the "self-referential character" of human rights. He contends, and rightly so, that the "discourse of human rights is also set up to provide *every* voice with a hearing. Consequently, this discourse itself sets forth the standards in whose light the latent violations of its own claims can be discovered and corrected."[48] From the moment when American revolutionaries utilized the discourse of rights to voice their opposition to British rule and to establish principles that would govern the terms of their new polity, there has been a contest over how to understand the meaning and implications of rights. Yet due to the resilience of replies to more inclusive interpretations of natural rights, similar to replies that vexed antebellum social critics, in keeping with the spirit of contestation, I have recommended that contemporary social critics contest

---

[47] For a classic psychological analysis of racist thinking, see Gordon W. Allport's *The Nature of Prejudice* (Garden City: Doubleday Anchor Books, 1958).
[48] Jürgen Habermas, "Remarks on Legitimation Through Human Rights," *Philosophy and Social Criticism* 24 (1998), 157–71, 162.

the very idea of natural rights, understood as rights that individuals possess merely on account of having a certain nature—human or otherwise. In place of the prevailing ontological conception I have proposed that they embrace an externalist conception of rights possession on the grounds that it would block attempts to move directly from modern versions of the black inferiority thesis to the claim that blacks lack certain rights. While this is not the only or clearly the best justification for embracing externalism, it partly accounts for why I favor a socially oriented conception of moral rights, and why Allen and others who long for a more "black-friendly" philosophical conception of rights should do so as well. The only task that remains, to which I now turn, is to demonstrate that our ability to wage normative argument against slavery (and other moral atrocities) can survive the demise of natural rights.

CHAPTER 5

What's wrong with slavery?

Slavery seems to us horrible: it is contrary to nature, it violates the feelings that God and Nature have implanted in our breasts, and so on. It used not to seem horrible or contrary to nature, even to many people who talked loudly about the inalienable right of liberty.

D. G. Ritchie, *Natural Rights*

[S]laves are human beings who are not counted as sources of claims, not even claims based on social duties or obligations, for slaves are not counted as capable of having duties or obligations. Laws that prohibit the abuse and maltreatment of slaves are not founded on claims made by slaves on their own behalf, but on claims originating either from slaveholders, or from the general interest of society (which does not include the interests of slaves). Slaves are, so to speak, socially dead; they are not publicly recognised as persons at all.

John Rawls, "Justice as Fairness: Political Not Metaphysical"

W. D. Ross describes T. H. Green's thesis that moral rights depend on social recognition for their existence, and not just for their effectiveness, as plainly wrong. He poses a purported *reductio ad absurdum*: "[It] would imply that slaves, for instance, acquired the moral right to be free only at the moment when a majority of mankind, or of some particular community, formed the opinion that they ought to be free."[1] He concludes that this is absurd and cannot be consistently maintained. To assess this criticism we must consider the precise formulation of the thesis that all rights are made by social recognition. Ross contends that for Green the relevant recognition consists "simply in a general state of public opinion." But this is uncharitable. While Green does indeed appeal to such an opinion in his account of rights, a more charitable formulation of his position notes that he does not tie recognition solely to the formation of

---

[1] W. D. Ross, *The Right and the Good* (Oxford: Clarendon Press, 1930), p. 51.

public opinion but also to concrete socially established ways of acting and being treated. To determine whether a subject actually has rights we must consider not only what people think but also, and more importantly, what they do. So insofar as public opinion bears on whether the requisite social recognition is forthcoming, withheld, or sustained but does not suffice to establish the existence of moral rights, Ross attacks a straw man.

Moreover, the appeal of this objection diminishes considerably if we deny that appealing to an unrecognized moral right to be free is either the only or best way to make a normative argument for why a slave's freedom ought to be recognized legally. It could turn out that the majority opinion on this matter was defended not by appeal to unrecognized moral rights at all but by other kinds of moral considerations. Indeed, a cursory review of actual arguments made against slavery in antebellum America will show that a variety of arguments were deployed for this purpose and that many of them were not at all rights-based arguments, at least in the sense of presuming that natural rights were the foundational or basic normative category. Bearing this in mind, consider Ross's additional observation: "Some may think that slavery is not wrong; but everyone will admit that there are certain forms of treatment of others which are wrong and which the sufferer has the right to have removed, whether this right is recognized by society or not."[2]

Although many people would eagerly second this observation, it begs the question. While many might agree that certain forms of treatment such as the enslavement of human beings are morally wrong, clearly not everyone will explain why they are morally wrong by appealing to unrecognized moral rights; nor is it obvious that they ought to. We could even agree with Margaret MacDonald's observation that the postulation of natural or unrecognized moral rights was meant to solve the problem of explaining how a slave could hold that he had a "right" to be free even if the laws of every existing society condemned him to be a slave.[3] Yet we need not believe that this is the only way for the slave or the abolitionist to make the case for why the slave ought to be free, or why his freedom should be legally recognized. A Benthamite certainly would not argue for the immorality of slavery in these terms, nor would anyone else who eschewed the existence of such natural or unrecognized rights altogether. I agree that this point seems to be too obvious to need stating, but critics of

---

[2] *Ibid.*

[3] Margaret MacDonald, "Natural Rights," in Jeremy Waldron (ed.), *Theories of Rights* (Oxford University Press, 1984), p. 23.

rights externalism, who continue to find the slavery objection compelling and even decisive, routinely overlook this point.

But be that as it may, if we eschew natural or unrecognized moral rights-based arguments, we still need an alternative normative framework for morally condemning slavery or any other social practice that we believe ought to be abolished. We still need an alternative means of making the moral case for why a slave's freedom ought to be legally recognized. As a first step toward understanding Green's solution to the problem of slavery, which will be reconstructed in this chapter, it is useful to appreciate that he could accept MacDonald's imagined possibility of a slave having a right to be free independently of the laws and government of every existing society without renouncing rights externalism. Admittedly, the following point is somewhat less obvious than the point that appealing to unrecognized moral rights is not the only way to argue for the immorality of slavery; nevertheless, agreeing with MacDonald's observation about the rationale for postulating the slave's right to be free does not compel us to understand this right as one that the slave possesses independently of all forms of community or society. In other words, a natural right need not be a presocial right, though it may certainly be a prepolitical one. This point will be crucial for appreciating how Green is able to account for the wrongness of slavery in general, and to make a case for why the slave's freedom ought to be legally recognized, without making recourse to the idea of natural rights in the traditional sense. I think that his argument is a good one, and that it can be deployed by anyone who wants to rely upon a rights-based argument but without being committed to the existence of rights that preexist all forms of community or society.[4]

How, then, can moral rights externalists establish the immorality of slavery (or other forms of treatment that most people would deem immoral) if they take some form of social recognition to be necessary for the existence of moral rights? More precisely, how can they do so without making recourse to unrecognized moral or natural rights? In this final chapter I shall address these pressing questions and demonstrate that moral rights externalists can indeed salvage normativity without appealing to natural rights in the orthodox sense, that is, in the sense of being rights that persons possess prior to and independently of all forms of social

---

[4] For another response to Ross's slavery objection to Green, see Gerald Gaus, "Green's Rights Recognition Thesis and Moral Internalism," *The British Journal of Politics and International Relations* 7 (2005), 5–17.

recognition. This will suffice to rebut what is arguably the most potent and widely espoused objection to a socially grounded conception of what possessing moral rights amounts to. An important implication will be that if we wish to retain the language of rights, we can make sense of the claim that a slave has a "right" to be free even if the laws of every existing society condemn him to be a slave without thereby holding that this is a natural right in the traditional sense, in which case we have a very different and more appealing solution to the problem that MacDonald identifies.

MORAL RIGHTS AND MORAL ARGUMENT

Even if we acknowledge the merits of moral rights externalism that I have identified in this book, people will be loath to embrace it as an alternative conception of the source of rights if it appears to be too costly. Some critics will follow Ross's lead by arguing that rights externalism is indeed too costly insofar as it appears to leave us with a moral vacuum and unable to conduct our normative business. They will contend that the most significant cost is that embracing rights externalism precludes us from making moral arguments against a social institution or practice (e.g. slavery) that proceed from the premise that subjects possess unrecognized moral rights that preexist all forms of community. These critics simply cannot see how we can get on morally without such rights serving as a basic or foundational moral category, or, alternatively, why we would want to get on morally without them in our moral arsenal.[5] Obviously anyone who is not prepared to forsake such arguments will not welcome this implication of rights externalism; these critics will lament that it deprives us of certain kinds of moral arguments that many people rely upon quite often and have come to value. But careful reflection shows that matters are not as bleak as these critics would have us think.

To avoid a possible misunderstanding, let me emphasize that at no point in this book have I claimed that one cannot embrace a normative theory that takes unrecognized moral rights that preexist all forms of community to be a basic or foundational normative category. Although one might attempt to argue for the strong conclusion that such a theory is incoherent or implausible, this has not been my strategy. To the contrary, I have conceded that advocates of a such a theory can indeed deploy

---

[5] For a defense and a critique of right-based moral theory, see J. L. Mackie, "Can There Be a Right-Based Moral Theory?" and Joseph Raz, "Right-Based Moralities," respectively in Waldron, *Theories of Rights.*

arguments that appeal to moral rights so understood as basic premises while those of us who impose a social constraint on moral rights possession cannot do so. However, the crucial question is what follows from this. Many critics of rights externalism hastily take this result to be sufficient to justify rejecting such a conception out of hand. But this is a serious mistake. Although imposing a social constraint on moral rights possession does indeed preclude us from deploying arguments for moral conclusions that appeal to unrecognized moral rights that preexist all forms of community, it does not preclude us from appealing to moral rights altogether in moral arguments, and as I have intimated throughout it certainly does not preclude us from arguing for moral conclusions from other more basic moral premises.

Consider the following argument. Dred the slave has a moral right to go and come as he pleases with impunity. It is morally wrong to violate his moral right. Enslaving Dred violates his moral right. Therefore, enslaving him is morally wrong. Those who reject the imposition of a social constraint on moral rights possession could interpret this argument as establishing a moral conclusion from premises that take certain rights to be morally basic. But moral rights externalists will deny that the moral rights adduced in this argument are morally basic. To be sure, we will have to bear the burden of explaining the function of appeals to moral rights in such arguments; however, this demand can be met with relative ease, as I demonstrated in chapter 3. We can contend that a moral right exists whenever the corresponding conventional right is morally justified. On this analysis, then, the requisite justification is provided not by a morally basic right but by the resources of a substantive moral theory that is not rights-based. So, for example, the claim that Dred has a moral right to go and come as he pleases with impunity is, on this view, logically equivalent to the claim that the policy of conferring upon Dred the corresponding conventional right to go and come as he pleases with impunity can be morally justified by a particular kind of moral argument. Hence the function of appeals to moral rights in such arguments is not to supply the requisite moral justification but to indicate or announce the existence of such a justification, which is ultimately provided in other, more basic, normative terms.

So although imposing a social constraint on moral rights possession does indeed preclude us from deploying arguments for moral conclusions that take unrecognized moral rights that preexist all forms of community to be basic or foundational moral posits, it does not preclude us from appealing to moral rights altogether in moral arguments. But when we do use moral rights in such arguments, it will always be an abbreviated way of indicating that a deeper moral justification can be given for the validity of some way of acting or being treated. Even if one ultimately disagrees with this particular explanation of the semantics of moral rights assertions, the fact remains that merely supplying it suffices to show that moral rights externalists can indeed explain the role of moral rights in moral arguments. From this vantage point, then, to deny that such rights are morally basic is to deny that they can serve as premises in the deeper argument morally justifying a socially recognized way of acting or being treated. For the deeper moral justification we must look beyond them in search of a substantive normative theory that does not regard such rights as morally basic.

Perhaps some critics will insist that the genius underlying the natural rights tradition going back to Locke and extending to contemporary appeals to human rights is precisely to postulate as morally basic a class of rights that can be used in a deep moral justification for the validity of some way of acting or being treated, or can be used to argue that some social practice or institution is morally wrong regardless of whether it has been recognized by conventional practices, legal or otherwise. But rights externalists can grant this point—understood as a point about what motivates some people to postulate the existence of natural rights—while insisting that the crucial question is what follows from the fact that natural rights are postulated for this reason. Surely one cannot infer from the utility of postulating the existence of a class of rights that are morally basic that such rights exist or that individuals actually possess these rights. While I do not mean to beg any questions against theism, this argument is certainly no more effective than inferring from the utility of postulating the existence of a Supreme Being who gives humanity the moral law to the conclusion that such a Supreme Being exists. Both of these arguments are suspect insofar as they infer from the usefulness of their posits to their actual existence. Although belief in natural rights and belief in a Supreme Being could be motivated by an attempt to provide moral resources for a deep justification of our moral beliefs, this consideration does not constitute an evidentiary basis either for the existence of natural rights or for the existence of a Supreme Being.

The foregoing argument notwithstanding, some critics may contend that looking beyond unrecognized moral rights that preexist all forms of community in search of a substantive normative theory that does not regard such rights as morally basic would be futile since moral rights are the only way to establish the moral validity of ways of acting or being treated. But this is clearly false. In addition to appealing to a Supreme Being (as I do in the foregoing example), which takes the existence of a Supreme Being who gives the moral law to be morally basic, one can embrace other substantive normative theories that do not take these rights to be morally basic. Any of the following principles would supply the resources for such a normative theory: principles having to do with the maximization of some impersonal value such as happiness (utilitarianism); principles derived from the hypothetical consent of ideally situated agents or principles derived from the rationally motivated consent of actual agents (versions of contractarianism); principles having to do with respect for the dignity of persons (Kantianism); principles having to do with living virtuously (virtue ethics). To be sure, these do not exhaust the available options. And although substantive normative theories built upon these or other nonrights-based foundations must be assessed (and will undoubtedly have their own shortcomings), until we have reason to think otherwise they certainly constitute substantive alternatives to a rights-based moral theory. I suppose that if one could convincingly argue that all substantive nonrights-based moral theories could be reduced to an unrecognized moral rights-based moral theory, then the claim regarding the futility of looking beyond these rights in search of a substantive normative theory could be salvaged. But whether such an argument can be given remains to be seen.

More plausibly some critics may contend that looking beyond these rights in search of a substantive normative theory that does not regard unrecognized moral rights that preexist all forms of community as morally basic would be wasted effort since such rights are not the only but the best way to justify our moral beliefs. In other words, defenders of these rights could assert that if they existed (leaving this question open to be settled by other means) they would be the best way to justify our moral beliefs, or to argue for the moral validity of ways of acting or being treated. The explanation for this point goes roughly as follows. An unrecognized moral rights-based normative theory would be best suited for these normative purposes because the natural or moral rights that are taken to be morally basic according to this theory are suitably independent of existing social practices to serve as appropriate moral norms. Indeed, it seems obvious that the moral force of moral rights—that which makes it possible for them to serve as moral justifiers—is precisely the fact that they are suitably independent of existing social practices to serve our various normative purposes. In circumstances where subjects have not been afforded a certain kind of social recognition, where ways of acting and ways of being treated have not been recognized, maintained, and enforced—formally or informally—we are most apt to talk about violations of natural, human, or moral rights. And this is because their existence is not tied to the activities of social actors, which makes them uniquely fit for critical normative use in these circumstances.

Without being overly enamored of the rhetorical force of this appeal, moral rights externalists can certainly grant the point that unrecognized moral rights that preexist all forms of community are indeed suitably independent of existing social practices and the activities of social actors to serve as moral justifiers; this will be true by hypothesis. Furthermore they can even grant that the same must be true of all potential moral justifiers. In other words, any substantive normative theory must be such that the norms it takes to be morally basic must be suitably independent of existing social practices to serve as moral justifiers or to serve as normative standards, especially in circumstances where social practices do not reflect how things ought to be from the moral point of view.

Yet even if we grant these points, the problem is that unrecognized moral rights defenders have failed to show that such rights are best suited to serve this function. In other words, they have not shown that of all the possible substantive normative theories that we have to choose from an unrecognized moral rights-based moral theory is superior insofar as its morally basic posits are the best ones. Presumably what makes basic moral rights suitable is that they are appropriately independent of existing social practices. But by this standard any moral norm that is appropriately independent of existing practices would also be suitable. While this may rule out some substantive moral theories on the grounds that their morally basic posits are not suitably independent of social practices, or the activities of social actors, to serve as appropriate normative standards, it certainly does not rule out all of them.

For instance, principles having to do with maximizing general utility appear to be suitably independent of social practices to be fit to serve as appropriate normative standards. Perhaps one might propose that basic moral rights are superior in that they would be "most" independent of social practices or the activities of social actors. But in addition to doubts about whether this point can be convincingly argued for, it leaves open the possibility that, if another moral posit were even more independent than rights, then this posit would be a more superior normative standard. But then one wonders whether a Supreme Being whose commands constitute the moral law would best fit this description thereby making a divine command moral theory the frontrunner for the title of "supreme" normative theory.

A last-ditch effort to salvage the case against imposing a social constraint on moral rights possession by attending to the impact that this has on the role of rights in normative argument takes the form of an apparent dilemma. If nonrights-based moral norms (the existence of which rights externalists appear to be committed to insofar as they assign moral justification a role in grounding rights) are to serve as moral justifiers or as bases for normative criticism, then they must be suitably independent of the social practices or the activities of social actors as well. If we deny that there are moral norms that are suitably independent of practices, then it is unclear how moral justification or moral criticism can proceed on our view. But if we contend that there are such norms (ones that are suitably independent of practices but do not regard unrecognized moral rights that preexist all forms of community as morally basic), then it is unclear why we are reluctant to regard unrecognized moral rights as morally basic and not these other moral norms as well. In other words, it is not clear why our skepticism about unrecognized moral rights that preexist all forms of community does not ultimately force us to be skeptics about other moral norms in particular, or even morality in general, insofar as some norms must be regarded as rock-bottom morally basic to serve as moral justifiers or as normative standards.[6]

While it may turn out in the final analysis, after all of the available substantive moral theories along with their various basic moral posits have been scrutinized, that a sweeping skeptical conclusion about all of them and morality in general is warranted, I myself have not done the work to make a case for this conclusion. Furthermore, I do not see why we are forced to a sweeping skepticism about morality in general by refusing to regard unrecognized moral rights that preexist all forms of community as morally basic, anymore than those who refuse to regard the commands of a Supreme Being as morally basic are forced to a sweeping skepticism about morality in general. Hence the reasoning underlying this criticism entails that all moral and political philosophers who are either atheist or agnostic would also be forced to be skeptics about morality in general, and, presumably, this is a conclusion that many of them would reject out of hand.

Suppose, therefore, that the critics of moral rights externalism agree begrudgingly that appealing to unrecognized moral rights that preexist all

---

[6] For this criticism, see Lyons, *Rights, Welfare, and Mill's Moral Theory.*

forms of community is neither the only nor the best way to conduct our normative business. It still remains to be shown how a rights externalist can account for the immorality of slavery and other practices without making recourse to moral rights so understood. For this purpose I shall advance an interpretation of Green's argument against slavery. My ultimate concern is not to make a novel contribution to Green scholarship. Rather the point of this exercise is to demonstrate with a concrete example how a moral rights externalist can argue that slavery is immoral without making recourse to moral rights that preexist all forms of community. Before considering Green's argument against slavery, we must briefly consider his conception of moral rights and the problems that the slave case raises for it.

GREEN ON RIGHTS AND SLAVES

Green's conception of rights appears in his posthumously published "Lectures on the Principles of Political Obligation."[7] What distinguishes it from conceptions of rights advanced by some social contract thinkers as well as other liberal thinkers who preceded him is the idea that "rights have no being except in a society of men recognizing each other as *isoi kai homoioi* [equals]."[8] According to Green, all rights, including moral ones, are constituted by such mutual recognition. It is important to note, however, that this mutual recognition is not sufficient for the existence of moral rights on Green's account. He maintains that in analyzing the nature of any right we must identify two distinguishable but inseparable elements: (1) a claim of the individual; and (2) the concession or recognition of this claim by society. I shall refer to the former as the claim element and the latter as the recognition element. On Green's account these two elements are individually necessary and jointly sufficient for the possession of what

---

[7] I believe that one must have some familiarity with Green's ethical views as expressed in the *Prolegomena to Ethics* to fully understand his conception of rights. In particular, one needs some familiarity with the perfectionist dimensions of his ethical thought, a core idea of which is that societal assistance is needed to enable some of its members to realize freedom in a positive as well as a negative sense. I expand on some of his ethical views below in my reconstruction of his argument against slavery. But for more detailed attention to his ethical views, one must turn elsewhere. For a concise overview of some themes for his ethics, see David O. Brink, *Perfectionism and the Common Good: Themes in the Philosophy of T. H. Green* (Oxford: Clarendon Press, 2003). And for more extended treatments of Green's ethical thought, see Geoffrey Thomas, *The Moral Philosophy of T. H. Green* (Oxford: Clarendon Press, 1987), Terence Irwin, "Morality and Personality: Kant and Green," in Allen Wood (ed.), *Self and Nature* (Cornell University Press, 1984), and Peter Nicholson, *The Political Philosophy of the British Idealists* (Cambridge University Press, 1990), ch. 2.

[8] Green, *Lectures on the Principles of Political Obligation*, p. 139.

we would call conventional rights in general. And since he takes the recognition element to be necessary for the existence of all rights, a corollary of this analysis is that moral rights are a species of conventional or socially derived rights, or, as I have described them, a species of unnatural rights. In this regard Green can be considered a nineteenth-century proponent of moral rights externalism.

We must take care not to mistake Green's analysis of rights for the one proposed by his older contemporary John Stuart Mill, who contends:

> When we call anything a person's right, we mean that he has a valid claim on society to protect him in the possession of it, either by the force of law or by that of education and opinion . . . To have a right, then, is I conceive, to have something which society ought to defend me in the possession of. If the objector goes on to ask why it ought, I can give him no other reason than general utility.[9]

According to this analysis, the moral validity of an individual's claim is necessary and sufficient for the possession of a moral right. To be sure, one could disagree with Mill by appealing to moral considerations apart from general utility to establish the moral validity of the claim without thereby denying that having moral rights amounts to nothing more than having a morally valid or morally justified claim to act or be treated in a certain way that society ought to uphold. As noted in chapter 2, this Millean analysis has had tremendous influence on contemporary discussions of the nature of moral rights, although Green rejects it. From a Greenian perspective, in the absence of the concession or recognition of an individual's morally valid claim to act or be treated in a certain way, at most we can conclude that the individual has a claim which there is a morally valid basis for conceding or recognizing.

Hence to say that an individual possesses a moral right, as Green conceives it, it must be the case that the individual possesses a morally valid claim to act or be treated in a certain way that is conceded or recognized by society or, more precisely, by other individuals who participate in social relations of mutually recognizing and being recognized. This last qualification is crucial for understanding his argument against slavery and for appreciating the ineffectiveness of Ross's objection to moral rights externalism.

As is the case with other versions of moral rights externalism, Green's conception yields the following implications: (1) it is possible for individuals

---

[9] John Stuart Mill, *Utilitarianism*, p. 52.

to have morally valid claims that are unrecognized by their government, or even society at large; (2) it is possible for them to have claims that are recognized by their government or society at large though they are not morally valid. Somewhat misleadingly Green describes the former case, in which someone has a valid claim that is not legally recognized by government, as an "implicit" as opposed to "actual" or "explicit" right.[10] He then uses this contrast in his discussion of the slave case in a way that appears to be inconsistent with the recognition element of his conception of rights. At one point Green maintains:

> The claim of the slave to be free, his right *implicit* to have rights *explicit,* i.e. to membership of a society of which each member is treated by the rest as entitled to seek his own good in his own way on supposition that he so seeks it as not to interfere with the like freedom of quest on the part of others, rests, as we have seen, on the fact that the slave is determined by conceptions of a good common to himself with others, as shown by the actual social relations in which he lives.[11]

But this attribution of implicit rights to slaves poses a quandary for Green: either he believes in unrecognized rights after all (as these so-called implicit rights appear to be nothing more than that) or, if he really believes that these too are in some sense creations of society, then he is not entitled to appeal to them as a foundational normative basis for criticizing a slaveholding society. Thus insofar as Green's case against slavery seems to attribute to slaves rights that their society or legal system refuses to recognize—for the purpose of normatively criticizing this society—the folly of trying to ground moral rights in social recognition is made manifest.

There is a further complication raised by Green's treatment of the slave case. Preceding his discussion of this case he maintains: "In analysing the nature of any right, we may conveniently look at it on two sides, and consider it as on the one hand a claim of the individual, arising out of his rational nature, to the free exercise of some faculty."[12] But this seems to indicate that Green grounds rights (understood as valid claims) not in considerations having to do with social recognition but in human nature in particular or ontological considerations in general. If this is not the case, then one wonders exactly what role this appeal to rational nature (a fact about how subjects are constituted) plays in his overall analysis of

---

[10] Green, *Lectures on the Principles of Political Obligation,* §8, §143, and §144; also see Nicholson's very useful discussion of this distinction, *The Political Philosophy of the British Idealists,* ch. 3.

[11] Green, *Lectures on the Principles of Political Obligation,* p. 115.

[12] *Ibid.,* p. 108.

the source of moral rights. To be sure, insofar as Green takes moral rights to be constituted in part by mutual recognition he does not want to move from the mere fact that an individual has a rational nature to the conclusion that the individual possesses a moral right, since this would conflict with the claim that mutual recognition is a necessary element of moral rights possession. Accordingly, he adds that the other side of a right amounts to "a concession of the claim by society, a power given to the individual of putting the claim in force by society."[13] While this recognition is a necessary feature of any would-be right, elaboration on the precise role of ontological considerations is still in order.

Proponents of rights internalism can offer a ready account of the role of ontological considerations in grounding rights. To say that a subject possesses moral rights merely by virtue of having a rational nature or having a certain ontological constitution is a way of spelling out the view that individuals possess certain rights prior to and independently of all social relations, which, it is argued, allows them to provide a standard of normative criticism of individual conduct and political authority that is suitably independent of social practices. In this regard internalism seems to offer a normatively more attractive and more theoretically straightforward way of handling certain hard cases. For example, in cases where the social concession or recognition of a claim is not forthcoming from society, internalism allows us to claim that individuals nevertheless possess certain presocial rights that society can violate, which provides grounds for moral objection.

Hence insofar as Green's account deprives us of this particular response it is unattractive from the moral point of view. Moreover, as Green seemingly makes recourse to ontological considerations in his handling of the slave case, he demonstrates the serious normative deficiency of the social recognition approach to grounding moral rights. More generally, it demonstrates the futility and wrong-headedness of grounding moral rights in social relations. The slave case appears to be a serious problem for Green's theory of rights. Therefore, whatever shortcomings the prevailing conception of moral rights, a recognition-based conception of moral rights appears to face insurmountable obstacles to being embraced as an attractive alternative.

To the contrary, careful reflection, and a more sympathetic reading of Green, demonstrates that the slave case does not pose an insurmountable

---

[13] *Ibid.*

obstacle for a social recognition-based conception of rights. In particular, it does not establish the normative deficiency of this conception, nor does it demonstrate the futility or wrong-headedness of this conception. Obviously, if slaves have no natural rights prior to the state, then the state cannot be said to violate natural rights. But if we follow Green in holding that slaves have natural rights in the sense of being independent of, and in conflict with, the laws of the state in which he lives, but not in the sense of being independent of all social relations, then not only can we see that the foregoing criticisms miss their mark but we can appreciate how Green makes a case for the immorality of slavery precisely by relying on the idea that rights are constituted by social relations.

WHAT'S WRONG WITH SLAVERY?

The appearance that Green—contrary to his professed view that rights are made by social recognition—is working with the idea of rights prior to recognition to make the case against slavery is understandable given his misleading distinction between implicit and explicit rights. To dispel this appearance we must attend to a crucial distinction that he draws in his reply to the slave case.

He presents his response to this case in a section bearing the title "Has the Citizen Rights Against the State?" According to the classical natural rights tradition, the familiar answer is that individuals do indeed have rights against the state, which they are taken to possess prior to and independent of the establishment of the state. One of the general aims of Green's political philosophy is to reject the Lockean social contract account of the basis of political authority according to which the authority of the state over its members and the ground of their duty to obey is having consented to do so for the preservation of these so-called preexisting natural rights. Historical and contemporary defenders of natural rights usually make the further point that these rights exist prior to the existence of all social relations, not just prior to the establishment of political authority. As I have already discussed, both the valid claims approach and rights internalism constitute ways of accounting for the existence of presocial rights in this sense. And the obvious virtue of arguing that natural rights exist prior to all social relations is so that they can be taken to mark the scope and limits of all conduct, not just state conduct, and thereby provide a normative basis for condemning such conduct that is suitably independent of all social relations, political or otherwise. However, Green refuses to take this further step of asserting that natural rights exist prior to and independent of all social relations. And appreciating this distinction between having rights prior to relations within a political community and having them prior to relations in a nonpolitical community is the key to understanding his response to the slave case.

To give content to this point, let us consider a specific right, the right to freedom or to a free life. In the tradition of those positing rights that preexist all forms of recognition, Kant observes: "An innate right is that which belongs to everyone by nature, independently of any act that would establish a right; an acquired right is that for which such an act is required."[14] He further maintains: "*Freedom* (independence from being constrained by another's choice), insofar as it can coexist with the freedom of every other in accordance with a universal law, is the only original right belonging to every man by virtue of his humanity."[15] While Green departs from Kant by rejecting the innateness thesis, he follows Kant in singling out the right to freedom for special attention. Green maintains: "If there are such things as rights at all, then, there must be a right to life and liberty, or to put it more properly, to free life."[16]

While we can indeed suppose that individuals have a moral right to conduct their own affairs or to make their own lives in pursuit of their interests or ends, we need not take this to be an innate or "natural" right in the sense of being a right that the individual possesses prior to and independently of social practices. Furthermore, we need not take this right to be grounded in human nature itself as if we could infer from the appeal to humanity (or some more specific power or capacity that human beings typically but not always possess) that an individual has this right. Of course, we may certainly appeal to human nature in mounting an argument for why individuals ought to be afforded the freedom to make their own lives in pursuit of their ends, but this is radically different from taking the mere possession of humanity to settle the matter of whether they actually possess this moral right to freedom.

On a more mundane level, individual life-making—conducting affairs in the pursuit of ends—is a way of acting that may or may not be realized in particular social contexts where individuals find themselves in some form of community. So what exactly is required for this particular way of acting to be realized in a particular social context? From a Greenian

---

[14] Immanuel Kant, Mary J. Gregor (trans.) and (ed.), *Practical Philosophy* (Cambridge University Press, 1996), p. 393.

[15] *Ibid.*

[16] Green, *Lectures on the Principles of Political Obligation*, p. 117.

perspective, to make one's life requires, in addition to having knowledge of oneself and one's ends, that an individual be able to reckon on a certain freedom of action and acquisition for the attainment of those ends. But an individual can only reckon on a certain freedom of action within a particular social milieu if other individuals within the community of agents are prepared to afford him the opportunity to make his own life either by not interfering with his pursuit of these ends or by assisting him in various ways in attaining them. Human nature being what it is, however, an individual cannot count on others to afford him this opportunity unless he is prepared to do likewise. Consequently, being able to reckon on the freedom to act in the pursuit of one's ends can only be secured when members within a particular social community mutually recognize that affording others the freedom to make their own lives is necessary for the common good of all. Hence, within a community of individuals, each must realize that being afforded the freedom to make one's life is dependent in large measure upon affording others an equal opportunity to do the same.[17]

So from this vantage point we see that the moral right to conduct one's own affairs (or to make one's own life) in particular, as well as rights in general, owe their existence—as morally valid ways of acting and being treated—to this social recognition. As Green puts it: "rights have no being except in a society of men recognising each other as *isoi kai komoioi* [equals]. They are constituted by that mutual recognition."[18] If we take this mutual recognition to be a necessary condition for the possession of any right, we must explain what it comes to. With respect to the right to make one's own life—the having of which requires that an individual be able to reckon on the opportunity to do so—the individual must be viewed as having a morally valid claim to act in pursuit of his own ends, and others with whom he finds himself in community must concede the claim by not interfering with him or by assisting him in various ways. It is a further question as to what makes the claim morally valid, and here is where rights externalists typically part ways depending upon where they turn for normative guidance. Yet none of us will turn to the idea of

---

[17] *Ibid.*, §114. While this point clearly brings Hegel to mind, it also brings to mind the structure of the argument underlying the great social contract theorists Hobbes and Locke. For an illuminating discussion of the connection between Green and the social contract thinkers, see Rex Martin, "T. H. Green on Individual Rights and the Common Good," pp. 49–68. For a useful discussion of Hegel on freedom, see Frederick Neuhouser, *Foundations of Hegel's Social Theory: Actualizing Freedom* (Harvard University Press, 2000).

[18] Green, *Lectures on the Principles of Political Obligation*, §139.

natural or basic rights as understood by the prevailing view to establish the moral validity of claims.

Thus Green is squarely within the "rights are made by social recognition" camp. For him, one of the most basic rights of individuals—the moral right to make a life of one's own in the pursuit of one's ends—is not a right that individuals actually possess *qua* their status as human beings *pace* Kant; rather it is, as with other rights, one that they possess by virtue of having been afforded a certain sort of social recognition by others, which affords them concrete opportunities to make their lives with non-interference or assistance from others where appropriate. Hence to understand why the slave case does not pose a problem for Green in particular, notwithstanding his attribution of implicit rights to slaves, or for moral rights externalists in general, we must appreciate the obvious point that individuals participate in various forms of community with others.

This is significant for at least two reasons. For one thing, all of these communities can be a source of rights to the extent that they can afford (or withhold) the social recognition that is partly constitutive of having rights. What is more the social practices in these various communities can be in conflict with one another so that an individual could be afforded the relevant social recognition that allowed him to be able to reckon on the opportunity to act or be treated in certain ways in one community but not in others, with the most significant conflict arising between the state and all of the other communities. And this is precisely the predicament of slaves according to Green:

> The slave thus derives from his social relations a real right which the law of the state refuses to admit. The law cannot prevent him from acting and being treated, within certain limits, as a member of a society of persons freely seeking a common good . . . A man may thus have rights as a member of a family or of human society in any other form without being a member of a state at all—rights which remain rights though any particular state or all states refuse to recognize them;[19]

So, for instance, while the state may not recognize the slave as having property rights or control over his family, it cannot stop him from living in some form of community with his family in which he acts and is treated as a father, husband, son, or brother, and thus derives rights which are involved in his so acting and being so treated. The same can be said of

---

[19] *Ibid.*, p. 109; also see pp. 90, 110, 112, 115, and 152.

the slave's social relations with friends and even with the family of his master if not also the master himself.

Of course, such a situation is far from ideal. Although the slave may gain rights from social relations within these more informal prepolitical communities, there is no substitute for having these rights recognized within social relations in the larger political society. But we need not assume a form of positivism as strong as Bentham's by supposing that all of our rights are products of positive law and political authority. According to Green, the political state is the society of societies and its chief function is to sustain, secure, and harmonize the rights that arise not out of human nature as such, or merely out of individuals having morally valid claims, but out of their various prepolitical social relations. And these rights are neither natural in the sense supposed by the prevailing view nor merely derived from the state. If we insist on using the language of natural rights (as Green unfortunately does) and ascribing such rights to slaves, we can say that they are "natural" in the sense of being independent of and prior to the positive laws of the state in which the slave lives, though they are not independent of and prior to all social relations in which the slave finds himself. But to avoid the misunderstanding that Green invites it is best to leave the term "natural" in the hands of the defenders of the prevailing view, and to use the term "unnatural," or "externalism" as I have done, to capture the view that all rights are products of social relations.

So if we cannot account for the immorality of slavery on account of it being a violation of natural rights in the traditional sense, then how exactly can we account for it? Although Green is content to argue that slavery is wrong because it violates natural—or implicit—rights (though not "natural" in the way that is typically supposed), it should be clear by now there must be more to the argument than this for a moral rights externalist since such rights cannot be morally basic. And indeed there is more. There are three kinds of normative considerations that Green brings to bear in making the case against slavery, considerations having to do with the nature of slaves, the common good, and fairness. But these must be viewed alongside his grounding of natural rights in the activities of individuals in various forms of prepolitical community with one another to appreciate how a moral rights externalist can salvage normativity without positing rights that preexist all social relations.

It is uncontroversial to assume, as Green does, that actual states will fall short, some falling farther short than others of course, of giving fuller reality to rights established out of the social relations of individuals within prepolitical communities. Actual states do not always reconcile, sustain, and harmonize the rights arising out of these other forms of community that precede and are independent of the formation of the state. So we have in the case of slaves individuals who have rights arising out of participating in these various forms of community that are not given this fuller reality by the state, and this is normatively objectionable in several respects.

At least one important reason why individuals enter into any form of community with others is to seek forms of cooperation for mutual advantage or benefit, as well as opportunities for self-development. And, for Green, the formation of family communities in particular is singled out for special attention, as he maintains that "the idea of a true good first took hold of men in the form of a consideration of what was needed to keep the members of a family alive and comfortably alive."[20] An important prerequisite for such mutual cooperation, however, is being able to limit one's conduct according to commonly agreed upon constraints just in case others are willing to do the same with all recognizing this as a means to securing the common good of making their own lives in cooperation with others and living well. But to participate in such a community individuals must have certain capacities or powers, such as the powers of reason, thought, and judgment, and the capacity to understand and act on the basis of normative constraints or ideals, along with the capacity to form and pursue a conception of one's own good.

Philosophers have held widely divergent views about the nature of these capacities. For Green, the normative ideal that guides conduct is the capacity for conceiving of a better state of oneself as an end to be attained by action. For John Rawls, to participate in a modern constitutional democratic society in particular, individuals must have what he calls a capacity for a sense of justice. However these capacities or powers are understood, others coming to be aware of them, or to acknowledge that one has them, suffices to morally validate one's claim to being an individual with whom others can enter into community for the common good of life-making and the pursuit of well-being in cooperation with others. In short, the claim is morally validated to the extent that the possession of these powers or capacities is taken to be a moral reason for acting toward and treating subjects that possess them in certain ways. Hence they may be aptly called moral powers and capacities due to the moral significance assigned to them.

[20] *Ibid.*, p. 274.

In nonpolitical social relations in which slaves finds themselves, e.g. relations with other slaves and perhaps relations with the slaveholding family, we see that they are thus acknowledged as having certain moral capacities or powers. At the same time, they acknowledge others as having these same moral capacities. And this mutual recognition accounts for how slaves can find themselves in community with others despite the fact that slaves may not find themselves in community as citizens within the larger political community. Others' awareness and acknowledgment of the slave as having these moral capacities suffices to establish the moral force or validity of the slave's claim to be free to make his own life in cooperation with others conditionally upon allowing like activity in others. To be sure, this is only part of what is required for the establishment of the claim as a right, even within these nonpolitical social relations. In addition, as we have seen, the claim must also be recognized or conceded by those against whom it holds in a way that allows the holder of the claim to reckon on the exercise of free activity to make a life of one's choosing in cooperation with others. To the extent that both of these elements (the moral validity and the social recognition of claims) can be and are satisfied in prepolitical social relations, slaves can and do have moral rights prior to and independently of the laws and practices of political society, but not prior to and independently of all social relations, as is supposed by proponents of the prevailing view.

A foundational normative consideration for why the larger political society ought to give fuller reality to the slave's prepolitical rights should be readily apparent. Within these prepolitical social relations such mutual recognition is extended insofar as it is held to contribute to the common good or general social well-being of all to enter into community with those possessing certain moral capacities. Both the slave and those with whom he finds himself in various forms of community realize that allowing one another free activity will be to the benefit of their common good of making their own lives in relative security, as well as to the benefit of their pursuit of individual self-development, provided that they allow others to do the same. But if the possession of these moral capacities provides a moral reason for making the slave's freedom real (i.e. something he can reckon on in ways of acting and being treated) in prepolitical social relations, for the pursuit of mutual advantage in cooperation with others, then it also provides such a reason in political social relationships between citizens joined together in broader political relationships for the same general reason: namely, the collective pursuit of a common good through mutual cooperation in community with others displaying the same requisite moral capacities.

Although political society must be distinguished in many respects from other forms of community in which individuals organize themselves, a shared element is that it too is established for the purpose of enabling individuals possessing certain moral powers to pursue a common good of reckoning on a certain freedom of action, acquisition, and self-development, as Green puts it. Yet a distinctive element of political society is that it enables individuals so constituted to reckon on such freedom on a much broader scale. For instance:

> A family or a nomad horde could not be called a political society, on account of the narrow range of the 'freedoms' which they severally guarantee. The nomad horde might indeed be quite as numerous as a Greek state or as the sovereign canton of Geneva in Rousseau's time; but in the horde the range within which reciprocal freedom of action and acquisition [and self-development] is guaranteed to the individuals is exceedingly small.[21]

Nevertheless, in both nonpolitical and political forms of community—in the horde and in political society—the possession of certain moral powers validates each individual's claim to be recognized and, for Green, such recognition is warranted for the sake of mutually pursuing the common good. So to withhold from the slave, who is a participant in these nonpolitical forms of community, the relevant right-conferring recognition within broader political society would not only be morally inconsistent, given that slaves clearly possess the requisite moral powers, it would also be contrary to the common good and unfair.

One final normative consideration emerges in Green's case against withholding political recognition from slaves. He assumes: "The political society is more complete as the freedom guaranteed is more complete, both in respect of the persons enjoying it and of the range of possible action and acquisition over which it extends."[22] In the most complete political society the range of persons to whom the common good is conceived as common will extend to all, or at least all individuals possessing the requisite moral powers as evidenced by their participation in nonpolitical forms of community. In the most complete political society, therefore, the fuller reality that comes from political recognition would extend to slaves. Somewhat charitably, Green contends that a basic

---

[21] *Ibid.*, p. 73.
[22] *Ibid.*

intuitive idea of late Victorian modern society, a virtual axiom of popular ethics, is that there is at least a potential duty of every man to every man though there are plenty of pretexts, philosophical and otherwise, for evading this duty such as taking race, religion, or status to be a bar to participation in this wider form of community.[23] Therefore, in addition to the argument from moral capacity and fairness for giving the prepolitical rights of slaves fuller reality, there is the argument that doing so moves society closer to the ideal of complete freedom by extending the range of persons to whom the common good is conceived as common to include those held as slaves.

To summarize: the normative argument against slavery is that slaves' possession of moral powers (as recognized in their participation within nonpolitical forms of community) serves to validate morally their claim to be recognized within the larger political community, and such recognition is taken to be for the common good of all, and so to withhold it would be morally inconsistent, unfair, and would undermine the pursuit of a complete political society. This multifaceted normative argument for the legal recognition of slaves, which does not appeal to natural rights in the traditional sense, strikes me as powerful an argument as one can hope to have in the aftermath of eschewing the idea of natural rights that preexist all social relations.

RAWLS ON SLAVERY AND SOCIAL DEATH

In working out his political conception of justice as fairness for specifying the terms of social cooperation that can serve as a public basis of informed and willing political agreement between citizens in a particular kind of society, Rawls identifies several closely related basic intuitive ideas assumed to be implicit in the public culture of a modern constitutional democratic society. The overarching and most comprehensive of these is that of society as a fair system of cooperation over time from one generation to the next between free and equal persons for mutual advantage. Closely associated with this foundational intuitive idea is the idea of a person as a citizen, that is, one who can cooperatively participate in social life over a complete life by participating in rights relations by exercising and respecting various rights and duties. And these ideas are, in turn, connected with another basic intuitive idea assumed to be latent

---

[23] *Ibid.*, pp. 268–70.

in the public culture of a constitutional democratic society: namely, the conception of persons as having two moral powers that render them both free and equal.

Rawls reasons as follows. If we start with the intuitive idea of society as a fair system of cooperation, and we assume that persons are individuals who can cooperatively participate in social life (e.g. by exercising and respecting rights and duties), then we must assume that they have all the capacities that would enable them to be "normal" and fully cooperating participants in social life. Hence within the public culture of a constitutional democratic society it is assumed that persons have two moral powers: first, what Rawls calls "a capacity for a sense of justice," namely "the capacity to understand, to apply, and to act from the public conception of justice which characterizes the fair terms of social cooperation." And, second, they have what he calls "a capacity for a conception of the good," namely "the capacity to form, to revise, and rationally to pursue a conception of one's rational advantage, or good." By virtue of having these two moral powers, as well as the powers of reason, thought, and judgment connected with them, persons are said to be free. And by virtue of having them to the requisite degree to be fully cooperating members of society persons are said to be equal.

Taking stock of these intuitive ideas and their connectedness affords us what Rawls describes as a "clear" and "uncluttered" view of the fundamental question of political justice in a modern constitutional democratic society. What is the most appropriate conception of justice for specifying the terms of social cooperation between citizens regarded as free and equal persons, and as normal and fully cooperating members of such a society over a complete life?

Against this background we can situate Rawls's remarks about the predicament of slaves (quoted at the beginning of this chapter), and use them as a foil to sharpen the contrast between rights externalism and the prevailing view. Rawls's statement of the "slavery as social death" thesis serves to contrast the political conception of the person that underlies his political conception of justice as fairness with a political conception that allows slavery. A further respect in which persons, as citizens, view themselves as free in a constitutional democracy, according to Rawls, is that when questions of justice arise they actually think of themselves as self-originating sources of valid claims. And they believe that these claims have independent weight apart from any connections they may or may not have with duties or obligations specified by the political conception of justice. Given the longstanding and familiar way of elucidating what having rights amounts to in terms of having valid claims, we can plausibly translate Rawls's point here as the point that citizens within a constitutional democratic society actually regard themselves as holders of certain rights, which they take themselves to possess independently of those specified by the public conception of justice, or, more broadly speaking, independently of all forms of political authority or public recognition of the validity of these claims.

Assuming, therefore, that this is a plausible observation that certainly applies to many citizens in such a society and, moreover, certainly captures a basic assumption of the prevailing theory of rights, consider how it applies to the slave case. To say that slaves are not viewed as self-originating sources of valid claims from the point of view of certain political conceptions that allow slavery, and hence are socially dead, can be taken to deny that they have prepolitical rights at all. From this perspective slaves are not taken to be self-originating sources of rights that they possess independently of all forms of political authority or public recognition. This is, of course, consistent with saying that others within such a society could have obligations to treat slaves well, just as they may have obligations to treat nonhuman animals well; however, these obligations will not be grounded in any correlative prepolitical rights of slaves, any more than our obligations to treat nonhuman animals well are grounded in such rights.

One way, though not the only way, to defend this conclusion (for those inclined to do so) would be to argue for it from a particular understanding of the point or function of rights. Suppose, for instance, that we assume that the essential function of rights is to distribute freedom and control between the possessor of a right and one or more second parties against whom the right holds.[24] Furthermore, we assume that it would be idle and inappropriate to ascribe rights to any being incapable of actually exercising such freedom and control. It would be idle because no purpose would be served by allocating freedom and control to those incapable of taking advantage of them. And it would be inappropriate because it might mislead us into believing that freedom and control could be exemplified by those incapable of acting freely or exercising control. From here one might conclude that since only beings with the two moral powers, and the powers of reason connected with them, can act freely or exercise control, it is only to beings that possess these powers that the distribution of freedom

---

[24] Wellman, *Real Rights*, p. 107.

and control could be justified. Hence only beings possessing these powers can be self-originating sources of valid claims, or rightholders, which they might conclude rules out slaves since they are devoid of such powers.

We can easily construct similar arguments that might be used to defend the conclusion that slaves have no rights by adopting a different account of the function or point of rights, associating this with the possession of certain properties that are taken to be compatible with this function, and arguing that ascribing rights to slaves runs afoul of this function to the extent that they lack these rights-qualifying properties. But, by the same token, defenders of the prevailing view can use this same strategy to challenge the "slaves have no rights" thesis (a point that I have already developed at length in chapter 4). In response to the present case, they can of course simply reject the claim that slaves lack the two moral powers and the powers of reason, in which case the allocation of freedom and control to them could be justified, and they could thereby be viewed as self-originating sources of valid claims, or rightholders, even under a political society that allows slavery. Alternatively, they could propose that the function and point of rights is not to distribute freedom and control but more generally and more liberally to promote the interests of beings that are capable of being harmed or benefited by the conduct of others. And assuming that only beings that can be viewed as having a good of their own can be harmed or benefited, defenders of the prevailing view could conclude that slaves were self-originating sources of valid claims insofar as they clearly had a good that could be harmed or benefited by the conduct of others. Hence this strategy will serve equally well to draw the conclusion that slaves do indeed possess rights even under a political society that allows slavery.

Thus, in response to Rawls's "slavery as social death" thesis, defenders of the prevailing view will claim that we cannot imagine a scenario where slaves are not viewed as self-originating sources of valid claims and thereby lacking any rights whatsoever. While it may be true that they lack legal rights within a political society that allows slavery, and are thus socially dead in that sense, they will still remain self-originating sources of valid claims, and thus possessors of prelegal or prepolitical rights, by virtue of having the moral powers and powers of reason that qualify a subject for the possession of such rights. In sum, defenders of the prevailing view will reject Rawls's description of the predicament of slaves under a society that allows slavery on the grounds that all beings with the requisite moral powers and powers of reason are self-originating sources of claims even when their political society does not legally or socially recognize them as such. And this accounts for why they have rights even when such recognition is not in the offing.

In contrast, as a rights externalist, my assessment of the "slavery as social death" thesis is different. For one, I am certainly prepared to concede the description (in a manner of speaking) of the predicament of slaves within a political society that allows slavery. Indeed, as it stands, Rawls's statement plausibly could be viewed as an accurate description of slaves in the antebellum United States, which ironically viewed itself as a modern constitutional democracy and presumably shared the intuitive ideas Rawls associates with such a society, yet still managed to designate slaves differently. But an important qualification is in order. Specifically, a more accurate description would distinguish between being socially dead and being politically dead, where the latter applies to being excluded from membership in political society.

Recall Green's useful distinction between formal and informal recognition. Informally slaves were recognized in various communities much smaller than the community of members in a common political society precisely because they manifested moral powers and powers of reason, and this, for Green, was integral to understanding why we could ascribe prepolitical rights to slaves, though not presocial rights. All rights are partly the product of subjects being afforded recognition by some community or other. And thus, while slaves within a political society that allowed slavery may have been politically dead, they were far from being socially dead. Indeed, it seems beyond the realm of possibility to imagine any human being living in some form of community with others ever being socially dead.

Given the analysis in this chapter, this informal form of recognition suffices to establish that even slaves are originating sources of valid claims no matter what political conception of the person or justice we envision. And this is not merely because the slave has moral powers and powers of reason; rather, it is because even within a political society that allows slavery, slaves will be in some form of community with others, and thus, while they may be politically dead, they are never socially dead. Of course, as Green himself argues, the manifestation of the moral powers and powers of reason accounts for why others enter into a relation of mutual recognition with the slave, which is constitutive of having rights.

Hence defenders of the prevailing view would contend that Rawls's description of the predicament of slaves is necessarily false in all cases, in all societies real or imagined, as slaves are the kinds of beings that cannot fail to have rights since they too possess the requisite right-endowing powers. I maintain, however, that it can and has been true in some cases, and in some societies where the laws of the land have failed to fall in line with existing nonlegal social practices. But, at the same time, given the fact that even slaves have community with other slaves, it unlikely that this thesis applies all the way down to all levels of social relationships that the slave might be party to including his relationship with his family and with other slaves. If the thesis is false, it is contingently so. Of course, for reasons that I made clear in chapter 3 and in this one, being politically dead in a political society is perhaps the worst form of social death.

To conclude, the upshot of Green's argument against slavery may be put in these terms. The slave's moral powers account for why he gets recognition in smaller communities, and as these are prerequisites for participation in any community, consistency requires that the slaves be afforded recognition under the law of society. But it is clear that this recognition itself constitutes the status rather than the mere possession of the moral powers, even in a liberal democratic society that has a history of slaveholding. Defenders of the prevailing view would argue that the moral powers give rise to rights even when they are not recognized. But externalists contend that if slaves' moral powers are not acknowledged and they are otherwise without recognition and cannot reckon on action, then they are without rights. Fortunately, given our social nature, it is impossible without considerable imaginative dexterity to imagine a plausible situation in which even the slave does not participate in some form of community that acknowledges his moral powers. Hence, while Rawls's description may apply to slaves under political society, it surely does not apply in all societies. And the social practices within these societies afford us ample resources to make as strong a normative argument against slavery as we can hope for. Indeed, yet another way to capture the genius of Frederick Douglass's political philosophy is as calling our attention to the blatant inconsistencies between these patterns of recognition within larger political society and within smaller communities within political society.

Let me assuage one last concern in bringing this final chapter to completion. A primary motivation that leads to the postulation of rights prior to all forms of community is to establish what is taken to be a secure foundation for the protection of individual persons from the acts or omissions of a community of individuals. This is an admirable goal and it is easy to see why many think that grounding at least some of our rights in human nature itself will supply this secure foundation. But students of history will not be misled here. When the common humanity of particular persons is called into question, or when humanity (in a Kantian sense, for instance) is lost, say, in a tragic accident for example, rights grounded this way will go by the board; they will be useless to those on the short end of this stick.

Grounding rights in the activities of communities of individuals acting in concert by mutually affording one another the opportunity to reckon on certain ways of acting and being treated—as I have proposed in this book—seems to be as solid a foundation as any, and perhaps even more solid in the case of slaves. Although they may have their humanity called into question or rendered less relevant within an insufficiently progressive political society on account of racial thinking, they will nevertheless participate in other nonpolitical forms of community in which their humanity, or moral powers, are thoroughly acknowledged by at least some people. And given the practical impossibility of removing any person—enslaved or not—from all forms of community with others, I see no reason at all to assume with Kant and many others that grounding rights in community renders persons any less secure than grounding them in humanity as such.[25]

This is not to suggest that we cannot want more, indeed much more, for slaves and other politically dead individuals. Quite the contrary, I have argued that we should want more and that we can provide weighty normative reasons for why politically dead individuals such as slaves ought to be afforded political recognition in the form of being granted legal rights to reckon on certain ways of acting and being treated. But I have done so in a way that does not contravene the main thesis of this book, which is that all rights—legal and otherwise—are products of social recognition.

---

[25] For a detailed defense of this claim that grounding rights in social practices is no less secure than grounding them in ontology, see my article "Rights Externalism," *Philosophy and Phenomenological Research* 68 (2004), 620–34.

Conclusion

The idea that we have certain natural or presocial moral rights—ones that we possess prior to and independently of all forms of social recognition—has been a powerful resource for arguing against all manner of moral wrongdoing, as we observed in the first two chapters. Some advocates of these rights maintain that the case for believing in them is perhaps strongest when we consider their role in facilitating arguments against one of the most infamous instances of moral wrongdoing, namely black chattel slavery as practiced in the United States of America for well over two hundred years. They claim that this case perhaps more than any other demonstrates the normative value of affirming the existence of rights without recognition. And the worry that we would be rendered unable to argue against slavery in particular and other instances of moral wrongdoing in general, or to argue effectively against them, accounts for why many people will be loath to give up the idea that we possess certain presocial moral rights despite the fact that positing such rights and providing a plausible account of how we come to have them has proven to be far more challenging than is usually supposed, which I argue in chapter 2 by taking on rights internalism and the valid claims approach—the two predominant ways of accounting for how we come to acquire rights without recognition.

Anticipating this reluctance to give up the idea that we possess certain unrecognized rights notwithstanding the challenges of adequately grounding them, I further questioned the purported normative credentials of such rights by considering their bittersweet legacy with respect to black Americans. Specifically, in chapter 4 I argue that when we pause to consider the question of how we come to acquire these unrecognized rights, and when we consider the widely espoused view that they are grounded ontologically in facts about human nature alongside the long history within the United States of calling the full humanity of blacks into question, the espousal of these ontologically grounded unrecognized rights not only becomes less compelling but proves to rely upon a rather one-sided view of the historical facts regarding the legacy of slavery and its justification. And this one-sided view of the historical facts in large part explains why the normative value of possessing rights without recognition is usually overstated. Hence I have maintained that by taking a broader view of these historical facts—however unflattering and disconcerting this might be—we are able to reflect on the ways in which the purportedly irreproachable idea of natural rights was used not only to argue for the abolition of slavery but to argue against its abolition and to justify the continued subordination of blacks and their descendants during and long after the demise of slavery. And when we come to terms with the fullness of this historical legacy, only then can we appreciate the wisdom behind the view that what rights we do have, legal, moral, and otherwise, are neither natural nor the gift of a supreme creator but are instead the result of individuals being afforded a certain kind of social recognition by a community of persons.

In a speech about the infamous legacy of slavery delivered on Goree Island in Senegal (2003), the President of the United States, George W. Bush, contended:

Down through the years, African-Americans have upheld the ideals of America by exposing laws and habits contradicting these ideals. The rights of African-Americans were not the gift of those in authority. Those rights were granted by the author of life and regained by the persistence and courage of African-Americans themselves.

One could of course follow Bush and many others in embracing the view that the rights of African Americans are the gift of the author of life, the ultimate authority, so to speak; however, a clear implication of my conception is that moral rights are instead the product of struggle by persistent and courageous people to establish recognized ways of acting and being treated that are sometimes fought for and that can be won or lost. Indeed, one of the great lessons of a fuller study of the legacy of slavery and its aftermath is an appreciation of the active role of black people themselves in fighting for their own rights, which was tantamount to fighting for being able to act and being treated in certain ways by a much larger community of persons. US Democratic presidential candidate Barack Obama followed a similar strategy in a campaign speech on race by placing the emphasis on the role of successive generations of struggle and protests, from the streets to the courts, and through a civil war and civil disobedience, to secure the full measure of rights for slaves and their descendants and thereby narrow the gap between American's self-proclaimed ideals of freedom and equality and its prevailing social realities.

My socially grounded (or some would say positivistic) conception of moral rights, as developed in chapter 3 and further qualified in chapter 5, aims to take account of both the formal and more informal manner in which ways of acting and being treated are afforded the social recognition relevant to converting mere ways of acting and being treated into rights. Although I resist building a commitment to a particular normative theory into my general account of what possessing moral rights amounts to, in chapter 5 I indicate the contours of my preferred way of salvaging normativity without positing presocial moral rights. And the normative considerations introduced there, namely ones having to do with the normative significance of recognizing and developing certain human powers, would be instrumental in determining whether a socially recognized way of acting or being treated was a moral and not merely some sort of conventional right.

Chapter 5 has an auxiliary purpose: it sets up the next important project. A way to put the question, in very general terms, taken up in this final chapter is to ask how we get on with our normative business without presocial moral rights. I propose a way of getting on with this business by developing an argument against slavery that is not rooted in the idea that slaves possess certain presocial moral rights. But given the longstanding association of such rights with (at least some) versions of liberalism, this rejection of natural or presocial moral rights raises a further question. How to understand the primary role of a liberal society without positing such rights? Though I have already addressed this question at some length (chapter 1), a final reflection would be useful.

In *Liberalism and Social Action*, John Dewey reminds us of this association of presocial rights with liberalism by observing that one of the salient features of Locke's version of liberalism is that "governments are instituted to protect the rights that belong to individuals prior to political organization of social relations."[1] And drawing further inspiration from Locke many people have added that governments—particularly liberal ones—are instituted to protect certain rights belonging to individuals prior to any form of organization of social relations, not just political

---

[1] John Dewey, *Liberalism and Social Action* (New York: Prometheus Books, 2000), p. 15.

organization.[2] A further feature of Locke's version of liberalism is that the relevant presocial rights mandate non-interference on the part of others, or, as it is sometimes stated, they impose negative duties of non-interference. Hence from this perspective the primary role of a liberal society is to protect or uphold these presocial rights to be left alone. To be sure, this perspective represents an important school of thought concerning the nature of a liberal society but it is not the only one from which we might draw inspiration. Drawing on Thomas Hill Green in particular, as I do, Dewey credits Green with contributing to the displacement of the idea that individual freedom was something that individuals have as a ready-made possession, and with proposing instead that freedom (and ultimately having rights) was something to be achieved. So from this vantage point, according to Dewey, the primary role of a liberal state is to "use its powers to establish the conditions under which the mass of individuals can possess actual as distinct from merely legal liberty."[3] Working out a fuller articulation and defense of some such account of the primary role of a liberal society is the next natural step to take in showing how we can get along just fine without embracing the view that we possess natural or presocial moral rights. Hence not only can we eschew such rights in waging moral arguments against slavery and other instances of moral wrongdoing; moreover, we can also eschew them in working out an account of what a liberal society owes its citizens and citizens of the world.

I suspect that some critics of my socially oriented conception of what having moral rights amounts to will continue to recite a litany of objections, including that this conception is simply not true, that it does not capture contemporary philosophical common sense, that it is counterintuitive, that it does not pay sufficient attention to history, that is not adequately grounded in the history of philosophy, that it is morally pernicious, that it leaves us morally bankrupt, and that it is illiberal. But I hope that more sympathetic critics will appreciate the ways in which I have attempted to answer these objections. There is one last concern, however, that I shall briefly address. How should we determine which of the two conceptions of how we come to acquire moral rights, the

---

[2] Indeed, Dewey himself captures this more general construal of the impact of Locke's liberal legacy:

> In serving the immediate needs of England—and then those of other countries in which it was desired to substitute representative for arbitrary government—it bequeathed to later social thought a rigid doctrine of natural rights inherent in individuals independent of social organization.

See *Liberalism and Social Action*, p. 16.

[3] *Ibid.*, p. 35.

prevailing one or my alternative, is more attractive? In other words, how do we determine which side to choose? Of course, anyone who shares my methodological concern with coming up with a solution to the moral rights ascription problem that takes a wider view of the historical facts regarding the legacy of black chattel slavery for purposes of philosophical reflection will see this as a strong reason in favor of rights externalism over the prevailing conception, or so I hope to have shown. Yet it is worth addressing this question of how we should choose sides more generally speaking before concluding.

Let me begin by identifying an unpromising way of defending these conceptions that is quite commonplace in the philosophical debate.[4] Proponents of these conceptions sometimes proceed by invoking a distinction, showing that their conception falls on one side of the distinction, and leaving us to think that this alone is enough to make a case for embracing their view. For example, Joel Feinberg, arguably the most influential contemporary defender of the prevailing conception explicated by appealing to the idea of moral rights as morally valid claims, distinguishes between moral rights that are exercisable even prior to social or legal recognition and enforcement and those rights that cannot be exercised prior to such recognition and enforcement. The right to vote and the right to sell one's labor for a wage are examples of the latter, whereas the right to picket peacefully "until the police arrive to haul one away,"[5] the right to practice one's religion "secretly,"[6] and the right to commit suicide are cited by Feinberg as examples of the former.[7]

Obviously this distinction is compatible with the prevailing conception, as it allows us to speak of rights that exist prior to and independently of legal recognition and enforcement regardless of whether they are exercisable. But merely invoking this distinction does not tip the scales in favor of this conception; it does not give us any reason to choose this conception instead of an externalist one. In the first place, merely invoking this distinction does not preclude one from rejecting the presumption that a subject can possess moral rights prior to and independently of social recognition and enforcement. Without a prior case being made for postulating a class of rights that can be possessed prior to and independently of social recognition and enforcement, the distinction between

---

[4] The foregoing observations are taken from my essay "Feinberg and Martin on Human Rights," *Journal of Social Philosophy* 34 (2003), 199–214.

[5] Feinberg, "In Defence of Moral Rights," p. 153.

[6] *Ibid.*

[7] *Ibid.*

exercisable and non-exercisable rights does not lend any support at all to the prevailing conception of moral rights, although it certainly makes clear where proponents of this conception stand.

What is more, this distinction may actually tell against the prevailing conception. When one considers the examples that Feinberg gives of non-exercisable moral rights and the qualifications he makes (which I flagged above with quotation marks), it seems rather odd to call these ways of acting (e.g. picketing peacefully, practicing religion secretly, and killing oneself) rights. And if this does not seem odd to some observers, they must at least admit that, if these ways of acting are rights (in some sense or other), they are certainly not rights that we really care about. I suspect that many of us would be unwilling to engage in life-threatening social and political struggle to have these ways of acting socially recognized and enforced. Hence one could maintain that a more illuminating conception of moral rights is one that accounts for the existence of rights that we really care about and are willing to fight for, and perhaps even die for, to get socially recognized and enforced. Such a conception would, therefore, have to focus on ways of acting and being treated that are not exercisable prior to such social recognition and enforcement, e.g. being able to vote or to sell one's labor for a wage. But then the issue becomes whether to characterize non-exercisable ways of acting and being treated as "rights." A defender of an externalist conception will respond by claiming that only ways of acting and being treated that are exercisable—socially recognized and maintained in law or in prelegal social arrangements—count as rights.

Although simply invoking the distinction between rights that are exercisable prior to and independently of social recognition and enforcement and ones that are not does not suffice to tilt the scales in favor of the prevailing conception of moral rights, on behalf of this conception I admit that this distinction can play a part in a broader defense of the prevailing conception. For instance, one could claim that a criterion of adequacy for any conception of moral rights was that it was able to accommodate this distinction. It could then be argued that insofar as the prevailing conception of moral rights can accommodate this distinction and an externalist conception cannot then we have reason to favor the former instead of the latter. Although I concede that this constitutes a more workable defense of the prevailing conception, it is unpersuasive. I see no point in demanding that a conception of moral rights be able to classify ways of acting (or being treated) as "rights" despite the fact that we do not really care about them in our everyday lives and in the social and political sphere. If practicing one's religion secretly and committing suicide (which can be done relatively easily without a physician or any-one's assistance) are to be classified as "rights," then so must masturbating secretly, whispering one's dislike of a neighbor, and scratching an itch in public or private. Perhaps some of us want to be able to speak of having a right to masturbate secretly, a right to whisper one's dislike of a neighbor, or a right to scratch an itch in public or private; however, I think that demanding that a conception of moral rights satisfy the proposed criter-ion of adequacy generates a needless proliferation of moral rights. And in addition to devaluing the currency of rights discourse this will contribute to growing skepticism about rights that is directly linked to concerns about rights inflation, a matter I addressed earlier. Hence proponents of an externalist conception of moral rights can argue that reserving the term "rights" for ways of acting and being treated that are exercisable will curb the problem of rights inflation and remove a popular source of skepticism about rights discourse.[8]

But rights externalists must take care not to make the same mistake of relying too heavily on a distinction to make a case for this conception. Rex Martin, an influential advocate of an externalist conception of rights, distinguishes between nominal and real rights. He characterizes the former as "paper" rights or rights that exist in name only but not in fact.[9] Consider Viola's right to sell her labor for a wage. Suppose that the relevant governmental authority promulgated Viola's being able to sell her labor for a wage. In other words, suppose that this way of acting was afforded the relevant sort of social recognition. Further suppose that this way of acting was not maintained or enforced by government. One could capture Viola and force her to work without a wage with impunity. In this case, Martin would claim that Viola's right to sell her labor was a nominal one at best. And if Viola's being able to sell her labor for a wage was not promulgated by government, then she could not be taken to possess a moral right at all. Hence, according to Martin, real rights are those that exist both in name and in practice.

---

[8] I argue for this point at length in my article "Two Conceptions of Rights Possession," *Social Theory and Practice* 27 (2001), 387–417, and revisited this argument in ch. 2. For other philosophers who also use the problem of rights proliferation as their point of departure for theorizing about the source of rights, see Sumner, *The Moral Foundation of Rights*, and Lomasky, *Persons, Rights, and the Moral Community*. And for an illuminating exploration of the proliferation of rights since World War II, see Carl P. Wellman, *The Proliferation of Rights: Moral Progress or Empty Rhetoric?* (Boulder: Westview Press, 1999).

[9] Martin, *A System of Rights*, p. 83.

Obviously this distinction between real and nominal rights is compatible with moral rights externalism, since it prevents us from characterizing as "rights" ways of acting or being treated that are not recognized and maintained by governmental action. But this by itself does not tip the scales in favor of this conception. In particular, contrary to what Martin suggests, it does not constitute an argument for imposing a social constraint on moral rights possession.[10] Feinberg and other defenders of the prevailing conception of moral rights will simply claim that there are rights that are possessed prior to and independently of whether they are socially recognized and maintained and, moreover, that these rights are no less real. Moreover, they will contend that to insist that ways of acting or being treated which are not promulgated and maintained, or not promulgated at all, are nominal rights or not rights at all, is question begging since another way to frame the issue that divides these sides is over whether the only real rights are ones that are socially promulgated and maintained. Therefore, without a prior case being made for the claim that real rights only result when ways of acting or being treated are socially promulgated and maintained, the distinction between real and unreal rights does not lend any argumentative support to an externalist conception of moral rights.

The foregoing observations show that merely invoking a distinction and showing that one's conception comes down on a certain side of it is not sufficient to justify taking one side over the other. I suspect that the temptation to proceed this way is connected with the idea that the ultimate way of deciding how the source of moral rights is to be understood is by showing that one conception is correct or true and that the alternatives are incorrect or false. Feinberg is especially guilty of this. After noting that proponents of an externalist conception of rights share the premise "that there can be *no* rights without an institutional base for them" he claims to have shown that this view is false.[11] On behalf of Feinberg, I admit that some defenders of the externalist conception also carry on as though they can give a truth-preserving argument for the thesis that the concept of a moral right includes within it practices of recognition and promotion, and so they too must also be criticized. Nevertheless, Feinberg has not shown that this thesis is false. To be sure, he has postulated the existence of moral rights that do not have an institutional base, but this is not tantamount to showing that the opposing thesis is

---

[10] Rex Martin, "Human Rights and Civil Rights," *Philosophical Studies* 37 (1980), 394.
[11] Feinberg, "In Defence of Moral Rights," p. 168.

false. The general problem, therefore, is failing to appreciate the fact that both sides constitute plausible conceptual alternatives. Accordingly, the way to justify taking sides is not by trying to show that one view is true and the other false, or by trying to give a truth-preserving argument for one's preferred thesis. A more fruitful way to justify taking sides is to review the respective virtues and shortcomings of each conception and to decide which is more attractive on balance.

This book had provided an extended argument for the thesis that a social recognition-based conception is indeed more attractive on balance than the prevailing conception of what having moral rights amounts to. In the final analysis I have dislodged the prevailing conception from its lofty perch, and defended an alternative one that takes a wider historical view of the past and present social realities of race and racism as a point of departure for philosophical reflection. And this, along with the fact that my social recognition-based conception does not suffer from various alleged shortcomings, the most significant of which is leaving us unable to salvage normativity, suffices to establish it as formidable contender among competing conceptions of how we come to acquire moral rights. Even with my argument in hand many readers will undoubtedly find it difficult—perhaps even painful—to give up the view that we possess certain moral rights prior to and entirely independent of any form of social recognition whatsoever. But be that as it may, we now have ample reason to maintain that if we possess any moral rights at all they are partly conferred upon us by the hands of a community of persons.

Bibliography

Alcoff, Linda Martín, *Visible Identities: Race, Gender, and the Self* (Oxford University Press, 2005).

Allen, Anita L., "Legal Rights for Poor Blacks," in Bill Lawson (ed.), *The Underclass Question* (Philadelphia: Temple University Press, 1992).

Allport, Gordon W., *The Nature of Prejudice* (Garden City: Doubleday Anchor Books, 1958).

Appiah, Kwame Anthony, *In My Father's House: Africa in the Philosophy of Culture* (Oxford University Press, 1992).

Babbitt, Susan E. and Campbell, Sue (eds.), *Racism and Philosophy* (Cornell University Press, 1999).

Bell, Derrick A. (ed.), *Civil Rights: Leading Cases* (Boston: Little Brown & Company, 1980).

Faces at the Bottom of the Well: The Permanence of Racism (New York: Basic Books, 1992).

Bentham, Jeremy, in John Browing (ed.), *The Works of Jeremy Bentham* (Edinburgh: William Tait, 1843).

Blassingame, John W. (ed.), *Slave Testimony* (Baton Rouge: Louisiana State University Press, 1977).

Blumer, Herbert, "Race Prejudice as a Sense of Group Position," *Pacific Sociological Review* 1 (1958), 3–7.

Bobo, Lawrence, "Race and Beliefs about Affirmative Action: Assessing the Effects of Interests, Group Threat, Ideology, and Racism," in David O. Sears, Jim Sidanius, and Lawrence Bobo (eds.), *Racialized Politics: The Debate About Racism in America* (University of Chicago Press, 2000).

Bobo, Lawrence and Hutchings, Vincent L., "Perceptions of Racial Group Competition: Extending Blumer's Theory of Group Position to a Multiracial Social Context," *American Sociological Review* 61 (1996), 951–72.

Bobo, Lawrence, Kluegel, James R., and Smith, Ryan A., "Laissez-faire Racism: The Crystallization of a Kinder, Gentler, Antiblack Ideology," in Steven A. Tuch and Jack K. Martin (eds.), *Racial Attitudes in the 1990s: Continuity and Change* (Westport: Praeger Publishers, 1997).

Boucher, David, *The British Idealists* (Cambridge University Press, 1997).

Boxill, Bernard, *Blacks and Social Justice*, rev. edn. (Lanham: Rowman and Littlefield, 1992).

Boxill, Bernard (ed.), *Race and Racism* (Oxford University Press, 2001).

Brink, David O., *Perfectionism and the Common Good: Themes in the Philosophy of T. H. Green* (Oxford: Clarendon Press, 2003).

Cartwright, Samuel, "The Prognathous Species of Mankind," in Eric L. McKitrick (ed.), *Slavery Defended: The Views of the Old South* (Englewood Cliffs: Prentice-Hall, 1963).

Cochran, David Carroll, *The Color of Freedom: Race and Contemporary American Liberalism* (Albany: SUNY Press, 1999).

Cranston, Maurice, "Are There Any Human Rights?" *Daedalus* 112 (1983), 1–17.

Daniels, Norman, "Wide Reflective Equilibrium and Theory Acceptance in Ethics," *Journal of Philosophy* 76 (1979), 256–82.

Darby, Derrick, "Are Worlds without Natural Rights Morally Impoverished?" *The Southern Journal of Philosophy* 37 (1999), 397–417.

"Two Conceptions of Rights Possession," *Social Theory and Practice* 27 (2001), 387–417.

"Grounding Rights in Social Practices: A Defence," *Res Publica* 9 (2003), 1–18.

"Unnatural Rights," *Canadian Journal of Philosophy* 33 (2003), 49–82.

"Feinberg and Martin on Human Rights," *Journal of Social Philosophy* 34 (2003), 199–214.

"Rights Externalism," *Philosophy and Phenomenological Research* 68 (2004), 620–34.

"Blacks and Rights: A Bittersweet Legacy," *Law, Culture, and the Humanities* 2 (2006), 420–39.

Darwall, Stephen, "Two Kinds of Respect," *Ethics* 88 (1977), 34–49.

Deigh, John, "Rights and the Authority of Law," *The University of Chicago Law Review* 51 (1984), 668–99.

Den Otter, Sandra M., *British Idealism and Social Explanation: A Study of Late Victorian Thought* (Oxford: Clarendon Press, 1996).

De Vos, Pierre, "Pious Wishes or Directly Enforceable Human Rights? Social and Economic Rights in South Africa's 1996 Constitution," *South African Journal on Human Rights* 13 (1997), 67–101.

Dewey, John, *Liberalism and Social Action* (New York: Prometheus Books, 2000).

Dillion, Robin S., "Toward a Feminist Conception of Self-Respect," in Robin S. Dillon (ed.), *Dignity, Character, and Self-Respect* (New York: Routledge, 1995).

Douglass, Frederick, *Narrative of the Life of Frederick Douglass, An American Slave* (New York: The Library of America, 1994).

"What the Black Man Wants," in Manning Marable and Leith Mullings (eds.), *Let Nobody Turn Us Around: Voices of Resistance, Reform, and Renewal* (Lanham: Rowman and Littlefield, 2000).

D'Souza, Dinesh, *The End of Racism* (New York: Free Press, 1995).

Dworkin, Ronald, *Taking Rights Seriously* (Harvard University Press, 1977).

Feinberg, Joel, *Rights, Justice, and the Bounds of Liberty* (Princeton University Press, 1980).

Freedom and Fulfillment: Philosophical Essays (Princeton University Press, 1992).

"In Defence of Moral Rights," *Oxford Journal of Legal Studies* 12 (1992), 149–69.

"The Social Importance of Moral Rights," *Philosophical Perspectives* 6 (1992), 175–98.

Finkelman, Paul, *Slavery and the Founders: Race and Liberty in the Age of Jefferson* (Armonk: M. E. Sharpe, 1996).

Frederickson, George M., *The Black Image in the White Mind: The Debate on Afro-American Character and Destiny, 1817–1914* (New York: Harper and Row, 1971).

Freeden, Michael, *The New Liberalism: An Ideology of Social Reform* (Oxford: Clarendon Press, 1978).

Frey, Raymond, *Interests and Rights: The Case against Animals* (Oxford: Clarendon Press, 1980).

Foner, Eric, *The Story of American Freedom* (New York: W. W. Norton, 1998).

Gabel, Peter, "The Phenomenology of Rights-Consciousness and the Pact of the Withdrawn Selves," *Texas Law Review* 62 (1984), 1563–99.

Gaus, Gerald, "Green's Rights Recognition Thesis and Moral Internalism," *The British Journal of Politics and International Relations* 7 (2005), 5–17.

Gewirth, Alan, "Are All Rights Positive?" *Philosophy and Public Affairs* 30 (2002), 321–33.

Glendon, Mary Ann, *Rights Talk: The Impoverishment of Political Discourse* (New York: The Free Press, 1991).

Gordon, Robert W., "New Developments in Legal Theory," in David Kairys (ed.), *The Politics of Law: A Progressive Critique*, rev. edn. (New York: Pantheon Books, 1990).

Green, T. H., in P. Harris and J. Morrow (eds.), *Lectures on the Principles of Political Obligation* (Cambridge University Press, 1986).

Guess, Raymond, *The Idea of a Critical Theory: Habermas and the Frankfurt School* (Cambridge University Press, 1981).

History and Illusion in Politics (Cambridge University Press, 2001).

Habermas, Jürgen, "Remarks on Legitimation Through Human Rights," *Philosophy and Social Criticism* 24 (1998), 157–71.

Harris, Cheryl, "Whiteness as Property," in Kimberlé Crenshaw, Neil Gotanda, Gary Peller, and Kendall Thomas (eds.), *Critical Race Theory: The Key Writings that Formed the Movement* (New York: The New Press, 1995).

Hart, H. L. A., *The Concept of Law* (Oxford: Clarendon Press, 1961).

Essays on Bentham: Studies in Jurisprudence and Political Theory (Oxford: Clarendon Press, 1982).

"Are There Any Natural Rights?" in Jeremy Waldron (ed.), *Theories of Rights* (Oxford University Press, 1984).

Herrnstein, Richard J. and Murray, Charles, *The Bell Curve: Intelligence and Class Structure in American Life* (New York: Free Press, 1994).

Higginbotham, Jr., A. Leon, *Shades of Freedom: Racial Politics and the Presumptions of the American Legal Process* (Oxford University Press, 1996).

Hill, Thomas, "Self-Respect Reconsidered," in Robin S. Dillon (ed.), *Dignity, Character, and Self-Respect* (New York: Routledge, 1995).

Hochschild, Jennifer L., "Lumpers and Splitters, Individuals and Structures," in David O. Sears, Jim Sidanius, and Lawrence Bobo (eds.), *Racialized Politics: The Debate about Racism in America* (University of Chicago Press, 2000).

Hohfeld, Wesley N., *Fundamental Legal Conceptions* (Yale University Press, 1919).

Holmes, Stephen and Sunstein, Cass, *The Costs of Rights: Why Liberty Depends on Taxes* (New York: W. W. Norton, 1999).

Horton, Carol A., *Race and the Making of American Liberalism* (Oxford University Press, 2005).

Husak, Douglas, "Why There Are No Human Rights," *Social Theory and Practice* 10 (1984), 125–41.

Irwin, Terence, "Morality and Personality: Kant and Green," in Allen Wood (ed.), *Self and Nature* (Cornell University Press, 1984).

Itzkoff, Seymour, *The Decline of Intelligence in America* (Westport: Praeger Publishers, 1994).

Jenkins, William Sumner, *Pro-Slavery Thought in the Old South* (Chapel Hill: University of North Carolina Press, 1935).

Jordan, Winthrop, *White Over Black: American Attitudes Toward the Negro, 1550–1812* (Chapel Hill: University of North Carolina Press, 1968).

Kant, Immanuel, in Mary J. Gregor (trans. and ed.), *Practical Philosophy* (Cambridge University Press, 1996).

Kinder, Donald R. and Sears, David O., "Prejudice and Politics: Symbolic Racism versus Racial Threats to the Good Life," *Journal of Personality & Social Psychology* 40 (1981), 414–31.

Kinder, Donald R. and Mendelberg, Tali, "Individualism Reconsidered: Principles and Prejudice in Contemporary American Opinion," in David O. Sears, Jim Sidanius, and Lawrence Bobo (eds.), *Racialized Politics: The Debate About Racism in America* (University of Chicago Press, 2000).

Klare, Karl, "Labor Law as Ideology: Toward a New Historiography of Collective Bargaining Law," *Industrial Relations Law Journal* 4 (1981), 450–82.

Klinkner, Philip A. and Smith, Rogers M., *The Unsteady March: The Rise and Decline of Racial Equality in America* (University of Chicago Press, 1999).

Lawson, Bill (ed.), *The Underclass Question* (Philadelphia: Temple University Press, 1992).

Leach, Robert, *British Political Ideologies* (London: Philip Allan, 1991).

Levin, Michael P., *Why Race Matters: Race Differences and What They Mean* (Westport: Praeger Publishers, 1997).

Levin, Michael P., and Pataki, Tamas (eds.), *Racism in Mind* (Cornell University Press, 2004).

Liebenberg, Sandra, "The Value of Human Dignity in Interpreting Socio-economic Rights," *South African Journal on Human Rights* 21 (2005), 1–31.

Locke, John, in Peter Laslett (ed.), *Two Treatises of Government* (Cambridge University Press, 1960).

Lomasky, Loren E., *Persons, Rights, and the Moral Community* (Oxford University Press, 1987).

Lyons, David, "Rights, Claimants, and Beneficiaries," *American Philosophical Quarterly* 6 (1969), 173–85.

  Rights, Welfare, and Mill's Moral Theory (Oxford University Press, 1994).

  "Rights and Recognition," *Social Theory and Practice* 32 (2006), 1–15.

MacDonald, Margaret, "Natural Rights," in Jeremy Waldron (ed.), *Theories of Rights* (Oxford University Press, 1984).

MacIntyre, Alasdair, *After Virtue: A Study of Moral Theory* (University of Notre Dame Press, 1981).

Mackie, J. L., "Can There Be a Right-Based Moral Theory?" in Jeremy Waldron (ed.), *Theories of Rights* (Oxford University Press, 1984).

Martin, Rex, "Human Rights and Civil Rights," *Philosophical Studies* 37 (1980), 391–403.

  "Green on Natural Rights in Hobbes, Spinoza and Locke," in Andrew Vincent (ed.), *The Philosophy of T. H. Green* (Hants: Gower Publishing, 1986).

  A System of Rights (Oxford: Clarendon Press, 1993).

  "T. H. Green on Individual Rights and the Common Good," in Avital Simhony and David Weinstein (eds.), *The New Liberalism: Reconciling Liberty and Community* (Cambridge University Press, 2001).

Martin, Rex and Nickel, James, "Recent Work on the Concept of Rights," *American Philosophical Quarterly* 17 (1980), 165–80.

McCloskey, H. J., "Moral Rights and Animals," *Inquiry* 22 (1979), 25–54.

McConahay, John B., "Modern Racism, Ambivalence, and the Modern Racism Scale," in John F. Dovidio and Samuel L. Gaertner (eds.), *Prejudice, Discrimination, and Racism* (Orlando: Academic Press, 1986).

Melden, A. I., *Rights and Persons* (Berkeley: University of California Press, 1977).

Mill, John Stuart, in George Sher (ed.), *Utilitarianism* (Indianapolis: Hackett Publishing Company, 1979).

Miller, Fred D., *Nature, Justice, and Rights in Aristotle's Politics* (Oxford University Press, 1995).

Mills, Charles W., *Blackness Visible: Essays on Philosophy and Race* (Cornell University Press, 1998).

Milne, A. J. M., *The Social Philosophy of English Idealism* (London: George Allen & Unwin, 1962).

Milo, Ronald, "Contractarian Constructivism," *The Journal of Philosophy* 92 (1995), 181–204.

Meyers, Diane T., "Self-Respect and Autonomy," in Robin S. Dillon (ed.), *Dignity, Character, and Self-Respect* (New York: Routledge, 1995).

Nelson, William, "On the Alleged Importance of Moral Rights," *Ratio* 18 (1976), 153–4.

Neuhouser, Frederick, *Foundations of Hegel's Social Theory: Actualizing Freedom* (Harvard University Press, 2000).

Nicholson, Peter, *The Political Philosophy of the British Idealists* (Cambridge University Press, 1990).

Nozick, Robert, *Anarchy, State, and Utopia* (New York: Basic Books, 1974).

Nussbaum, Martha, *Women and Human Development: The Capabilities Approach* (Cambridge University Press, 2000).

Olivier, Marius, "Constitutional Perspectives on the Enforcement of Socio-economic Rights: Recent South African Experiences," *Victoria University of Wellington Law Review* 33 (2002), 117–52.

Omi, Michael and Winant, Howard, *Racial Formation in the United States: From the 1960s to the 1990s* (New York: Routledge, 1994).

Outlaw, Jr., Lucius T., *On Race and Philosophy* (New York: Routledge, 1996).

Panichas, George E., "The Rights-Ascription Problem," *Social Theory and Practice* 23 (1997), 365–98.

Paton, G. W., *A Textbook of Jurisprudence*, 4th edn. (Oxford: Clarendon Press, 1972).

Patton, Paul, "Foucault, Critique and Rights," *Critical Horizons* 6 (2005), 267–87.

Polan, Diane, "Toward a Theory of Law and Patriarchy," in David Kairys (ed.), *The Politics of Law: A Progressive Critique* (New York: Pantheon Books, 1982).

Rawls, John, "Outline of a Decision Procedure for Ethics," *Philosophical Review* 60 (1951), 177–97.

    A Theory of Justice (Cambridge: Belknap Press, 1971).

    "The Independence of Moral Theory," *Proceedings and Addresses of the American Philosophical Association* 47 (1974–5), 5–22.

    "Kantian Constructivism in Moral Theory," *The Journal of Philosophy* 77 (1980), 515–72.

    "Justice as Fairness: Political not Metaphysical," *Philosophy and Public Affairs* 3 (1985), 223–51.

Raz, Joseph, "Legal Rights," *Oxford Journal of Legal Studies* 4 (1984), 1–21.

    "On the Nature of Rights," *Mind* 93 (1984), 194–214.

    "Right-Based Moralities," in Jeremy Waldron (ed.), *Theories of Rights* (Oxford University Press, 1984).

    Practical Reason and Norms (Oxford University Press, 1999).

Rise, Arthur, *Race, Slavery and Liberalism in Nineteenth-Century American Literature* (Cambridge University Press, 2006).

Ritchie, D. G., *Natural Rights: A Criticism of Some Political and Ethical Conceptions* (London: Swan Sonnenschein, 1895).

Robbins, Peter, *The British Hegelians 1875–1925* (New York: Garland Press, 1982).

Ross, W. D., *The Right and the Good* (Oxford: Clarendon Press, 1930).

Rushton, J. Phillippe, *Race, Evolution, and Behavior: A Life History Perspective* (New Brunswick: Transaction Books, 1995).

Sandel, Michael, *Liberalism and the Limits of Justice* (Cambridge University Press, 1982).

Sayre-McCord, Geoffrey, "The Many Moral Realisms," *The Southern Journal of Philosophy* 24 (1986), 1–22.

Scanlon, Thomas, "The Aims and Authority of Moral Theory," *Oxford Journal of Legal Studies* 12 (1992), 1–23.

Schuman, Howard, Steech, Charlotte, Bobo, Lawrence, and Krysan, Maria, *Racial Attitudes in America: Trends and Interpretations* (Harvard University Press, 1997).

Scott, Craig and Macklem, Peter, "Constitutional Ropes of Sand or Justiciable Guarantees? Social Rights in a New South African Constitution," *University of Pennsylvania Law Review* 141 (1992), 1–148.

Sears, David O., "Symbolic Racism," in Phyllis A. Katz and Dalmas A. Taylor (eds.), *Eliminating Racism: Profiles in Controversy* (New York: Plenum Press, 1988).

Sears, David O. and Kinder, Donald R., "Racial Tensions and Voting in Los Angeles," in Werner Z. Hirsch (ed.), *Los Angeles: Viability and Prospects for Metropolitan Leadership* (New York: Praeger Publishers, 1971).

Sears, David O., Kinder, Donald R., Hetts, John J., Sidanius, Jim, and Bobo, Lawrence, "Race in American Politics: Framing the Debates," in David O. Sears, Jim Sidanius, and Lawrence Bobo (eds.), *Racialized Politics: The Debate about Racism in America* (University of Chicago Press, 2000), pp. 1–43.

Sears, David O., van Laar, Colette, Carrillo, Mary, and Kosterman, Rick, "Is it Really Racism? The Origins of White Americans' Opposition to Race-Targeted Policies," *Public Opinion Quarterly* 61 (1997), 16–53.

Sen, Amartya, "Elements of a Theory of Human Rights," *Philosophy and Public Affairs* 32 (2004), 315–56.

Shelby, Tommie, *We Who Are Dark: The Philosophical Foundations of Black Solidarity* (Harvard University Press, 2005).

Simhony, Avital and Weinstein, David (eds.), *The New Liberalism: Reconciling Liberty and Community* (Cambridge University Press, 2001).

Smith, Bryant, "Legal Personality," *Yale Law Journal* 37 (1928), 283–99.

Smith, Rogers M., *Civic Ideals: Conflicting Visions of Citizenship in US History* (Yale University Press, 1997).

Smith, William A., *Lectures on the Philosophy and Practice of Slavery, as Exhibited in the Institution of Domestic Slavery in the United States* (New York: Negro Universities Press, 1969).

Sowell, Thomas, *Race and Culture: A World View* (New York: Basic Books, 1994).

Stone, Christopher, "Should Trees Have Standing? Toward Legal Rights for Natural Objects," *Southern California Law Review* 45 (1972), 450–501.

Sumner, L. W., *The Moral Foundation of Rights* (Oxford: Clarendon Press, 1987).

Sunstein, Cass, "Social and Economic Rights? Lessons from South Africa," *Public Law and Legal Theory* Working Paper no. 12 (2001), 1–15.

Sweet, William, *Idealism and Rights: The Social Ontology of Human Rights in the Political Thought of Bernard Bosanquet* (Lanham: University Press of America, 1997).

Taylor, Charles, *Sources of the Self: The Making of Modern Identity* (Cambridge University Press, 1989).

Taylor, Marylee C., "The Significance of Racial Context," in David O. Sears, Jim Sidanius, and Lawrence Bobo (eds.), *Racialized Politics: The Debate about Racism in America* (University of Chicago Press, 2000).

Thomas, Geoffrey, *The Moral Philosophy of T. H. Green* (Oxford: Clarendon Press, 1987).

Tise, Larry E., *Proslavery: A History of the Defense of Slavery in America, 1701–1840* (Athens: University of Georgia Press, 1987).

The American Counterrevolution: A Retreat from Liberty, 1783–1800 (Mechanicsburg: Stackpole Books, 1998).

Tuck, Richard, *Natural Rights Theories: Their Origin and Development* (Cambridge University Press, 1979).

Tucker, William H., *The Science and Politics of Racial Research* (Urbana: University of Illinois Press, 1994).

Valls, Andrew (ed.), *Race and Racism in Modern Philosophy* (Cornell University Press, 2005).

Van Evrie, J. H., *White Supremacy and Negro Subordination or, Negroes A Subordinate Race, and (so-called) Slavery Its Normal Condition*, in John David Smith (ed.), *Anti-Black Thought: 1863–1925*, vol. III (New York: Garland Publishing, 1993).

Warren, Mary Ann, *Moral Status* (Oxford: Clarendon Press, 1997).

Wellman, Carl P., *A Theory of Rights* (Totowa: Rowman & Allanheld, 1985).

Real Rights (Oxford University Press, 1995).

The Proliferation of Rights: Moral Progress or Empty Rhetoric? (Boulder: Westview Press, 1999).

West, Cornel, "Philosophy and the Urban Underclass," in Bill E. Lawson (ed.), *The Underclass Question* (Philadelphia: Temple University Press, 1992).

Keeping Faith: Philosophy and Race in America (New York: Routledge, 1993).

Weston, Murray, "Grootboom and Beyond: Reassessing the Socio-Economic Jurisprudence of the South African Constitutional Court," *South African Journal on Human Rights* 20 (2004), 284–308.

Westra, Laura and Lawson, Bill (eds.), *Faces of Environmental Racism: Confronting Issues of Global Justice*, 2nd edn. (Lanham: Rowman and Littlefield, 2001).

Young, Robert, "Dispensing with Moral Rights," *Political Theory* 6 (1978), 63–74.

Zuckert, Michael P., *The Natural Rights Republic* (University of Notre Dame Press, 1996).

Index

187